ESSAYS ON SOCIALISM AND WAR

The Era of Tyrannies

BY

ÉLIE HALÉVY

TRANSLATED BY R. K. WEBB

WITH A NOTE BY FRITZ STERN

NEW YORK UNIVERSITY PRESS
1966

The Era of Tyrannies was originally published by Librairie Gallimard in 1938 as *L'ère des tyrannies: études sur le socialisme et la guerre.*

This edition is published by arrangement with Librairie Gallimard, and was first published by Anchor Books (Doubleday & Co., Inc.).

The publisher wishes to thank The Clarendon Press, Oxford University, for granting permission to reprint three lectures by Élie Halévy that appeared as The Rhodes Memorial Lectures in 1929 and were published in 1930 by The Clarendon Press with the title *The World Crisis of 1914–1918: An Interpretation.*

The publisher also thanks The Royal Institute of International Affairs for granting permission to reprint Élie Halévy's Chatham House lecture of April 24, 1934, "Socialism and the Problem of Parliamentary Democracy," which appeared in *International Affairs,* July 1934, Volume XIII.

These lectures, originally given in English, appeared in a French translation in the original edition of *L'ère des tyrannies.*

The Principal Works of Élie Halévy

La théorie platonicienne des sciences. Paris, Felix Alcan, 1896.

La formation du radicalisme philosophique. Paris, Felix Alcan, 1901–1904. Translated by Mary Morris as *The Growth of Philosophic Radicalism*. London, 1928.

Thomas Hodgskin, 1787–1869. Paris, Rieder, 1903. Translated by A. J. Taylor, London, 1956.

"La naissance du Methodisme en Angleterre," *Revue de Paris*, 1906, IV, 519–539, 841–867 (August 1 and 15, 1906).

Histoire du peuple anglais au XIXe siècle. Paris, Hachette.

    I. *L'Angleterre en 1815*, 1913. Translated by E. I. Watkin and D. A. Barker, London, 1924.

    II. *Du lendemain de Waterloo à la veille du Reform Bill, 1815–1830*, 1923. Translated by E. I. Watkin, London, 1926.

    III. *De la crise du Reform Bill à l'avènement de Sir Robert Peel, 1830–1841*, 1923. Translated by E. I. Watkin, London, 1927.

    IV. *La politique libre-échangiste, 1841–1852*, edited by Paul Vaucher and published posthumously, 1947. Translated by E. I. Watkin, London, 1947.

Epilogue, I: *Les impérialistes au pouvoir, 1895–1905*, 1926. Translated by E. I. Watkin, 1929.

Epilogue, II: *Vers la démocratie sociale et vers la guerre, 1905–1914*, 1932. Translated by E. I. Watkin, London, 1934.

(Note: In the first edition of the English translation, the title of each volume is *A History of the English People*, with the dates of the years covered. In the new edition of the translation, published 1947–1952, the titles are: I, *England in 1815;* II, *The Liberal Awakening;* III, *The Triumph of Reform;* IV, *The Age of Peel and Cobden* (1947) or, with an additional chapter covering 1852–1895 by R. B. McCallum, *The Victorian Years;* Epilogue, I, *Imperialism and the Rise of Labour;* Epilogue, II, *The Rule of Democracy.*)

L'ère des tyrannies. Published posthumously. Paris, Gallimard, 1938.

Histoire du socialisme européen. Published posthumously. Paris, Gallimard, 1948.

TRANSLATOR'S PREFACE

Élie Halévy (1870–1937) is best known to American
and English readers for his contributions to our knowledge of English history from the end of the eighteenth
century to the twentieth century, contributions with a
scope, power, and influence unmatched by the work of
any English historian of the period. But the English-speaking world has remained largely unaware of Halévy's
equally strong interest in socialism. His brief early study
of the English Ricardian socialist Thomas Hodgskin
(1787–1869), though published in 1903, appeared in
translation only in 1956. The lectures on the history of
European socialism which Halévy alternated with his
lectures on nineteenth-century England at the École des
Sciences Politiques were published posthumously in 1948
and then only by way of reconstruction from his students'
notes; the book has not been translated. Since its publication in 1938, the present volume has been the only way
for a reader to gain a general appreciation of Halévy's
interpretation of socialism in a form that bears the war-
rant of his own words. This translation will perhaps serve
to bring this interpretation a wider reputation and to provide, as well, an essential perspective on Halévy's seminal
work in English history.

The importance of *The Era of Tyrannies* will not seem
evident from a first glance at its contents. The book may
well seem miscellaneous, even disjointed. There are some
scholarly articles, an introduction to a collection of extracts, a handful of lectures, a set of propositions intended
to provoke discussion, and a summary of the discussion.
The pieces range in time from 1902 to 1936. Some of

them lay claim to authority and justify it; others are tentative, almost occasional, inquiries into contemporary events. In actuality, the book reflects a remarkable unity of intellectual concern. That unity will gradually become apparent to a reader, especially if he already has some acquaintance with Halévy's work; it is reinforced in the recapitulation of Halévy's argument by his close friend Célestin Bouglé in the preface to the original edition, which is reprinted here. Little can be added to what Bouglé and Halévy himself have said about the emergence of this historical concern—at once single-minded and profound—from the circumstances of Halévy's youth and from his rare temperament and personality. There is, however, something to be said about the significance of Halévy's work, particularly as it is revealed in this volume, for our understanding of what might be called, to borrow some appropriate Benthamite jargon, the "art-and-science" of history.

At one level, these essays can stand as models of what usually passes for the history of ideas. In the essays on the Saint-Simonian school, especially, Halévy is engaged in a common variety of historical writing: he is tracing the origins and descent of ideas and trying to isolate the influence of one thinker or group of thinkers on others. His technical skill is, however, most uncommon.

Historians of ideas too frequently suffer from the sin of pride, the dangerous pride that grows from a little learning. Having acquired a certain facility—not unrelated to some present-day emphases of undergraduate education, especially in the United States—in ranging freely through the whole of western culture, they are tempted to place their subject in a vast context of thought and feeling assembled from the writer's own, often accidental, store of learning, more by means of analogy and metaphor than by the harder, drearier task of genetic reconstruction. Such writing can be valuable, when it is not fraudulent: it can provide startling juxtapositions and novel insights which we should be poorer for not having. But the process is literary, not historical. In Halévy—who tried rigorously to be as objective as possible and who, as Bouglé tells us, had only contempt for "mere literature" —such presumption, even such useful presumption, had no place.

Halévy was never satisfied with easy explanations. He nicely balanced respect for and skepticism about a writer's own explanation of his intellectual obligations, a balance admirably shown here in his construction of intellectual genealogies for Saint-Simon and Auguste Comte. He had an incomparable knowledge of books and writers whose importance for their time has been obscured by their failure to survive to our own day, but he was extremely careful to avoid casual ascriptions. As certain passages and some of the longer footnotes in the Saint-Simonian essays show, he undertook the kind of careful detective work essential to a proper history of ideas: no mere invocation of a catalogue of names, no simple resort to *post hoc ergo propter hoc,* but close analysis of historical situations and of turns of phrase and rhetoric to reveal conscious or unconscious obligation.

Turning from Halévy's technical competence in dealing with ideas to his perception of the importance of ideas in history, we move to an aspect of his work that is more profound and more generally appreciated. Readers of his *History of the English People* will readily recall the central part played by ideas, both religious and secular, in his account of the nineteenth century in Britain; in this volume, his awareness of the autonomous and creative role of ideas is most explicitly stated in his original and influential interpretation of the first World War. Halévy maintained these views rigorously throughout a generation during which, consciously or unconsciously, most historians were ruled by a more or less simplistic Marxist bias. It is a tribute to his authority that he was admired in that generation as well as now, when historians are wary—sometimes too wary—of the Marxist taint. But there is little need to comment further on this aspect of Halévy's interest in ideas; his whole work is a commentary on it.

There is, however, a third, less immediately evident way in which ideas are involved in Halévy's writing of history. Why do so many of his analyses and interpretations, one or two generations later, continue to inform our thinking, when later and more elaborate studies often serve only to confirm or correct in detail? The answer surely lies in Halévy's inability to write anything without giving it a structure of astonishing clarity and strength, a structure that remains when details have been forgotten and that, in one way or another, underlies and directs whatever reconstructions might subsequently be made. An architectural metaphor may not be out of place. In the historiography of the subjects on which he wrote, Halévy's constructions are not like those Saxon or Frankish churches on the foundations of which Gothic cathedrals were raised, foundations that can be uncovered only by archeological research. The architectural parallel is to be found, rather, in the old New England house, with its massive central chimney and its elegant proportions, to which later generations have made useful or doubtfully decorative additions: the woodshed, the new kitchen, the gingerbread porch, and the asbestos siding. Restoration of the house to its original purity of design may, indeed, be undesirable on grounds of utility; but, changed though the building is, the basic structure stands and determines the life that is lived inside its walls.

The structure that Halévy invariably provides is not pieced together from the obvious succession of chronology or by the topical divisions of the filing system and the catalogue card. It is a structure of ideas, arrived at by penetrating analysis and arduous thought. Historians usually, and understandably, take easier paths, in good part because they have not been trained to take the harder ones; that may account for the remark once made to me by an economist that history is too important to be left to historians. But Halévy was trained as a philosopher, and in everything he wrote the philosopher underlay the historian. Bridging a separation of disciplines which has gone much further now than it had done in Halévy's youth, one might say that his concern and his method were scientific. Certainly he thought so. Having finished his work on Methodism, he began to ponder his project for the *History*. More history? he asked his friend Bouglé; then he answered: "Yes, because it is unfortunately the only way for me to do science. Better physics or astronomy. But I can't do them, and I look where I can for explanatory connections."[1] As an historian, Halévy did what a good scientist does: he reduced refractory evidence to a consistent intellectual structure. His narrative was more than chronicle, that useful but pedestrian historical analogue to the old amateur natural history. He did not surround himself with the more modern trappings of tables, graphs, and calculations. Nor did he try to formulate elaborate and futile laws, like Spengler's or Toynbee's. Rather, he saw through his material to a radical principle of organization, intellectually satisfying, genuinely explanatory, and suggestive of a thousand further explorations. This is not to say that his construction or explanation is final or the only one possible; it says no more than that his explanation is satisfying and that it works—it saves the appearances. One can imagine a number of different constructions that would also work, even though done with less intellectual brilliance, less style, and a smaller grasp. But it is precisely because of the inner strength, coherence, and authority of Halévy's constructions that he cannot be destroyed by competing explanations, criticism in detail, correction in fact, or carping around the edges. He was the master of a rare talent: the bold apprehension of historical reality. His first book dealt with the Platonic

[1] September 12, 1905, in Alain (Émile Chartier), *Correspondance avec Élie et Florence Halévy* (1958), pp. 332–333.

theory of the sciences; as historians are natural Aristotelians, he is a valuable reminder that it may not be only in the physical sciences that great leaps forward have been made from the Platonic, not the Aristotelian, position.

This point was made cogently in a perceptive analysis of Halévy's method published some years ago by Professor Charles Gillispie of Princeton.[2] "Except that he was never mystical," Professor Gillispie writes:

> his own cast of mind was Platonic: austere, analytical, and logical, always seeking to penetrate to the central idea or conception, moral or intellectual, which gave form not only to bodies of doctrine but also to concrete political and social movements. Halévy always accorded primacy to systems of values, ideas, beliefs, and morals, rather than to material interests in explaining human motives and social actions. . . . But his idealism was not of the romantic variety. He was, if anything, even less sympathetic to Hegelians than to Marxists.

Professor Gillispie describes Halévy's use of "almost a dialectical method." He would cut through successive layers of conceptions until he came to what seemed to him the core of the doctrine or the historical situation he was trying to expound. There, at the core, he would almost always find a contradiction, and around that contradiction he would organize his exposition and criticism. Whether his subject was Utilitarianism or classical political economy or the social structure of early nineteenth-century England, whether it was socialism in a sect or socialism as a century-long movement, whether it was a trade union or a Whitley Council, his method gave nearly everything he wrote something of the quality of inevitability: it is still possible to disagree, but one cannot fail to respect a conclusion that has been arrived at with the utmost rigor

[2] "The Work of Élie Halévy: A Critical Appreciation," *Journal of Modern History*, XXII, 232–249 (September 1950).

and complete honesty. Halévy's work is conclusive justification for the centrality of thesis and argument in historical writing.

There are other virtues to the method. In the first place, the clarity of Halévy's perception of central ideas provides criteria for paring away the irrelevant. Here, again, the Saint-Simonian essays are particularly instructive. They deal only with certain economic ideas of Saint-Simon and of his disciples; even within those limits, they are not exhaustive. An historian coming to the Saint-Simonians with less stringent criteria or with a less disciplined curiosity may, for example, be led to write a long, general study in which the foolish or amusing vagaries of the school would inevitably bulk too large; or, in a brief study, he might be led by the preponderance of nonsense to form an unfavorable, even a sarcastic judgment.[3] Either result may be useful, but to understand the importance of the Saint-Simonians, in their own time and for the future, Halévy's narrower approach is the more rewarding and ultimately the more far-reaching.

A second virtue of the method may be illustrated by the three essays in this volume on the social situation in Great Britain immediately following the first World War. Had Halévy himself prepared this volume for the press, he might have been tempted to eliminate the slightest and most occasional of the pieces—the second—incorporating what did not appear elsewhere into the remaining articles. Or, to avoid the repetitiveness which is certainly a fault of the articles as they stand, he might have reworked them into a single essay, with much the same conclusion, so far as the argument is concerned. But had he done so, we should have lost something for which a little repetitiveness

[3] Frank Manuel's general survey of the career of Saint-Simon, *The New World of Henri Saint-Simon* (1956) may stand as an example of the first approach; the second result is evident in the amusing perverseness of Sir Alexander Gray in *The Socialist Tradition: Moses to Lenin* (1946).

and a few blighted prophecies are a small price to pay. For one thing, the three articles as they stand document an important biographical fact—the dashing of Halévy's English hope, a disillusion that had deepened by the time of his Chatham House lecture in 1934 and that ended in the pessimism of "The Era of Tyrannies." From the skeptical optimism of the long article on the Whitley Councils, he arrived three years later at the ironic conclusion of the third article, with its exasperated postscript—the only occasion I know when Halévy allowed his self-control to slip, almost to petulance, certainly to a sneer.

But the present form of these articles has more to offer than biographical interest. Of all kinds of historical writing, contemporary history is the most evanescent; in most hands, it is little more than chronicle, destined to lose its usefulness as soon as the hindsight of a few years makes interpretation possible. In these articles Halévy is writing about events of only a few months before, even at the very time of writing; but, by the steady application of his method, he presses continually to interpretation within a significant framework of ideas. He seeks out what seems to have been the central intention of the framers of the Whitley Report, sets it into a pattern of the quest for industrial peace over the preceding generation, and points up the conflict of this intention with the idea at the core of the trade-union movement onto which the Whitley Councils were unsuccessfully grafted; similarly he isolates the contradictory and unassimilable ideas within the postwar demand for worker control. And he relates these seemingly insignificant and certainly forgotten movements to English socialism in a way to illuminate the internal contradiction that he found to be the chief characteristic of all socialism. One need only look at the dreary administrative histories that touch on these movements or at more recent pedestrian histories of the Labour Party and of socialism to appreciate the brilliance of Halévy's accomplishment.

So far, I have dealt only with the "science" or the "technology" of Halévy's "art-and-science" of history. A third virtue of his sovereign method lies in its literary effect. Halévy was as skillful at narrative as at analysis and interpretation. In the larger scale of the *History,* long narratives move with pace and clarity because the systematic structure beneath them makes both course and significance plain. In the essays in this book, narrative necessarily forms a much smaller part, but when he turns to it, it is masterful. The accounts of Lloyd George's maneuverings around the Sankey Commission and the National Industrial Conference or of the rapid demolition of the apparatus of wartime socialism in Britain are models of swift, lean prose, informed by the complementary senses of drama and irony. So much any reader may grant. But there are other passages where the going is harder, where sentences are awkward and style turns gritty. Whatever difficulties these analytical passages may present—one must blame them more, perhaps, on the barbarousness of his subjects' prose or the obscurity of their thought than on Halévy himself—careful reading or rereading reveals not only the explanatory strength arising from the steady application of his analytical method, but also the literary tension sustained by it.

The more widely one reads in Halévy, the more impressive and moving those tensions become. Looking back from the Rhodes Lectures on the first World War or from "The Era of Tyrannies," small incidents or notions, touched on almost in passing in articles of thirty years before, fall into place. Setting the implications of these essays against his larger work on English history, one grows more and more aware of the grand contradiction, central to everything he did, between the liberal and the authoritarian, a contradiction he was to resolve regretfully in favor of the authoritarian. In his pessimistic apprehension that a new era of tyrannies, in the classical Greek sense of the word, had begun with the war and revolution of 1914–1918, there was no sudden disillusion, none of the violence that has made embittered reactionaries today from sanguine liberals of yesterday. He was, in a word, not surprised. In fact, in a light-heartedly serious letter in 1900, Halévy caught the conflict of liberal and authoritarian in metaphor. Taking up Taine's suggestion of a monkey-man, he proposed a fanciful construction of the history of the world: it was the struggle of the monkey and the elephant. When the gorilla won out over the mammoth, the victory assured that man would be a supermonkey, not a superelephant. But though the monkey won the primeval victory, the history of the human race was the history of the struggle against the elephant's revenge. The monkey had not won because it was more thoughtful or nobler, but because it was more supple; then, ashamed of its suppleness, the supermonkey lost its prehensile tail and gave up two of its four hands. Relentlessly, the people of the elephant won out over the people of the monkey— the West over the East, the Romans over the Greeks, the barbarians over the Mediterranean peoples. "And in every one of us, the monkey is continually at war with the elephant—the real moral life of the individual." He told his friend gaily to take it from there.[4] Halévy himself took it from there. The classically calm propositions of "The Era of Tyrannies" are the utterances of the Greek chorus, recognizing what it foresaw but could not prevent —the victory of the elephant.

The incidents and arguments of the smaller units of Halévy's work enter into and heighten the grandeur of the whole; the drama of the whole intensifies the effect of the parts. But tension cannot last forever in a work of art. At his greatest, when all the elements of his method are in full operation—in the first volume of the *History*, in the study of philosophic radicalism; here, in the articles on the Saint-Simonians, and in the first and third articles

[4] To Bouglé, May 14, 1900, Alain, *Correspondance*, p. 326.

on the social situation in postwar England—we are led to another analogy, not architectural now, but musical. In the development of the immediate argument and in the larger implications, the conflict of ideas grows more intense; the intensity may even be heightened by difficulties in the prose. The mounting tension is like the interweaving of contrapuntal voices and the piling up of dissonances towards the end of a Bach organ fugue. But, as certainly as in the fugue, a resolution begins to emerge and ends in a clear chord in the dominant key—the conclusions of the books, the last paragraphs of the articles: ". . . England is a country of voluntary obedience, of an organization freely initiated and freely accepted"; the triumph of Manchester over Westminster; the prophecy in the Saint-Simonian vision; the hope that parliamentary methods might tame England's class war as they had tamed her religious and civil wars; the irony that a Labour Party which had helped to defeat its own ends could find no program but that of Manchester liberalism. In the last of these resolutions there is a new, more pessimistic tone. "The World Crisis" ends, not with a resolution, but with warning questions, with a *caesura*. Seven years later, with "The Era of Tyrannies," the dissonance was at last resolved, and the great fugue came to an end—in a minor key.

R. K. Webb

PREFACE TO THE ORIGINAL EDITION[1]

The problems of socialism attracted Élie Halévy's attention very early. A liberal to the marrow of his bones, by personal temperament as much as by family tradition, he had an instinctive horror of the encroachments of the state, even of the democratic state. He quickly realized, however, that in certain cases—as a very consequence of the economic dislocations that followed the Industrial Revolution—state intervention might be needed to safeguard the essential rights of the individual. His family's wealth put every conceivable means of culture within his grasp, but he vowed, while still very young, that he would not be a prisoner of his privileges. He wrote in his notebook at the *lycée:* "I more and more dislike having a fortune that I have neither earned nor deserved." To make sure of his liberation, he thought at one point of learning some manual trade. In any event, he urgently warned that the demands then spreading among the manual workers had to be taken as seriously as the systems of the thinkers who became their defenders. As early as 1888 he made this note: "Socialism, a great, powerful, and formidable doctrine which we in France cannot appreciate." When he entered the École Normale Supérieure[2] the next year—as he explained to the Société Française de Philosophie—he did not experience the thrust

[1] [The opening paragraphs of this preface, which deal largely with plans for publishing Halévy's uncompleted work, have been omitted.]

[2] [The École Normale Supérieure is a school for the training of teachers in secondary and higher education. Students are selected by a rigorous competitive examination.]

towards socialism of which so much has been said. It was not until some years later that Lucien Herr and Charles Andler brought their full influence to bear in the Rue d'Ulm[3] and helped to create there the corps of militant intellectuals who formed so impressive a phalanx around Jaurès. But Élie Halévy was part of no phalanx. He owed fealty to no one. He approached the enigma of socialism without prejudice, favorable or unfavorable, with the complete freedom of mind of one who wanted no more than to be an historian.

* * *

As far as doctrines are concerned, the most important of these articles are those dealing with Saint-Simonianism. They stand as a counterpart to Élie Halévy's work on Benthamism, the most characteristic philosophy of the England to which he was to return so often.

They are a counterpart and also an antithesis. In the system worked out by Jeremy Bentham and his disciples, Élie Halévy found a kind of confirmation of the individualist tendencies imprinted, so to speak, in his own temperament; he admired the Utilitarians for providing us, in their account of the harmonization of individual interests, not only with a method of explanation, but also with the standard of the most rational orientation he could have wished. At the same time, he was aware that, even for the Utilitarians, the identification of interests did not take place spontaneously. Occasional nudges, compensatory or corrective interventions were needed and could, in certain instances, justify the response of organized society.

After an experience of industrialism that gave pause even to the most optimistic, the Saint-Simonians came to insist on precisely that need for action, dictated by a sense of the general interest. Sismondi was the first herald of the crises of abundance, the white bird that preceded the storm in fleeing it; with that calm analytical ability

[3] [Where the École Normale is located.]

for which he was noted, he had already called attention to the damage done by production that was both unregulated and intensified, and that could only dangerously worsen the inequality of conditions. Saint-Simon and especially the Saint-Simonians took up and expanded these themes, opposing a complete philosophy of history to the liberal conception of society, insisting on the necessity of correcting individualism by a dose of "collectisme" opposing inheritance, limiting competition, appealing to the state as an "association of workers" to take over, and calling not only on better organized factories but also on the banks under the stimulus of a new spirit to bring about at last a world in which the exploitation of the globe would no longer be predicated on the exploitation of man by man. Both the criticism and the program were developed in the lectures devoted in 1829 to an *Exposition de la doctrine de Saint-Simon* (*An Account of Saint-Simon's Doctrine*); in them Bazard, Enfantin and their associates were writing a kind of *summa* of the industrial age, what one might call the Bible of socialism. Only the word was lacking; all the essential ideas were there in force.

Which of us proposed to the other that we collaborate on editing this remarkable document? I really no longer know. Since I had succeeded M. Espina in lecturing on social history at the Sorbonne, our research ran in parallel channels. Our judgments very often coincided. Month after month, before going to lecture at the École des Sciences Politiques, Élie Halévy would come to the Centre de Documentation Sociale in the Rue d'Ulm to tell me about his discoveries or to set me problems. What confidence and at the same time what pleasure I derived from his utter sincerity, the impartiality he could assume, his hatred of the vague, his contempt for everything that was "mere literature". . . .

Patiently and enthusiastically we pursued our painstaking work as editors, convinced that, in carrying out the work of M. Charléty, M. Weill, and M. Maxime Leroy,[4] we were helping to bring about a fully deserved resurrection. No work could have been more fruitful in every kind of suggestion.

At the end of the second article on the Saint-Simonians, we shall see Élie Halévy's demonstration that the seeds of everything, or nearly everything, are present in Saint-Simonianism. Did not Auguste Comte pass on its characteristics to his disciples, just as Karl Marx transmitted them to his? But what Élie Halévy praised above everything else in the school was their having made it clear that modern socialism is a doctrine with two faces. "It is a doctrine of emancipation which aims at abolishing the last traces of slavery remaining in industrialism, and it is a doctrine of organization which, to protect the freedom of the weak against the strong, needs a restored and strengthened social power." Emancipation or organization? The distinction is pregnant with consequences. It lies at the root of the antithesis that the worried author of "The Era of Tyrannies" developed with the utmost rigor in his last communication to the Société Française de Philosophie, in what was, one might say, his political and social testament.

❊ ❊ ❊

What speeded the pace of the evolution and paved the way in Europe for an authoritarian *étatisme*, socialist in character, was the war of 1914–1919. The war was the grim harbinger of "tyrannical" socialism.

As Élie Halévy saw it, the causes of the war, the causes of wars, were by no means all economic. But it was clear to him that, by inciting and forcing each of the belligerent

---

[4] [Sébastien Charléty, *Essai sur l'histoire du Saint-Simonisme* (1896) and *Histoire du Saint-Simonisme, 1825–1864* (1931). Georges Jacques Weill, *Un précurseur du socialisme: Saint-Simon et son oeuvre* (1894) and *L'école Saint-Simonienne, son histoire, son influence jusqu'à nos jours* (1896). Maxime Leroy, *Henri de Saint-Simon* (1924) and *La vie véritable du comte Henri de Saint-Simon* (1925).]

nations to concentrate its productive power, in order to bring it to the highest pitch, the war of 1914 had an unexampled influence on the entire economic organization of those nations. Events counted for more than doctrines. The catastrophe of 1914 did more for socialism than the spread of the Marxist system.

In the essays published here the criticisms of the Marxist ideology that Élie Halévy never ceased to make will be found again, notably his criticism of that historical materialism—Hegelianism turned upside down—that explains everything by the movement of a dialectic in which the material interests of the classes, not ideas or feelings, are the moving forces. As a historian, Élie Halévy was ready to try this theory as a working hypothesis. He certainly did not deny that industrialism had been one of the most powerful revolutionary elements in the modern world. He agreed that it could have a profound effect on the movement of ideas, notably on the progress of the sciences. Knowing that the needs of the metal-working or textile industries in England at the beginning of the nineteenth century had led to many a discovery by physicists or chemists, he agreed that "the thesis of historical materialism, questionable when applied universally, is to this extent true of England at the opening of the nineteenth century. Scientific theory was the offspring of industrial practice."[5] But in many other instances the hypothesis is not verified, and it is impossible to make it a generalization, even for societies today. Élie Halévy's study of England in 1815 showed him the moral forces, pietist in origin, whose strength accounted for the "English miracle." Throughout a whole century, and in spite of the relative weakening of those forces by the spread of customs arising from industry, he was aware that it was beliefs, not interests, that drove men. Even when interests were at stake, they were dependent on the

[5] [*England in 1815* (1949 ed.), p. 559.]

support of common emotions, as it was granted or withheld. Do we not find, even in the revival of British imperialism, elements that are sentimental rather than economic, patriotic rather than utilitarian?

In any case, as he saw it, it would be entirely useless to try to explain the origins of the Great War, which he had studied very closely, by abstracting from these elements. On that point especially he opposed the simplistic interpretation of traditional Marxism. Would war be the natural and constantly reappearing result of capitalism? The very experience of the prewar years leads us to believe that, where only their interests were at stake, the capitalists of different countries would have been completely capable of concluding international agreements, with a system of mutual concessions certainly less costly to them than war. If, nevertheless, war broke out, it was because intense collective feelings were there, ready to enter the vicious circle. In Asia as in Europe, oppressed peoples believed they would find an issue, a means of immediate salvation, in their rediscovered or newly claimed independence. Here political motives counted for more than economic motives. The principal cause of the war was certainly an effort to free nationalities. For that reason the war of 1914 was in actuality a revolution, a breakdown of the equilibrium, which resulted in the quest through violence for a new equilibrium; but this revolution has slowed and lessened the force of the classical revolutionary emotions. "From what happened in 1914, it appeared that national warlike emotions influenced the human mind more deeply than international revolutionary emotions."

*　*　*

To carry this struggle for survival to its end, governments in every land were led more or less quickly to take over not only manufacturing and transport, but all forms of industry and commerce. Wanting, no doubt, to secure the goodwill of the workers on the home front, they entered into negotiations with the leaders of working-class organizations and agreed with them on conditions of labor. In their own way they favored a kind of syndicalism. But it was a syndicalism reduced to its barest elements, forcibly sobered and, one might say, tamed by *étatisme*. More and more the state came to be relied upon for the centralization of production, as it was for the distribution of goods. More, indeed, than the spread of Marxist doctrines, the extension of these wartime methods into peacetime opened the way to socialism. But it was a Caesarist socialism.

Because of the war, Élie Halévy saw the kind of economic policy that for a long time he had feared most taking form. Long before the war, I recall, in one of the letters that he regularly wrote me after we left the École Normale, he wondered whether the world would see the establishment of a kind of federal democracy, on the Swiss model, or of a generalized Caesarism. The war chose: the Caesars prevailed.

To bring other methods to success, or at least to demonstrate their effectiveness, could one count on the common sense of England, that England so dear to Élie Halévy, where he went every year—so it seemed—to regain courage and hope? It was a country where systems counted for less than they did elsewhere, a country more attached to precedent than principle, a country ready, moreover, to take historical necessity into account in making transitions and accustomed to the spirit of compromise and to parliamentary methods. Could not freedom co-exist with organization there?

But all the social reforms tried by England since the war, which Élie Halévy studied with the greatest care in the essays reprinted here, did not bring about a new equilibrium. The parliamentary methods with which the representatives of English trade unionism themselves willingly complied produced no lasting change in the economic structure. Guild Socialism suffered defeat after defeat. And Sidney Webb could laugh a mephistophelian laugh—that same Sidney Webb in whom Élie Halévy, soon after his arrival in England, detected sympathies for the Hegelian conception of the state and Prussian methods of organized bureaucracy.

The program implied by this conception and these methods is being carried out, Élie Halévy seems to have thought, in countries where men of action have understood that the modern structure of the state puts almost unlimited powers at their disposal or where armed sects, "fasces," have seized the legal machinery, as Jules Guesde put it, either to stop its working or to bend it to their will. In Russia, they have moved from a complete socialism towards a kind of nationalism. Elsewhere, in Germany and Italy, they have moved towards a kind of socialism. The result is the same as far as freedom is concerned. It is destroyed. And one asks if socialism can come about in any other way. Thus the contradiction that Élie Halévy had long sensed at the core of socialism between the need for freedom and the need for organization has, with the help of the war, been resolved for us only by a negation. *Finis libertatis?*

* * *

The pessimism of these conclusions surprised many of Élie Halévy's friends in the Société Française de Philosophie. He was at once reminded that there are socialisms and socialisms, that in France one could set Fourier and Proudhon against Saint-Simon; that, moreover, the democracies in America, England, and France had yet to be heard from; that it was still possible for them to work out a juster economic organization, without being forced either to subjugate the unions or to stifle all spirit of criticism.

A thousand questions were raised. To try to answer them, it was decided to hold another meeting, to devote

another session of the Société to a careful examination of
Élie Halévy's propositions. . . .

In presenting them now for public discussion, we are
not only fulfilling a pious duty towards the memory of
the friend who has been taken from us: his example—of
the freest, most systematic, and best informed thought
possible—is one that no one in these days can undervalue.

C. Bouglé[6]

[6] [Célestin Bouglé, 1870–1940. A student of Durkheim, he
taught social philosophy at the Sorbonne from 1901. In 1920
he became director of the Centre de Documentation Sociale at
the École Normale Supérieure. He became co-director of the
École Normale in 1928 and subsequently director. He was one
of Élie Halévy's closest friends.]

CONTENTS

CONTENTS

Appendices

A NOTE ON THE TRANSLATION

L'ère des tyrannies appeared in 1938. Opportunity has been taken to correct a few minor editorial and typographical errors in the original edition. An occasional ambiguity or error of fact has been commented upon in footnotes, and from time to time references have been added to subsequently published works that throw some light on the subject under discussion. In the case of Halévy's translations of quotations from English, every effort has been made to trace the originals; where this has proved impossible, through lack of citation or unavailability of sources, the present text includes retranslations from Halévy's French, a necessity pointed out in footnotes. When possible, citations lacking in the original have been supplied, and footnotes have been made to conform to normal English usage. Footnotes or portions of footnotes enclosed in square brackets are the responsibility of the translator; footnotes without square brackets appear in the original edition.

Since the studies in this collection cover so wide a range of topics, most of them outside the immediate area of my own scholarly concerns, many substantive questions have arisen along with the inevitable problems of language and usage. While responsibility for any remaining errors is entirely mine, I must thank the many friends and colleagues who have borne my steady barrage of questions with such good humor. As always, some have been more put upon than others. Many references had to be tracked down in London; that in some instances they could not be found is not for want of tireless and resourceful pursuit by my student, Mr. Stephen Koss. Large parts of the translation have been read and helpfully criticized by my colleagues, Professors Peter Gay, Charles Issawi, and Orest Ranum. Professor Fritz Stern was not only a critic, but, at the very beginning, was responsible for my undertaking the task and, at the very end, has added a commentary which much increases the book's value. Finally, I want to express my deepest appreciation to Élie Halévy's niece, Dr. Henriette Noufflard Guy-Loé, whose warm encouragement of this enterprise and whose patient, rigorous and subtle criticism of the translation have been invaluable to me. I hope that this volume will lead others to a small share in what she described to me as *"un souvenir bien vivant de l'homme merveilleux qu'il était—noble, droit et bon, avec une intelligence lumineuse. . . ."*

R.K.W.

Columbia University
New York

THE ERA OF TYRANNIES

SISMONDI[1]

A Critique of Industrialist Optimism

Jean-Charles-Léonard Simonde (the original name of the man who was later to call himself Sismondi) was born in Geneva on May 9, 1773. Geneva, the old holy city of Calvin, humanized by the rival and nevertheless complementary influences of Voltaire and Rousseau, was the birthplace of liberal Protestantism. The meeting-place of the Latin spirit with the German, it was the home of a salutary moral and intellectual cosmopolitanism and the future seat of the League of Nations. Charles Simonde's family had fled to Geneva from the Dauphiné during the Wars of Religion. His father, Gédéon, was a Calvinist minister. When he was only fifteen, before he had completed the solid, cold education of the Genevans of his time, the financial ruin of his family forced him to go to work at once. Necker, the Genevan banker, had been summoned by Louis XVI to rescue French finances. He floated a large loan to which a host of his fellow citizens enthusiastically subscribed; Gédéon was one of them and lost his entire investment. So Charles Simonde went to Lyon to learn banking. But the Revolution broke out in Paris, then in Geneva. More and more pressed for money, fleeing from poverty, the whole Simonde family (a Swiss family is always ready to emigrate) crossed over to England. Charles learned to speak English like an Englishman, to love England as a kind of second country, to think

[1] The introduction to Élie Halévy's selection of extracts, *Sismondi* (1933), published in the series *Réformateurs sociaux*, edited by C. Bouglé.

through (and to adopt unreservedly) the principles of political liberalism and of economic liberalism as well. In 1803 he published a treatise, *De la richesse commerciale, ou principes d'économie politique appliqués à la législation du commerce* (*On Commercial Wealth, or Principles of Political Economy applied to Commercial Legislation*), an unoriginal work, a mere popularization of the ideas of Adam Smith, but one much noticed at the time, for Jean-Baptiste Say's treatise had not yet appeared and it met a need in French-speaking countries. It should be added that, at that time, Geneva had become a French city in spite of itself, and, under the cover of political economy, Simonde attacked the administrative despotism of consular France. In the last sentences of the book Simonde vigorously expresses the ideas he was later to do so much to undermine: "The Legislators of Europe are afraid that the manufactures of their countries lack buyers; they fail to see that the manufactures of their countries are not nearly enough to meet the needs of buyers. . . . They take precautions against abundance, when it is want that pursues them. Finally, they are simply unable to see the consoling truth, that whatever reversal any of our manufacturers may experience, the nation's capital will never remain idle in the hands of its owners, and that it will never be employed by them otherwise than, directly or indirectly, to maintain productive labor, to spread prosperity among workingmen, and, by opening a new industry, to make up for the collapse of those that adverse circumstances have struck down."

De la richesse commerciale was not, however, the first work young Simonde had published. Two years before, he had brought out a *Tableau de l'agriculture toscane* (*A View of Tuscan Agriculture*). Why Tuscan agriculture? Because, after his visit to London, a new foreign influence, Italian following on English, had taken hold of the young man from Geneva. In 1792 the Simonde family, brought back from London to Geneva by homesickness, had to take to the road again, pursued by the Terror. They crossed the Alps this time and bought an estate in Tuscany. Simonde developed a taste for this new country; he liked the simplicity of its ways and the happy balance of its wealth. He wanted to celebrate the happiness of the Tuscan peasant, and he did it poetically. He worked out a political philosophy, compounded of English liberalism, Genevan republicanism, and admiration for what remained in Italy, according to him, of the old autonomous spirit of the free communes of the Middle Ages. His whole family became half Italian; thereafter, he himself divided his time between the neighborhood of Geneva and the neighborhood of Pescia and undertook an *Histoire des républiques italiennes au moyen âge* (*History of the Italian Republics in the Middle Ages*), the first volume of which appeared in 1804, and which was to make him famous. From that time on, in his own eyes as in those of the entire western public, he was an Italian patriot as well as a citizen of Geneva. He even made, or thought he made, an important discovery in the course of his historical research. In the fifteenth century one of the "seven first families of Florence," the Sismondi family, fleeing from ruin and civil war, had taken refuge in the Dauphiné. And it was from the Dauphiné a century later that the Simonde family (then calling themselves Symond) had left to settle in Geneva. Beyond a doubt it was the same family. Charles Simonde became Simonde de Sismondi, S. de Sismondi, de Sismondi. People in Geneva laughed when they saw the respectable bourgeois come back from across the mountains decked out with a quaint title. But, naive as they are, such frauds are usually successful: it is only a matter of time. How many people suspect today that Sismondi did not bear that name from birth?

Having returned from Tuscany to Geneva, Charles Simonde (whom from now on we shall call Sismondi, like everyone else) came to know Mme. de Staël and, with Benjamin Constant, became one of the regular visitors to

3

Coppet. After England and Italy, was he going to discover Germany? The discovery seems to have made little impact on his mind. Possibly Johannes von Müller guided his historical research, but there was nothing specifically German in the outlook of Johannes von Müller. He loathed the very Germanic and bothersome Schlegel. While he was publishing the sixteen volumes of his monumental *Histoire des républiques italiennes,* he plunged into the study of comparative literature, planning to devote two separate works to the literature of the South and of the North, but he wrote only the first; he remained a prisoner of the Latin world.

Paradoxical though it seems at first glance, he had yet to discover France. Sismondi liked neither the France of former times—of the St. Bartholomew Massacre and the Revocation of the Edict of Nantes—nor Jacobin and imperial France, which, ever centralizing and despotic, had just robbed Geneva of her freedom. "I have never seen Paris," he wrote in 1809, "but I detest it even before seeing it, and, moreover, I am afraid of it, because I should not want what little pleasure I might perhaps find there to lessen my hatred for the city and its inhabitants and the nation of which it is the capital." But before long he had to go to Paris on publishing business. The salons of the Faubourg St. Germain at once began to fight over him and completely conquered the serious young man who very much liked the company of women. When he was hardly back in Geneva, he wrote: "After five months of so busy a life and of a continual feast of the mind, I think only of the friends I have left behind, I live on memories, and I understand more than ever before the deep nostalgia of my famous friend who found her exile such a cheerless desert." But was it merely that a "little pleasure" had weakened his will to resist? In actuality his reconciliation with French culture, the beginning of which was so overwhelming and the consequences of which were to be so lasting, grew from deep causes on which we must dwell for a moment if we want to understand the nature of the "conversion" that took place in his mind at this time.

He came to Paris at the moment when the disasters of the Grand Army began, and when western liberals realized—going like history itself from one extreme to the other—that they no longer had to hate France as the home of warlike arrogance, but must love her as the last refuge of liberty. The more disasters rained down, the more Sismondi felt himself French. "There is a man for whom I have a strong dislike which has not changed at all; but there is not one of his enemies for whom I have any affection or esteem." "I understand hatred for a monarch whose ambition has turned to madness, but it does not compare to the contempt I feel for imbecile rulers; I do not know which is stronger, indignation or grief, when I see so many kings and so many governments re-established only by virtue of their stupidity and their utter incapacity."

In spite of everything, his sympathy for England persisted. Wanting to render British opinion favorable to the liberties of his native land, he presented Geneva to the English as "an English city on the continent . . . , the champion of civil and religious liberty, of English liberty, wise and strong, both progressive and conservative." He declared, moreover, that among the nations he held only England "in high esteem." She seemed to him "without equal." France merely followed after. But when the Hundred Days came, when Sismondi, like Benjamin Constant and almost as explosively, rallied to the Napoleonic Empire of the Champ de Mai, how could he not be shaken in his worship of British civilization? One appreciates the profound revolution that was taking place at that time in many liberal minds when one sees Jean-Baptiste Say, the follower of the ideas of Adam Smith and the most obstinately anti-Napoleonic of the French ideologues, devoting the whole of a little book to a denunciation of the vices of British society: the contrast between extreme

5

wealth and extreme poverty, the decline of education among the working classes and of culture among the middle classes. But Jean-Baptiste Say remained faithful to the doctrines of Adam Smith and attributed so many evils to the fact that the ruling classes in England, betraying her genuine national traditions, had gone over to a policy of war and to agricultural protection. Let them cut down military expenditures, give up the conquest of colonies, lower and then abolish import duties on grain, and prosperity would again reign with liberty. It remained for Sismondi, two years later, to go further than Jean-Baptiste Say and to note the insufficiency of the remedies proposed by classical political economy and the theoretical weakness of that political economy.

The *Encyclopaedia Britannica* was a famous publication in England; it had become a sort of permanent institution, brought up to date by one new edition after the other. For the moment, to avoid the expense of a complete resetting, the editors decided to limit themselves to a six-volume supplement. To write the article on "Political Economy," they turned to the still popular author of *Richesse commerciale,* and Sismondi set to work. He returned to political economy for the first time in fifteen years during which he had been occupied with very different subjects; confronting his old ideas of fifteen years before and earlier with the facts, he became aware of a profound discordance between them. He wrote the article that had been commissioned in the spirit those who had asked for it wanted. But at the same time he was at work on the draft of a complete treatise in a different spirit; finished at the end of 1818, it appeared at the beginning of 1819. Perhaps in contrast to the subtitle of his work of 1803, *Principes d'économie politique appliqués à la législation du commerce* (*Principles of Political Economy applied to Commercial Legislation*), or to the title of the work published by Ricardo in 1817, *Principles of Political Economy and Taxation,* he called his book *New Principles*

6

(*Nouveaux principes d'économie politique, ou de la richesse dans ses rapports avec la population*) (*New Principles of Political Economy, or, On Wealth in relation to
Population*). Beneath the false appearance of England's
political liberalism he discerned an economic constitution,
the true name of which was not liberty but servitude, and
he thus found himself led to judge English civilization as
he would never formerly have dreamed of doing. "One
nation alone shows the unceasing contrast of its apparent
wealth with the frightful misery of a tenth of its population, reduced to living on public charity. But that nation,
so worthy of imitation in so many ways, so dazzling even
in her faults, has seduced all the statesmen of the continent by her example. And if these reflections can no longer
be useful to her, at least I shall consider that I have served
humanity and my countrymen by showing the dangers of
the course she is taking, and by establishing, through her
own experience, that basing all political economy on the
principle of unlimited competition is to justify the efforts
of every man against society and to sacrifice the interest of
humanity to the simultaneous action of all forms of industrial greed."

* * *

Let us try to define these "new principles" on which
Sismondi's political economy is based, and to do so, at the
outset, by comparing them to the economic "orthodoxy"
(using the expression he invented) that he proposed to
undermine.

First, at the base of this orthodoxy was a theory, latent
in the great work of Adam Smith, set out by Sismondi in
1803 in the final sentences of his *Richesse commerciale*
which we have quoted above, and which had just been
given classical form by Jean-Baptiste Say and James Mill:
the theory of markets. According to this theory, the glut-
ting of markets and the phenomena of a slump are facts
of little consequence, temporary and partial disorders that

7

would disappear when order is re-established. For goods are exchanged against goods, all goods against all goods. Every commodity brought into the market in itself constitutes the demand for another commodity. If, occasionally, there is general overproduction, it could never be general overproduction of the same article. That is to say, at one place in the world, certain goods cannot be sold, while elsewhere other goods cannot be sold, because customs duties constitute artificial obstacles to bringing them together. Abolish these obstacles; let everything obey the natural law of exchange. Liberty is abundance; equality is equality in abundance.

In 1817 Ricardo incorporated this law in his theory. But at the same time he based the theory on a law Adam Smith had not known: the Malthusian principle of population. According to the terms of this "principle," stripped of its pseudo-mathematical apparatus, the human race, which goes on steadily increasing, presses constantly on the means of subsistence, given that it lives in a world of limited extent and fertility. According to Ricardo's theory (the details of which need not concern us here), this results in the division of society into three classes—landlords, capitalists, and laborers—which are in conflict with each other, a conflict that, in some ways, grows worse as the human race progresses and multiplies. Did Sismondi retain this pessimistic aspect of Ricardian political economy to oppose it to the optimism of the theory of markets? Others would do so, but not he; he did not seem to see that it was possible to turn Ricardo back on himself. A strange oversight, but one common to many of his contemporaries, and it is in Sismondi's thought that we must seek the reasons for it.

At the outset Sismondi admitted that what repelled him in the modern economists, what repelled him to the point where he found Ricardo barely readable, was the abstract oversimplification of their speculations. "Our mind is incapable of admitting the abstractions they demand of us;

but this repugnance itself is a warning that we deviate from truth when in the social sciences, where everything is connected, we force ourselves to isolate a principle and to see nothing but that principle." Adam Smith proceeded quite differently, as an historian who repeatedly appealed to experience: that is why Sismondi never tired of declaring himself a disciple of Adam Smith, in spite of inevitable disagreements, while he appeared as an inveterate enemy of the economists after Smith who wanted to transform political economy into a science of principles. He liked to emphasize the complex nature of the subjects of social science; being complex, they are variable: hence one can vary them at will, within the limits of what experience shows to be possible. He hoped thus to escape from what he considered the second vice of Ricardian doctrine, its fatalism. In the hands of orthodox economists, the science "is so speculative that it seems detached from everything practical." Ricardo's system tended to prove "that everything is all the same, that nothing does harm to anything." Perhaps the fatalism and the oversimplification were tied together. In orthodox political economy, the division of society into classes is deduced from certain simple axioms; it is natural that it, too, should be simple, and that the appearance of three separate classes of landlords, capitalists and laborers, should have the same quality of necessity inherent in simple laws of nature. Sismondi took an entirely different point of view. He did not deny that a scientific political economy is possible; but the distinctions between classes, which are the ever-changing, infinitely complex product of history, are a point of departure for it, not a conclusion. Given a certain division of economic society into classes, and starting from the existence of those classes, one can establish the laws that necessarily govern the society made up of them and the effect of the operation of those laws on the happiness of the individuals who are members of it. If the effect is evil, one must find out, on the basis of experience, how it is possible to change

9

relationships that have nothing immutable about them. This is the art of politics—founded on science, but on a less abstract, and for that very reason less passive, science than that of the fashionable economists.

Now, according to Sismondi, we are members of a society that in contrast to all prior forms of society is characterized by its division into two classes: property-owners, whose income represents no labor, and workers, who possess no property; capitalists (under this rubric we must include the owners of land as well as of industrial capital) and proletarians. For the economist faced with such a society, the problem is both theoretical and practical. Theoretically, the problem is to understand the operation of the laws of exchange, the very basis of the science founded by Adam Smith, when they are applied to it. Practically, the problem is to know if the unhindered operation of those laws is favorable to the interests of the human race, and what institutional reforms could and should be introduced to correct the bad effects of laissez-faire.

Is this division of society into two classes such that the extension of free competition must constantly narrow the gap and correct its bad effects? This is the thesis upheld by the orthodox school. Let us suppose that a manufacturer has invented a process that allows him to produce his goods at lower cost. According to this school, what will happen? He will derive only a temporary advantage from this saving in the cost of production. Very quickly, knowledge of his process will spread; other producers will copy it; and the cost of production, on the one hand, and the price of the goods, on the other, will be lowered for everyone without distinction. But, according to Sismondi, things go quite differently. For manufacturers, the adoption of a new process implies the sacrifice of a quantity of fixed capital and also of acquired habits (by themselves and their workers), a sacrifice to which they will resign themselves only in the last extremity. It will be much easier for the inventor of the process to extend its application and to enlarge his factory: he alone will lower the price of his merchandise and, by turning out a quantity sufficient to satisfy an ever-growing demand, will ruin his competitors. In short, instead of tending finally to re-establish equality between him and his competitors, competition will make him master of the market. Thanks to large-scale production, the division of labor, and machines, competition will bring about the concentration of wealth in the hands of a smaller and smaller number of individuals and the concentration of business in larger and larger firms.

Although this society founded on inequality of wealth is not just, does it have the advantage of being stable? Not at all, according to Sismondi; that is the second point of his demonstration, and perhaps the more important. By cutting down the number of small producers, who are the representatives of the middle class, the system of concentration allows only a small number of very rich individuals to survive, facing a large number of very poor individuals. Now, by production on a large scale, these workers turn out a greater and greater quantity of goods with the same amount of labor. For whom? The workers? Thanks to the new distribution of wealth, they grow steadily poorer; their purchasing power is shrinking. The employers? If the goods are basic necessities, they cannot consume them in unlimited amounts, since they are very few in number; only luxury goods can be bought and consumed without limit. But the characteristic of the factory system is precisely to produce not luxury goods but goods of ordinary quality and general utility. In short, the effect of the factory system is to increase society's ability to produce at the same time that it restricts its ability to consume. The only way for manufacturers to get rid of their products is to seek out foreign markets not yet invaded by the factory system. After the first market has been saturated, or after the factory system has been forced on it, it will no longer be a market for exports, and a new crisis of overproduction will appear, until the discovery of some other outlet abroad. And so it will go until the whole world is overrun with the products of the factory system and the radical absurdity of it all becomes plain. Contrary to what is maintained in the theory of markets, glut is the characteristic trait of the economy in the present age, the usual result of the factory system.

According to Sismondi, the basic fault of orthodox political economy is that it is not concerned with society in its totality and complexity, but with the owner of wealth who gets rich by selling the products of his lands and factories. While it refuted the error of mercantilism once and for all, orthodox political economy has formed a new kind of mercantilism, looking only to the interests of the seller, fancying that, in doing so, it is assuring the interests of the whole of society, which would be true only if society were made up entirely of merchants. It is not true political economy—the art of managing society in the general interest—but the art of individual enrichment; to use the word Sismondi invented, it is "chrematistic." That is why it makes no sense. It is natural that what interests the owner of wealth is increasing the "net product" of human labor, while what concerns the human race is increasing the "gross product." It is natural that what interests the owner of wealth is, in the language of economic science, the "exchangeable value" of the goods he puts on the market—the price at which they will exchange for other goods —while what matters for society is their "utility," their "use value." The proponents of the theory of markets want to consider only the independent producer who will, once he has partially satisfied his own needs, exchange his surplus with others like him, in order to satisfy his remaining needs while also satisfying those of other men. In this the political economists fail to grasp the true character of the modern industrial society they boast they are the interpreters of; industrial leaders work, and employ others to work, only to sell. The world reflected by the theory of markets is, without its authors' realizing it, the old world, the outmoded world of "territorial wealth," in which production was undertaken only for a market limited and known in advance. The modern world is a world of commercial wealth, of blind, unbridled production for a market that, as it were, flees before the seller: its outlets are closed as a matter of course as the industrial leaders bring under their control a steadily growing number of poor workers, constantly thrown out of work.

*　*　*

What was the cure for these evils? Was it what would later be called the "socialist" cure? Sismondi knew the founders of socialism. We know that he saw Robert Owen in Paris in 1818, that is, at the exact moment when economic problems began to concern him again. Can we not conjecture either that he wanted to meet him because he had been struck by reading the numerous pamphlets in which Robert Owen maintained the reality of industrial overproduction, the urgency of legal limitation of the working day, and the need to substitute a society producing for use for a society producing for exchange, or even that a knowledge of these writings had brought about Sismondi's conversion and had led him to try to found political economy on "new principles"? The views of Robert Owen grew more consistent; and, under his influence, a group of disciples advocated replacing present-day society, based on exchange, by a "co-operative" society. In France, moreover, Fourier began to find admirers. But if Sismondi was interested in the propaganda of the disciples of Robert Owen and Fourier, it was only insofar as he agreed with their criticism of society as it was; he was never to accommodate himself to the remedies they advocated. He was too prudent an historian for that, too persuaded of the complexity of human affairs. "Who would be the man powerful enough," he wrote, "to conceive an organization that does not yet exist, to see the future when we already have such difficulty in seeing the present?" As for the

13

Saint-Simonians, whose propaganda was making a great stir, it goes without saying that they would never have Sismondi's sympathy. For there is a point on which these opponents of competition were in agreement with the theorists of unlimited competition; they did not admit the existence of the problem of overproduction. And Sismondi had nothing but suspicion and distaste for wild-eyed optimism of any kind.

He did not want a sweeping regulation of the conditions of labor. Although neither Fourier nor Saint-Simon nor their disciples were in any proper meaning of the word egalitarians, he was especially concerned in his criticisms with Owenism, which is egalitarian. He did not believe that an absolute equalization of wealth was possible without violence, which would render the new order odious and precarious. He was content with a moderate inequality of conditions, similar to that seen in certain regions where industrialism had not yet penetrated. Did he dream of a return to the past, of a "reaction," in the philosophical sense of the word? At times it seems so. Thus, in discussing the possibility of government intervention to remedy the ills of modern society, he came up against the standing objection of the orthodox economists that any legal interference with production is bad because it tends to cut down output. But his answer was to ask what that mattered, if the evil from which modern society suffers is an excess of production. His thought can, however, be interpreted in a less radically reactionary sense. He expressly declared that he was not opposed to the advance of mechanization, provided that it led to a decrease in the suffering of men, of all men, and not to the opulence of some, while the rest toiled in misery. He wanted the rich not to abuse the accumulated power the possession of machines gave them by increasing their profits while worsening the living conditions of the workers they employed. In this way, he wanted to protect the rich themselves against the thoughtlessness of greed—because better-off workers

14

would have greater purchasing power, and society would be less exposed to those periodic gluts of the market that are a permanent cause of insecurity for everyone, rich as well as poor. He wanted economic growth, not paralyzed but regulated by law, to follow the growth of consumption instead of preceding it by a giant step as happens, to everyone's misfortune, in our monstrous state of society.

So far as land goes, the legislator should favor the development of small holdings, less by new laws than by abrogation of old laws hindering such a development. He should do the same for movable property. Confronting a world in which a small number of rich men command an army of poor men, he should give the workers freedom to form combinations that, by uniting their individual weaknesses, would allow them to offer some resistance to oppression by the owners. He should, moreover—this time by positive laws—secure the limitation of the working day, the outlawing of child labor, and a weekly holiday; and he should work towards the organization of a new industrial system (inspired, he noted almost regretfully, by the old corporative regime) that would give the workers "a right of guarantee by those who employ them," requiring employers by law to protect their employees against the risks of their working lives, unemployment in particular. Sismondi suggested these remedies to his readers hesitantly, in a tone of extreme circumspection. "I confess," he wrote, "after having shown, in my view, where justice lies, I do not feel able to work out the means of execution." But although he almost came to think of the task as really "beyond human power," we should recognize that he was encountering a difficulty that stemmed from the very nature of his philosophy. His timidity was a reasoned timidity.

When he admitted the necessity of breaking with friends whose political opinions he shared, we should recognize that in his heart he always remained faithful to their liberalism. These liberals were not anarchists, enemies of all law. They wanted the laws to protect the individual against the excessive power of the sovereign, whether the sovereign was a man or a multitude. It was in the same spirit that Sismondi, having seen servitude born of free competition, wanted that freedom restrained, but always prudently and tentatively, since in the last analysis it was always to save liberty that restraints were imposed. When Sismondi proposed that the worker have the right to "guarantees" against his employer, was he not perhaps borrowing that word "guarantee" from the language of constitutional law? Are his basic assumptions not revealed in his denunciation of the capitalist's power over the proletarian as "unconstitutional"?

The *Nouveaux principes d'économie politique,* the first edition of which appeared in 1819, reached a second edition in 1827; at the beginning of this second edition Sismondi put a triumphant preface. A new crisis of overproduction had just burst on England after several years of prosperity; and France, which was beginning to industrialize, had just gone through her first crisis. So his predictions were borne out. Were years of fame, then, going to come for him? As certain of his economic doctrine as of his political doctrine, and, now that he was over fifty, having reached his full maturity, perhaps he hoped so. But the years that followed were, for him, years of decline.

He did not recapture the success of his *Histoire des républiques italiennes au moyen âge.* The dreary volumes (more than forty in all) of his *Histoire des Français (History of the French)* were swallowed up one after the other in general indifference. He plunged into causes dear to liberal opinion—abolition of the slave-trade, freedom for Italy. But the heterodox opinions advanced in his *Nouveaux principes* marked him as an eccentric thinker; everyone looked at him askance.

In 1834 the workers' insurrection at Lyon was crushed in blood. Sismondi, in Geneva, annoyed everyone by declaring "the massacre by the moderates and the friends of

order of people who had given no offense the most atro-
cious act of these forty-five years of revolution": the Genevan bourgeoisie classed him with the Jacobins. But the
Swiss radicals demanded that Switzerland be transformed
into a unitary democracy, and that was enough to throw
Sismondi, the enemy of all centralization and an impeni-
tent federalist, into the aristocratic camp. Ill, having made
a love-match which was good but hardly perfect—far from
it—he ended his days a lonely and hypochondriacal old
man. His neighbors recalled that, out of hatred for overproduction, he chose the slowest and oldest day laborer to
plough his land, and the least sought-after artisan to repair
his house. In France, in Paris, who understood him? Vil-
lermé, in a memoir on the state of the working classes,
did not mention his name, and Sismondi felt quite bitter
about it. De Villeneuve Bargemont, in his *Économie politique chrétienne* (*Christian Political Economy*), paid tribute to him; but it was tribute Sismondi could well have
done without. Sismondi had his own way of interpreting a
return to the Middle Ages. For Sismondi, the Middle Ages
meant weakness of the central power, federalism, and
town autonomy. For Villeneuve, as for many others, they
meant order, hierarchy, and the "sacerdotalism" Sismondi
detested. With a view to defining once and for all the
whole of his social philosophy, Sismondi had the happy
idea of bringing together and publishing, under the title of
Études sur les sciences sociales (*Studies in the Social Sciences*), an old treatise on political constitutions which,
forty years earlier, had not found a publisher, and a series
of extracts from his books, pamphlets, and articles on
political economy: the book seemed hardly to attract attention. "I am leaving this world," he wrote shortly before his death (he died on June 25, 1842), "without having made any impression, and nothing will be done."

"Without having made any impression." How much he
exaggerated, if he was really saying what he thought!
But did he not want, rather, to say that he had had a dif-

ferent influence from what he had hoped for, that his influence had made itself felt in the wrong way? For there developed in France what can be called a "Sismondism" of the left, which exploited his critical analysis of capitalism for the benefit of socialism, while Sismondi was as opposed to socialism as to capitalism, seeing in them only the two sides of the same form of centralizing and oppressive society. When Proudhon declared that "property is theft"—that it is, in other words, identical to its opposite and constitutes a contradictory idea, that it is not only "unjust" but "impossible"—he was influenced by Sismondi, without saying so, perhaps without knowing it. When Louis Blanc explained that "for the people competition is a system of extermination and for the bourgeoisie an ever-present cause of impoverishment and ruin," it was only Sismondism dramatized. How can Sismondi have read either the *Mémoire sur la propriété*[2] or the *Organisation du travail* (*Organization of Labor*), and not have been appalled to see his denunciations of industrialism lead to the triumph either of levelling anarchism or, still worse, of egalitarian Robespierrism?

Sismondi died, and a young philosopher of the Hegelian left, a young revolutionary named Karl Marx, came from Cologne to Paris to study the French socialists. The task he set himself was to apply to economic and social reality —to give it roots, so to speak—that grand philosophy that explained the development of the universe as the dialectical interplay of contradictions incessantly resolved and incessantly reborn. Sismondism gave him the key to the problem he was concerned about. Modern society was running to its ruin, driven straight to the communism that was at once its negation and its necessary result, thanks to the unbalanced, contradictory character of its material structure. It would not be paradoxical to argue that, in its critical aspect, Sismondism served as the basis for the

[2] [Better known as *Qu'est-ce que la propriété?* (*What is property?*)]

Communist Manifesto, published a little more than five years after Sismondi's death. Why should we not assume that Sismondi foresaw with dread this revolutionary interpretation of his doctrines, and that he was alarmed to see that "nothing would be done" to prevent society from going where it would inevitably go if left to itself, that is, as Sismondi saw it, towards catastrophe?

* * *

More than a century has gone by since the publication of the *Nouveaux principes,* nearly a century since Sismondi's death. An economic crisis, unprecedented in modern history, plagues the human race. It corresponds to the outline traced by Sismondi. There is a world-wide crisis of overproduction, agricultural as well as industrial, a glut in every market. The friends of peace blame the war for many of the evils, and they are not entirely wrong; but the relationship between the war and the economic troubles that have followed it is not so direct as they would have it. By itself, war destroys capital and lessens output; its direct effect must be and in fact is underproduction and scarcity. Should we conclude that, by creating new nationalities and intensifying national feelings, the war has multiplied customs barriers, raised their level, and brought about the glut of markets only by interfering with exchange? To say that would be to verify the old theory of markets, the thesis of J.-B. Say and Ricardo. But must we not say, rather, that if every country is surrounded by higher customs barriers, it is because, suffering from an excess of goods of all kinds at home, no nation wants to make the internal difficulty worse by letting in foreign goods? Must we not say that if war is the cause of the evils we suffer, it is so indirectly because, the art of war having been industrialized like the arts of peace, the last great war had the new effect in the military history of the human race of forcing the overindustrialization of the belligerent nations and of speeding up the coming of a crisis

19

which, by the normal progress of industrial technology, would not have broken until a half-century or a century later? How are the overindustrialized nations to be made either to go back, according to Sismondi's plan, or to be pushed forward towards a new system, which the western Marxists seem to have difficulty in bringing about? Whatever may be the issue of our troubles, there, it seems, is how the problem must be posed: it was Sismondi, not Jean-Baptiste Say, who formulated it for the first time, more than a century ago.

SAINT-SIMONIAN ECONOMIC DOCTRINE

I. *The Economic Doctrine of Saint-Simon*[1]

The nineteenth century is gone; we are beginning to understand it. Twenty years ago, we were not aware, as we are today, of the sources of two great movements—positivism and socialism—which kept the whole century in ferment. Littré was then thought to be the great man of positivism. Later, Auguste Comte was rehabilitated. Then we began to ask if, in tracing the origins of positivism, we did not have to go beyond Auguste Comte to the real originator, Saint-Simon. As for socialism, the name of Karl Marx seemed to sum up all theoretical socialism; even Proudhon had been forgotten. But the real inventors of Marxian socialism were all those theorists, dead before the middle of the century, whose varying doctrines Marx was able to bring together into a single system. So once again the attention of historians is directed to the French socialists in the time of Louis Philippe and, ultimately, to the members of the Saint-Simonian school. Once more we are led to the great precursor. To know positivism and socialism at their source, we must study the school in which the two words were first used; we must go back to the early years of the century when, in the words of Saint-Simon himself, "the Revolution had made Frenchmen enthusiastic about politics."

This essay will not deal with Saint-Simonian positivism; it is in connection with the economy under industrialism,

[1] An essay published in the *Revue du Mois,* IV, 641–676 (December 10, 1907).

21

as Saint-Simon and the Saint-Simonians saw it, that we believe we can bring a new precision on many points of detail to the results obtained in the past five or six years by a good number of students. Saint-Simon began to write and to have an influence really only after 1814; at that time, his social doctrine hardly differed from the liberalism of the classical economists. He died in 1825; five years after his death, when the July Revolution took place, a Saint-Simonian school had appeared, preaching a complete socialism. We shall return later to the history of Saint-Simonianism after the death of Saint-Simon. Here let us limit ourselves to examining the gradual changes in Saint-Simon's thought between 1814 and 1825 and the causes that determined those changes.

In 1812 Napoleon's armies evacuated Russia. In 1813 they evacuated Germany. In 1814 they fought on the very soil of France against the armies of the European coalition. The Emperor abdicated. In 1815, after a new and final convulsion, the dream of universal monarchy was gone for France. England had finally triumphed over France, the free power over the strong power, the commercial power over the military power: "Carthage" over "Rome." While the continent was being ruined by war, England expanded her industry, her commerce, and her merchant marine. The time finally came when the impoverishment of Europe went beyond what the English merchants desired; the people of the continent had become too poor to buy their goods. For the English to continue as the suppliers of Europe, the people of the continent had again to become prosperous enough to provide a market for English producers. An era of commerce and freedom had to succeed the era of conquest and despotism; war was bankrupt.

This was, at any rate, the moral a number of French publicists drew from events. In 1813, in Hanover, Benjamin Constant had published *De l'esprit de conquête et de l'usurpation, dans leurs rapports avec la civilisation* (*On the Spirit of Conquest and Usurpation, in Relation to*

Civilization). After the fall of the Empire, three men aspired to the leadership of pacific liberalism. There were, first, two young lawyers turned journalists, Charles Comte and Charles Dunoyer, who founded a periodical called *Le Censeur* (*The Censor*) to propagate their ideas. Then there was Count Henri de Saint-Simon, an older man who had not yet succeeded in satisfying the literary and scientific ambitions that consumed him. Having got rich by some lucky speculations, he lost everything. He deluged the Emperor and the Institute with memoranda proposing to bring out a "new encyclopedia," to organize the whole of human knowledge definitively on the "positive" basis of experience, to found a single science which would include, in addition to mechanics and physics, "physiology," the science of man as an individual and in society. From that time on, he was occupied exclusively with moral and political questions, and for three years, from 1814 to 1817, Charles Comte, Dunoyer, and Saint-Simon professed the same social philosophy and advocated the same policy. Sometimes one, sometimes the other, took the lead, so it is often difficult to disentangle the interlocking influences.

In 1814, assisted by Augustin Thierry, a young teacher of history whom he had just made his secretary, Saint-Simon published *De la réorganisation de la société européenne, ou de la nécessité et des moyens de rassembler les peuples de l'Europe en un seul corps politique en conservant à chacun son indépendance nationale* (*On the Reorganization of European Society, or, On the Necessity and Means of Bringing the Nations of Europe Together in One Body Politic, While Preserving the National Independence of Each*). As the title indicates, the problem was to re-establish order in a Europe "disorganized"[2] since the Reformation and to erect a system of international peace analogous to that which had existed in the Middle Ages, when European opinion thought it legitimate

[2] Saint-Simon, *Oeuvres* (1868–1875), I, 162.

for the Pope to arbitrate among rulers, but resting on new principles better adapted to modern times. To bring this about, all of Europe had first to become politically *homogeneous*, and all nations had to have the same institutions. Second, these institutions had to be "organized . . . in such a way that every question of public interest would be dealt with thoroughly and completely,"[3] and a liberal form of government adopted—a mixed government, made up of three powers, like the English: Saint-Simon offered England and its constitution as a model for all of Europe. "Separated from the continent by the sea, she ceased to have anything in common with the people who live there, while creating a national religion and a government different from all the governments of Europe. Her constitution was founded, not on prejudices and customs, but on what must be the basis of every constitution at all times and in all places, the freedom and happiness of the people."[4] Europe would have reached its ultimate organization "if all its nations, each one governed by a parliament, would recognize the supremacy of a general parliament superior to all national governments and invested with the power to settle their disputes."[5]

The necessary preliminary to this European organization was the alliance and federation of France and England, the two nations in western Europe that had already won their constitutional liberty. "Evils will begin to diminish, troubles to settle, wars to disappear": the veritable realization of the golden age that "the imagination of poets has put in the cradle of the human race along with the ignorance and grossness of earliest times," but that must be set "in the future . . . in the perfection of the social order."[6]

In short, according to Saint-Simon and Augustin Thierry, positive politics was parliamentary politics. The same at-

[3] *Ibid.*, I, 183.
[4] *Ibid.*, I, 163–164.
[5] *Ibid.*, I, 197.
[6] *Ibid.*, I, 247–248.

titude was also taken by the editors of the *Censeur;* and Charles Comte developed ideas very close to those Saint-Simon had just advanced in an article in the third volume, "Sur la situation de l'Europe, sur les causes de ses guerres, et sur les moyens d'y mettre fin" ("On the Situation of Europe, the Causes of Her Wars, and the Means of Putting an End to It").[7] There is no doubt that he was influenced by Saint-Simon. He was less optimistic; he did not proclaim the advent of the golden age, and, in spite of his pacifism, he feared the coming of new wars. He was less systematic and refused to go into detail as to "the form that must be given" to parliamentary government and as to "the constitutional machinery."

He was less confident than Saint-Simon that England would take the lead in the European federation. He was convinced, however, that an alliance of France, England, and (he added) Spain would benefit civilization as a whole. Like Saint-Simon, he believed that "this alliance can be lasting and advantageous only insofar as it is founded on a confederation based on justice, equality, moderation, and the sharing of the advantages of commerce and colonies."[8] Finally, like Saint-Simon, he set out the main characteristics "of the structure of a confederation of free peoples." "Only free peoples can come together in a confederation; moreover, they must have similar constitutions in order to be able to move steadily towards creating the central government which must unite them." This central government "must be representative and similar in kind to the separate governments of each federated state. . . . It must be placed so as to have no standpoint but the general interest of the confedera-

[7] *Le Censeur, ou examen des actes et des ouvrages qui tendent à detruire ou à consolider la constitution de l'État,* III, 1 ff. (*The Censor, or, An Examination of the Acts and Publications which Tend to Destroy or to Consolidate the Constitution of the State*).

[8] *Ibid.,* III, 26–27.

tion."[9] And he assigned to it the same functions that Saint-Simon had: "to concern itself with large-scale projects of general utility, to establish the main lines of communication, to build canals, to cut through isthmuses, to found colonies among uncivilized peoples, to spread civilization, and to extend the ties of commerce."[10]

Saint-Simon and the editors of the *Censeur* were concerned with political science, an effect of the great social upheaval of 1814. They were not yet concerned with economic science. They agreed in calling for free speech; free trade was not yet explicitly demanded. No doubt the transition is easy from political to economic liberalism. In his publication of 1814, Saint-Simon formulated the very principle that underlies the theories of the classical economists—the principle of identity of interests—and stressed its importance. "The less one thwarts the interests of others in promoting one's own," he said, "the less resistance one encounters from them, and the more easily one arrives at one's goal. Hence that old maxim—man finds true happiness only in seeking the happiness of others—is as certain and as positive as the law that says that a body moving in a certain direction is stopped or slowed in its path if it meets other bodies moving in the opposite direction."[11] In the *Censeur*, Charles Comte contrasted the interest of nations, which grow rich by trade, with the interest of governments, which grow rich by war. Dunoyer even sought "the origin of the ideas on which public opinion now rests" at the time "when letters, industry, and commerce arose in Europe." "The love of peace and liberty . . . must have been born in Europe at the same time as enlightenment and commerce. The more enlightenment progressed, the more commerce grew and spread its ties, and the more the two of them added to the happiness and prosperity

[9] *Ibid.*, III, 28.
[10] *Ibid.*, III, 30.
[11] Saint-Simon, *Oeuvres*, I, 238.

of the nations, the more this feeling must have developed, expanded, and grown in strength."[12] A long and detailed article in the *Censeur* was devoted to the *Traité d'économie politique* by J.-B. Say, the second edition of which appeared in 1814.[13] But the simultaneous conversion of the editors of the *Censeur* and of Saint-Simon to the doctrines of economic liberalism did not take place until 1817. Then all three of them dropped the problems of constitutional law and turned to other social questions that seemed to them to be more positive.

After two years of reconstruction, the French government, like the English, had to reckon with the problem of reorganizing the public finances, dislocated by twenty years of war. In both countries, statesmen had to deal with bankers and to take account of the interests of merchants and entrepreneurs. As a result, political economy became popular. In England in that same year, Ricardo published his *Principles of Political Economy and Taxation*. In France, Charles Comte, assisted as always by Dunoyer, began again to publish the *Censeur*, which had been suspended for two years, under the new title of *Le Censeur européen*. Saint-Simon, in collaboration with his secretary Augustin Thierry and with Saint-Aubin and Chaptal, undertook a similar publication called *L'Industrie*, which was praised by the editors of the *Censeur*. "We have already had occasion," they wrote, "to note how much political economy must have influenced the progress of ideas about politics, and how well adapted this science is to broaden the outlook of publicists. Here is an example that will prove the truth of that observation. In 1815 the Comte de Saint-Simon announced a work entitled *Le défenseur des propriétaires nationaux* (*The Protector of the Property-owners of the Country*), limiting himself to defending an article in the Charter. Now, M. de Saint-Simon has risen

---

[12] *Censeur*, VI, 143.
[13] *Ibid.*, VII, 43 ff.

to much more general ideas."[14] At the same time, Saint-
Simon, Augustin Thierry, Charles Comte, and Dunoyer
discovered that positive politics was political economy, the
principles of which had been set out by Adam Smith and
J.-B. Say.

Augustin Thierry, in *L'Industrie*,[15] and Dunoyer, in the
Censeur européen,[16] attacked the theory of the European
balance of power in almost identical terms; to this theory,
based on the rivalry of equally strong military powers,
they opposed the theory of the identity of the commercial
interests of all nations. From this came a new definition
of liberalism: "A constitutional government," wrote Augustin Thierry, "a liberal government in the true sense of the
word, is nothing but . . . a government founded on industry—*commercial government,* as an English writer calls
it."[17] The two publications never tired of pointing to the
conflict throughout Europe of two classes, one military and
feudal, the other industrial—the "class" or "nation" of the
industriels. Saint-Simon invented this new noun which took
hold.[18]

[14] *Censeur européen,* II, 371.

[15] *L'Industrie littéraire et scientifique liguée avec l'industrie
commerciale et manufacturière* (*Literary and Scientific Industry allied with Commercial and Manufacturing Industry*), I,
part 2, "Politique, par Augustin Thierry, fils adoptif de Henri
Saint-Simon," January 1817 (Saint-Simon, *Oeuvres,* II, 17 ff.).
In noticing the new publication, the editors of the *Censeur
européen* (I, 380–381) had reservations about the first part,
by Saint-Aubin, which they criticized for "including some ideas
of a rather ministerial color." The second part they praised
without reservation as "written with independence and often
with force."

[16] "Du système de l'équilibre européen," *Censeur européen,*
I, 93 ff. "Considérations sur l'état présent de l'Europe, sur les
dangers de cet état, et les moyens d'en sortir," *ibid.,* II, 67 ff.

[17] Saint-Simon, *Oeuvres,* II, 108.

[18] Enfantin (*Producteur,* V, 98) claimed the honor of having
invented the word for Saint-Simon. [Halévy gives two forms
of the word: *"industrieux,"* citing the *Censeur européen,* I,
115; I, 35, 76; and Saint-Simon, *Oeuvres,* I, 131, 198, 203, 215.

In the *Censeur européen,* Dunoyer explained this conflict by an historical theory. These two opposing classes,
though contemporaneous with each other, correspond to
two conceptions of social organization reflecting the needs
of two successive historical epochs. "The first way that
occurs to man to satisfy his needs is to take; plunder was
the first industry, as it was also the first end of human
association; history hardly knows a society that was not
first formed for war and pillage."[19] According to Dunoyer,
this was the primitive form of organized government, pre-
supposing perpetual war. "The first need of man," wrote
Charles Comte in the same vein, "is to provide his subsistence, and, as we have already seen, he can do so only
by the spontaneous produce of nature, or by what he seizes
from his fellows, or by the produce of his industry." The
first way presupposes no political organization and pro-
cures no wealth. The second way is suitable to peoples
whose structure is primitive. It divides society into masters and slaves, implying passive obedience of the latter
to the former and corrupting both. The third way is "that
best suited to man, because it abundantly supplies his
needs and because it is the only one that can keep him in
a state of peace and give his faculties all the development
of which they are susceptible." On the basis of these principles, Charles Comte boldly traced the whole history of
European civilization from the beginnings of the Roman
city to the present.[20]

Now, in the first volume of *L'Industrie,* Augustin Thierry
had just set out a theory very close to this. "In the savage
or primitive state," he tells us, "man has much to do with
men and little with things. . . . In a more advanced state,

The second form, *"industriels,"* regularly used hereafter, is
cited in *Oeuvres,* II, 58, 60.]

[19] *Censeur européen,* I, 93.

[20] "De l'organisation sociale considerée dans ses rapports avec
les moyens de subsistance des peuples," *Censeur européen,*
II, 1.

with greater capacity of observation and judgment, man brings himself into closer relationship with things. . . . The first tendency to opposition and hostility still survives, but man's interests change. The conqueror knows how to restrain himself; he ceases his depredations, he spares the fruits of the earth, he retains the slave to exploit him, he provides himself, as best he can, with machines for feeding man. . . . The peoples of antiquity were essentially military in character. The nation would have nothing to do with peaceable labor of any kind and abandoned it to slaves. . . . This order of things had to end with the moral state that had produced and maintained it. . . . The revolution came in the twelfth century. By the general enfranchisement of the commons throughout Europe, peaceful industry, which among the ancients had been outside the state, entered into the state, and became an active part instead of the passive part it had been originally."[21] In the following year—at a time when he had actually broken with Augustin Thierry—Saint-Simon declared expressly that it was from Charles Comte that he had taken the distinction, thereafter fundamental in his social philosophy, between two irreducibly distinct regimes, one "military or governmental," the other "liberal and industrial."[22] From Saint-Simon the distinction was transmitted to Auguste Comte, from Auguste Comte to Buckle, and from Buckle to Herbert Spencer, who gave it world-wide popularity.

History, interpreted by economic science, thus tells us in what direction we should, and can with some chance of success, guide our practical activity. In the stage of development at which mankind has arrived, we can properly consider a nation as nothing more than "a great society of industry."[23] "Society acquires wealth, produced

[21] Saint-Simon, *Oeuvres*, II, pp. 34 ff.

[22] *L'Industrie*, IV; *Oeuvres*, III, 157.

[23] Augustin Thierry, in *L'Industrie*, I, part 2; Saint-Simon, *Oeuvres*, II, 68–69.

value, in proportion to its capital and industry. . . . The share or income of each individual is measured by ratio of the capital or industrial service he has contributed to the whole."[24]

This state of things is, as yet, only partially realized. We must struggle to bring it to completion. "In their present state," wrote Dunoyer, "the nations can be compared to swarms made up equally of hornets and bees, swarms in which the bees agree to produce torrents of honey for the hornets, in the hope of keeping at least a few combs for themselves. Unhappily, there is not always even a small part left for them."[25] The next year, in his *Politique*, Saint-Simon took up the parable of the bees and the hornets in order to broaden it.[26] "We have already said it twenty times," wrote Dunoyer,[27] "and we shall repeat it a thousand times. Man's concern is not with government; he should look on government as no more than a very secondary thing—we might almost say a very minor thing. His goal is industry, labor, and the production of everything needed for his happiness. In a well-ordered state, the government must be only an adjunct of production, an agency charged by the producers, who pay for it, with protecting their persons and their goods while they work. In a well-ordered state, the largest possible number of persons must work, and the smallest possible number must govern. The peak of perfection would be reached if all the world worked and no one governed." Saint-Simon and Augustin Thierry had just put it in almost the same terms. "All by industry, all for industry. . . . The whole of society rests

[24] *Ibid.*, II, 68.

[25] *Censeur européen*, II, 102.

[26] "De la querelle des abeilles et des frelons," *Politique*, No. 11, April 1819, *Oeuvres*, III, 211. G. Dumas noted that on this point Auguste Comte borrowed from Saint-Simon. But, as we have seen, Saint-Simon himself was influenced by Dunoyer. See G. Dumas, *Psychologie de deux messies positivistes*, p. 263.

[27] *Censeur européen*, II, 102.

on industry. . . . What is best for industry is best for society."[28] "Society needs to be governed as little as possible, and there is only one way to accomplish that—to be governed as cheaply as possible."[29] And a little later: "To sum it up in a word, politics is the science of production."[30]

Since it would be a "liberal" society *par excellence,* founded on the free association of interests and not on allegiance to a common faith, would this new positive, industrial society then also be a society free of all intellectual discipline? Saint-Simon's doctrine rejects this conclusion. Ever since, long before, he wrote his fanciful *Lettres d'un habitant de Genève (Letters from a Resident of Geneva),* the problem Saint-Simon had set for himself was always to discover a new principle of order for European society, disorganized by the Revolution. We have seen him express this same conviction in 1814. In the prospectus for *L'Industrie* he wrote: "The eighteenth century has done nothing but destroy; we shall not go on with its work: on the contrary, what we will do is to lay the foundations of a new edifice."[31] Did not the editors of the *Censeur,* hostile to the idea of authority though they were, sometimes express themselves so as to suggest to Saint-Simon ways to link his philosophy of organization and the economic liberalism to which he had just been converted? Speaking of the struggle waged by the "nation of the *industriels*" against the "old aristocracy," Dunoyer added in language which would soon be that of Saint-Simon and his disciples: "We must not forget that its members are still few in number and isolated from each other, that there are few means of communication and defense; in a word, it is not organized, while, generally speaking, its enemies

28 *L'Industrie,* prospectus, April 1817, Saint-Simon, *Oeuvres,* II, 12–13.
29 *Ibid.,* II, 132.
30 *Ibid.,* II, 188.
31 *Oeuvres,* II, 13.

are organized."[32] "How will the nation of the *industriels,*" he asked, "be able to bring Europe out of the state of crisis in which we find her and to lead her easily to the desired goal?" Charles Comte asserted the existence of a new "hierarchy," different in theory from the old "military hierarchy," yet no less a fact: the "natural subordination" of workers to "those with the greatest ability and the largest capital," in other words, "to an aristocracy of farmers, manufacturers, and businessmen."[33]

So far, then, there was no disagreement between the editors of *L'Industrie* and of the *Censeur européen.* They were friends, almost collaborators. Today it is impossible to tell which one of them deserves the credit for one or another discovery. Nothing can be concluded from the fact that a theory or a new formulation first appeared in one or the other of the two publications. Saint-Simon was neither a reader nor a teacher; he was a talker. How can we know whether, in a chance conversation, the innovation had been suggested by one of the editors of the *Censeur* to one of the editors of *L'Industrie,* or vice versa? On one point, however, there is a clean separation between Saint-Simon and the men of the *Censeur:* in the important role that, as a literary man and philosopher, he assigned to literary men and scientists in the work of social reorganization.

Indeed, Charles Comte and Dunoyer showed a strong distrust of scientists and scholars, looking on them as "the people least likely to govern well, as their ideas and interests are directed towards a kind of speculation foreign to the business of the state."[34] Saint-Simon, on the contrary, called for "the collaboration of literary and manufacturing industry"[35] to bring the new principle of or-

[32] *Censeur européen,* II, 77.
[33] *Ibid.,* II, 49 ff., 57 ff.
[34] *Censeur européen,* II, 60.
[35] *Oeuvres,* II, 137. The original title of *L'Industrie* was *L'Industrie littéraire et scientifique liguée avec l'industrie commerciale et manufacturière,* p. 617.

ganization to victory: he was determined to find the basis of a new social organization in the collective acceptance of a new conception of the universe and of society, and thus both to complete and to abolish the revolutionary work of the eighteenth century. He attacked the theory of unlimited freedom of conscience, so dear to the eighteenth-century philosophers: "The philosophers of the nineteenth century will show the necessity of making all children study the same code of this world's morality, since the similarity of positive moral ideas is the one link that can unite men in society, and since nothing but the perfection of the system of positive morality can bring about the perfecting of the social state."[36]

Perhaps he refused to believe that there was any difference between these ideas and those maintained in the office of the *Censeur*. But he quarreled with his secretary, Augustin Thierry. Thierry, who had led him to discover first political and then economic liberalism, was disturbed to see an authoritarian conception of social organization reappearing in his conversation. One day Saint-Simon declared, "I cannot imagine association without government by someone." Thierry answered, "And I cannot imagine association without liberty." Saint-Simon broke with Augustin Thierry, probably towards the end of July 1817;[37]

[36] *L'Industrie,* prospectus for the third volume, June 1817, *Oeuvres,* II, 245.

[37] J. D. Guigniaut, *Notice historique sur la vie et les travaux d'Augustin Thierry* (1863), p. 50. A former secretary of Saint-Simon recalled the development of the row with Augustin Thierry as follows: ". . . It was the obscurity of his [Saint-Simon's] ideas, his uncertainty of the principle to which he should attach them, that led to the departure of M. Augustin Thierry. Tormented almost to tears by the urgent and ceaseless insistence of M. de Saint-Simon on his collaboration, the young scholar, who since has risen so high through his *Lettres sur l'histoire de France* and his *Conquête de l'Angleterre par les Normands,* preferred to leave him rather than work at what he could not understand. Since then, I can confess without shame that I have myself drawn back before the proposal that M. de

to fill his place as secretary, he chose another young man, Auguste Comte,[38] who had left the École Polytechnique two years before and was walking the streets of Paris, without money and without a job.

What part did Auguste Comte play in the later formulation of Saint-Simon's system? Could it be said that this eighteen-year-old boy had exercised a profound influence on the thought of his employer? It is quite true that, at about the time Auguste Comte became his secretary, Saint-Simon's theories underwent very considerable changes. But was Comte responsible for them? It was precisely because Augustin Thierry did not want to go in this new direction that Saint-Simon had just broken with his first secretary. All we can say is that Comte had no difficulty in entering into the views of his teacher. "By this joining of labor and friendship with one of the men who

---

Saint-Simon has made to me more than once to take part in the work. . . . More fortunate than we, M. Auguste Comte probably arrived at a time when the publicist had succeeded in clarifying his ideas and rendering them more intelligible. Besides, the pupil lacked neither knowledge nor talent to do honor to the master. . . ." (Notice sur Saint-Simon et sa doctrine et sur quelques autres ouvrages qui en seraient le developpement, par son ancien secrétaire, in the Bibliothèque de la Ville de Paris. M. Alfred Péreire brought this curious manuscript to our attention and provided us with a copy.)

[38] *Lettres d'Auguste Comte à M. Valat* (1870), April 17, 1818: "For three months I have been a political writer in the latest fashion, that is to say, as you well know, in the liberal style: I have been working with Saint-Simon. . . . Unfortunately, that has not lasted; the old man has suffered reverses which have forced him to break off financial relations at the end of three months. . . . I began as a publicist in August." G. Weill (*Saint-Simon et son oeuvre*, p. 93) says that the influence of Saint-Simon is still noticeable in an article by Thierry published in the *Censeur européen* in 1817 (II, 107 ff.). Actually, Thierry had not yet broken with Saint-Simon when the second volume of the *Censeur européen* appeared; the third volume was seized on June 6, even though the printing had not yet been finished.

sees farthest in philosophical politics," he wrote a few months later, "I have learned a lot of things that I would have sought in vain in books; my mind has made more progress during the six months of our association than it would have made in three years if I had been alone. So this job formed my judgment on political science and, as a result, it enlarged my ideas on all the other sciences, so I find that I have got more philosophy in my head and a more accurate and more elevated view of things."[39] It should be added that the new secretary must have had an instinctive feeling of intellectual jealousy towards the departing secretary: Auguste Comte must have felt himself naturally drawn to approve in Saint-Simon all the ideas that had separated him from Augustin Thierry.

In September 1817 Comte drew up the "third consideration" of the sixth article of *L'Industrie*, "Sur la morale" ("On Morals"), to develop the philosophical part of Saint-Simon's system and to demonstrate the necessity of going back to principles and of founding "politics" on "morals," for "no society is possible without common moral ideas."[40] It was necessary, then, to break with "theological morality"; to found a worldly, "positive," "industrial" morality; and to prepare for the future society a clergy, not of theologians, but of philosophers or scientists, by deciding that "no one can be ordained a priest if he has not shown by examination that he is abreast of the main conclusions in the positive sciences."[41]

This declaration of war on Christianity alienated the rich bankers and great merchants who had subscribed to the journal. They disavowed the publication, and Saint-Simon prudently decided to give up questions of principle and return to problems of applied politics. In two letters dated early in 1818, Auguste Comte reproached him for this decision and urged him to go back to questions of

[39] *Lettres à Valat*, April 17, 1818, p. 37.
[40] Saint-Simon, *Oeuvres*, III, 32.
[41] *Ibid.*, III, 41.

principle. Must we conclude that master and secretary had disagreed on this point, or that the secretary had already taken over the intellectual direction of his master? The two letters seem actually to have been written for publication, with the connivance of Saint-Simon, to prepare the public for a new statement of the principles that had caused the scandal in October 1817.[42] It must be said that the general morality on which, according to the author of the two letters, Saint-Simon's politics has to be founded does not seem very different from what the English call utilitarian morality, of which Bentham was the theorist and Ricardo a disciple, and which could have had a direct influence on the formation of Saint-Simon's system.[43] There was, therefore, no disagreement with the liberal economists. "You know better than anyone, Sir," wrote Auguste Comte to his master, "since you first said it clearly, that the only reasonable politics is political economy. Now, properly speaking, political economy is not yet a science; it lacks the basis for becoming one. . . . To give it such a basis is, in my opinion, the most important thing to do today for the progress of that science. As I see it, this aim is fulfilled by your fundamental idea: *Property is the most important of all institutions, and it must be ordered in the way most favorable to production.* It seems to me that all the truths of political economy can be linked to that beautiful idea; it provides a way to create at last a

[42] The two letters, already available in the *Revue occidentale* for September 1882, have been reprinted from the original texts by M. Alfred Péreire, "Des premier rapports entre Saint-Simon et Auguste Comte d'après des documents originaux," *Revue historique,* XCI, 1906. We entirely agree with M. Péreire's thesis, except on one point. We do not recognize Comte's style in the prospectus for the second volume of *L'Industrie;* besides, the prospectus appeared at the end of May or the beginning of June 1817, two months before Comte was in touch with Saint-Simon.

[43] Bentham is cited in *L'Industrie,* II, sixth article; Saint-Simon, *Oeuvres,* II, 13.

true political science founded on economic observations. What a great work it would be, Sir, to organize this complex of ideas and to bring positive politics into being!" Throughout the following year, in letters to his friend Valat, Comte never ceased to depict Saint-Simon as a great liberal.[44] The best reading he could recommend in social science was the treatise of Jean-Baptiste Say.[45]

Not until 1819 is the "organizational" character of their politics accentuated in the writings of Saint-Simon and Auguste Comte. This was the same year in which Joseph de Maistre published his treatise *Du Pape* (*On the Pope*), and Auguste Comte tells us that that work "had a salutary influence" on "the normal development of his political thought." The writings of the theocratic school, he said, made "a wise general appreciation of the Middle Ages" easier for him in his historical works and "thereafter fixed his attention directly on conditions of order eminently applicable to the present social state, although conceived for another state."[46] This influence is incontestable; Saint-Simon's judgments of the sixteenth-century Reformation and of the eighteenth-century Revolution are certainly more severe in his writings of 1819 than in those of 1817.[47]

Even more than Joseph de Maistre, de Bonald, whose name Comte does not mention, seems to have inspired the Saint-Simonian philosophy of history.[48] In 1817 he had

[44] See especially the letter of May 15, 1818, pp. 51–52.
[45] *Ibid.*, p. 55, and the letter of June 15, 1818, p. 63.
[46] *Cours de philosophie positive*, IV (1839), p. 184.
[47] Compare Saint-Simon's favorable judgments on Luther, in the third consideration of the second volume of *L'Industrie* (*Oeuvres*, III, 48), and on the American and French revolutions in "Objet de l'entreprise," *ibid.* (*Oeuvres*, II, 133–134), with the severe judgment of both Reformation and the Revolution in the *Système industriel*.
[48] On the other hand, de Bonald and not de Maistre is cited in *L'Organisateur*, November 1819 (*Oeuvres*, IV, 29): "The supremacy of the popes has ceased to exist since it is no longer recognized, and the ideas dominant in the Middle Ages have been replaced by other less erroneous ideas. So MM. de

published an *Essai analytique sur les lois naturelles de l'ordre social* (*Analytical Essay on the Natural Laws of the Social Order*), in which he summed up the principles of his great work of political philosophy, which was already twenty years old. He undertook to justify the theocracy of the Middle Ages as an historian and experimental philosopher. In the religious and political revolution of the last two centuries could be seen "a terrible and salutary crisis," after which Europe would recover "religious and political unity."[49] He defined the principles of this double revolution in terms that Saint-Simon and Comte borrowed from him almost literally. "As everything in this world," he wrote, "is being or nothing, algebra has its negative or impossible quantities . . . ; so too in the social or moral world, where everything is good or evil, there are false relations which divide men instead of true relations which unite them. For example, there are tyrants instead of true power, satellites instead of ministers, slaves instead of subjects, and, finally, there is a *negative* society, so to speak, leading to disorder and destruction, instead of a *positive* society, leading to order and preservation; the necessity of the latter is proved by the impossibility of the former."[50] This play on the meaning of the word *positive* was to seduce the inventor of positive philosophy. "Do you really believe, gentlemen," wrote Saint-Simon in his *Système industriel*, "that the critique of theological and feudal ideas, devised or at any rate completed by the eighteenth-century philosophers, can take the place of doctrine? . . .

Bonald and de Chateaubriand, although highly esteemed for their virtues and considered as men of much talent and learning, are generally regarded as extravagant because they seek to bring back an order of things that the progress of enlightenment has finished off." Cf. *Catéchisme des industriels* (*Oeuvres*, VIII, 172): "The writers of a reactionary tendency, such as MM. de Maistre, Bonald, Lamennais, etc. . . ."

[49] De Bonald, *Oeuvres*, I (1836), 29.
[50] *Ibid.*, I, 10–11.

Society can never exist on negative ideas, but only on positive ideas."[51]

To the extent that we have just indicated, Comte's testimony seems justified. We must beware, however, of attributing too great an importance to it: Comte's tendency all too plainly was scrupulously to note all the influences on him except the one that was truly decisive—Saint-Simon's. Without having read the theocrats, Saint-Simon had for a long time opposed his organizational philosophy to eighteenth-century criticism. In 1816 and 1817—influenced perhaps by Augustin Thierry, Charles Comte, and Dunoyer—he had gone as far along the liberal road as he would ever go. He had just broken with Augustin Thierry precisely because Thierry's intransigent liberalism was incompatible with Saint-Simon's views on the importance of ideas of authority and discipline in politics. Moreover, to construct this positive philosophy of history, historical knowledge was necessary, and the master was as ignorant of history as his new secretary. Thierry was a professional historian; and he was the one who had left. The writings of Joseph de Maistre and de Bonald gave Auguste Comte the explanation of Catholicism in the feudal age that he needed to complete the outline sketched by Saint-Simon. His was a vigorous mind, apt at speculation and generalization. It must be admitted that he accomplished the task that someone else had given him like a true inventor.

In *L'Organisateur*, Saint-Simon's new publication on which he collaborated, Comte tells us that if industrial society is, like feudal society, to be "organic," it must possess both a spiritual and a temporal power. But these two powers will differ from the older spiritual and temporal powers in principle and in form. Actually, there will not be two new powers, but rather two "capacities." The "action of principles" comes to supplant "human action," "reason to replace will."[52]

[51] *Oeuvres*, VI, 51.
[52] *L'Organisateur*, eighth letter, *Oeuvres*, IV, 85–86.

In the spiritual or intellectual sphere, the "scientific positive capacity" will replace the old ecclesiastical power. The scientists will play a role in society analogous to that played by the theologians. Like theological dogmas in the tenth century, their opinions will be accepted by everyone, not because this acceptance has been imposed by force, but because these opinions evoke the spontaneous confidence of mankind; not because they have been communicated to those who teach them by a mysterious revelation, but because everyone knows that the statements of scientists are always subject to experimental verification and are unanimously accepted by men with the necessary capacity to judge them. In any society, the organization of the temporal power must be modelled on the organization of the spiritual power. Here again there will be leaders: those who take over the effective management of industry will have demonstrated their "administrative" capacity by that very fact. Industrial society will be hierarchically organized in relationship to them.

Industrial society is a corporative society, and the history of its progress from the time when the commons were freed in the Middle Ages is the history of a corporation. Before Auguste Comte became his secretary, Saint-Simon had already called on the *industriels* to work with literary men to set up what he later called the alliance of "practical" and "theoretical" industry, and thus to form a vast antigovernmental corporation.[53] Under the influence of the historian Augustin Thierry, he had already recognized the importance of the enfranchisement of the commons in the history of western society. But the theory gained its full breadth and precision when Auguste Comte developed it in the ninth letter of *L'Organisateur*.[54] After that it was settled, and we find it set out later in the same form in the *Système industriel* of 1820 and in the *Catéchisme des in-*

[53] *L'Industrie, Oeuvres,* III, pp. 60 ff.
[54] *Oeuvres,* IV, 111 ff.

dustriels of 1822.[55] Saint-Simon and Comte recount "the
formation of the corporation of *industriels*."[56] They show
us the methods used since the Middle Ages to increase its
influence—not force, but contract, "the arrangements
which reconciled the interests of the contracting parties."
Its organization was completed in the seventeenth century,
when the "separate corporations" of agriculturalists, manufacturers, and merchants were linked financially and politically by the organization of credit. Then a new corporation was born, the corporation of bankers, mediating
between sellers and buyers, and between the *industriels*
as a whole and the rulers. Vis-à-vis governments, they
represented all the interests of the industrial class. Theirs
was a "general" or generalizing industry: they were the
"general agents of industry."[57] All that remains to be done
now is for that industrial society, the corporative organization of which has been completed, to assert its predominance over the governmental system, that survival of feudal times, and shortly thereafter to take the place of a
system drained of all life.

In industrial society, as formerly in feudal society and
as in all organized society, there will be a hierarchy of
functions. But this hierarchy will differ from the old hierarchy as the authority scientists exercise on opinion differs
from the authority formerly exercised by theologians. Auguste Comte first set down the formula by which the
school would characterize that difference: the new society,
he said, will not be *governed*, it will be *administered*. In
1818 Saint-Simon said that "the ability needed to make a
good budget is administrative ability; it follows that administrative ability is the most important ability in poli-

[55] *Oeuvres*, V–VII, VIII–X.
[56] *Catéchisme des industriels, Oeuvres*, VIII, 24.
[57] *Système industriel, Oeuvres*, V, 47. See also the discussion
of the important role of the bankers in modern society in *L'Industrie, Oeuvres*, III, 113.

tics."[58] But it was Auguste Comte who, in 1819, gave the formula its full philosophical strength. More rigorously than Saint-Simon, he defined the distinct principles of the two social systems—the military system and the industrial system, the one decadent, the other making steady progress. In the second, the aim is to act not on men, but on nature, "to modify it as much as possible in the best interests of the human race." The only action allowable on men is that strictly necessary "to make them concur in the general action on things."[59]

Following their emancipation, the commons had gradually developed the arts and crafts, in other words, the means at man's disposal for acting on nature; it was the only way for them to liberate and enrich themselves. But in a completely industrialized society, there will no longer be rulers—men who in their own interest impose passive obedience on others—but only administrators, managing the industrial association as their abilities entitle them to do. "In the old system, the people were *regimented* with respect to their leaders; in the new, they are *combined* with them. The military leaders *commanded;* the industrial leaders will only *manage.* Then the people were *subjects;* now they are *partners.*"[60] There will be no distinction between two classes, one idle, the other made up of workers, with the idle, who bring neither ability nor contributions to the association, rewarding themselves by means of the workers whom they command as masters do slaves. There will always be a hierarchy, but it will be a hierarchy in which each person will be ranked and rewarded according to his capacity and his contribution, in which everyone, wherever he may find himself, will feel that he is associated with the common task of production. "By its nature, the human race is destined to live in society; it has been called to live under *governmental* rule.

[58] *Le Politique* (1818), *Oeuvres,* III, 201.
[59] *L'Organisateur* (1819), *Oeuvres,* IV, 121.
[60] *L'Organisateur,* ninth letter, *Oeuvres,* IV, 150.

It is destined to pass from governmental or military rule to *administrative* or *industrial* rule."[61]

Still, must we not reckon with two important developments at the end of the eighteenth century—the French Revolution and the suppression of corporations—which the theory of Saint-Simon and Comte does not account for, and to which liberal historians attach great importance? According to Saint-Simon, to find the ultimate source of the French Revolution, we must go back to the time when the enfranchisement of the commons began and the empirical sciences began to be studied in western Europe. There lay the positive cause of the decadence of feudal society, and the French Revolution of 1789—the crisis of the violent dissolution of ancient institutions—was only a superficial effect of that deep-seated cause. The suppression of corporations must not, then, be seen as more than a transitory event, an accident in the history of the development of industrial organization since the Middle Ages. Here then is a new interpretation of the revolutionary crisis. This interpretation conforms to principles long since set down by Saint-Simon and explains the appeal the historical theories of Joseph de Maistre and de Bonald had for Saint-Simon and Auguste Comte in 1815. This brought about a clean break between Saint-Simon and the liberals properly so-called. In 1817 political economy was, for Saint-Simon, the friend of Comte and Dunoyer, the "science of liberty."[62] Now, to oppose his teaching for-

[61] *Catéchisme des industriels, Oeuvres*, VIII, 87. Before long, Auguste Comte would not hesitate to use the word "government" to indicate the systematic direction of society which he called for. See the *Système de politique positive* (1824), p. 11: "The government which, in every normal state of things, is the head of society, the guide and agent of general action . . ." and "Considérations sur le pouvoir spirituel," *Producteur*, II, 216: "Although it may be useful, and in some cases even necessary, to consider the idea of society apart from the idea of government, it is generally recognized that the two ideas are really inseparable."

[62] *L'Industrie, Oeuvres*, II, 213.

mally to the "liberalism" of Dunoyer, Saint-Simon was about to propose the new noun "industrialism."[63] Finally, this interpretation was the source of the famous theory worked out a little later by Auguste Comte to establish the law of the development of the human mind, the "law of the three stages." Again we see the influence of Saint-Simon's ideas on the formation of Comte's system.

In 1818, in the last numbers of *L'Industrie*, Saint-Simon began to attack not only the nobles and the military—in which he agreed with the editors of the *Censeur*—but the lawyers as well; in control of the administration of justice and all-powerful in the legislature, their actions were often prejudicial to the progress of industry. To be sure, "it is to the lawyers that we are principally indebted for the destruction of *military despotism;* they removed disputes among citizens from arbitrary judgment; they established complete freedom of pleading; and by these labors they certainly earned an honorable place in the history of the human mind."[64] But while the institution of "judicial order" was temporarily very useful, "today it is a hindrance." To the method of the civil courts, which consists in respecting certain juridical rules and certain notions of abstract law, Saint-Simon opposed the method of commercial tribunals, which seek to reconcile interests by arbitration. To a juridical philosophy he opposed an economic philosophy; he meant to show "the superiority of the principles of *political economy* to those of the *civil law.*"[65] In the third letter of *L'Organisateur*, Saint-Simon not only dealt with lawyers but metaphysicians, that is, "persons who, subject to blind beliefs and having only superficial knowledge, want to reason about generalities."[66] Saint-Simon considered both as belonging to the same social class: the metaphysicians, he said, "have set up their seminaries in

[63] *Catéchisme des industriels*, Appendix II, *Oeuvres*, VIII, 178 ff.
[64] *L'Industrie, Oeuvres*, III, 124–125.
[65] *Ibid.*, III, 126.
[66] *Oeuvres*, IV, 40.

the schools of law." Finally, the *Système industriel* set out at length the role played by lawyers and metaphysicians, as Saint-Simon saw it, in the history of modern society.

The transition from the feudal and theological system to the industrial and positive system could be brought about only gradually, spiritually as well as temporally. Two classes, derived from the old system of social organization but distinct from it, formed, Saint-Simon tells us, "what I call abstractly an intermediate and transitional system" in society.[67] These classes were the lawyers in the secular world and the metaphysicians in the spiritual world; they were closely associated in their political action, like feudalism and theology, or like industry and the sciences of observation. The principle on which the lawyers based themselves to destroy the old society in its temporal aspect was the principle of popular sovereignty. The principle on which the metaphysicians based themselves to destroy old beliefs was freedom of conscience. Useful in destroying an already decayed social system, these principles become sterile in that, being purely negative, they cannot serve as constituent principles for organizing the new society. In 1822, in the third part (*cahier*) of the *Catéchisme des industriels*, Auguste Comte generalized the theory and, for the first time, developed the law according to which human intelligence has passed through three successive stages: the theological or fictitious stage, in which "supernatural ideas serve to link up the small number of isolated observations of which science was then made up"; the metaphysical or abstract stage, in which the mind has recourse to "personified abstractions" to establish connections between facts; and, finally, "the scientific and positive stage," the definitive mode of all science whatsoever."[68] What Comte did was simply to extend to the general history of thought a theory by which Saint-Simon

[67] *Oeuvres*, V, 7.
[68] *Oeuvres*, IX, 75–76.

had tried to explain the transformations of western society over the last three centuries.

We know the course of human progress. What steps should be taken to move from theory to practice, "to speed up and to illuminate the necessary course of things,"[69] to hasten the transition from the military to the industrial system, and "to end the revolution"? It is necessary, Saint-Simon tells us, to defeudalize and industrialize the political constitution of the nations, and of France in particular. But, once again, what had to be done to accomplish that?

In the first place, the electoral law had to be changed. The *industriels* formed too small a part of the electorate, as then constituted, for the Chambre des Députés, the "House of Commons," to be considered truly representative of the interests of the producers. Through the Revolution, France made certain that rulers should be elected, not born. But who were the electors? They were not the *industriels*. They were the "idle rich," the "bourgeois," that is to say "the non-noble military, the lawyers who were commoners, and those unprivileged persons with private means."[70] In making the *patente* a direct tax, M. de Villèle had already helped to industrialize the electorate: thereafter all who paid the *patente* beyond a certain sum had become electors. Why not enact an analogous measure in favor of farmers? Why not decide that in future the land tax would be paid by the cultivator who works the land and not by the idle landlord who exacts the rent? In becoming taxable, the farmer, the rural *industriel*, would become an elector.[71] By such measures, the composition of the electorate could be altered and the concerns of the members of the legislature changed. Thereafter, Saint-Simon thought, they would practice the politics of industry, not the politics of abstract liberalism.

[69] *L'Industrie, Oeuvres*, II, 166.
[70] *Catéchisme des industriels, Oeuvres*, VIII, p. 11.
[71] *L'Industrie*, May or June 1818, *Oeuvres*, III, 90 ff. [The *patente* was a tax paid by merchants and professional men.]

Up to this point, however, the demands of the industrialist hardly differed from those of the ordinary liberal.

But Saint-Simon demanded more. According to him, it was necessary to make a profound change in the nature of the political constitution, to renounce the elective principle, and by means of the "ordinance," or decree, as we would say today, to give power to commissions made up of the managerial elements in the world of industry, representing, in other words, the higher levels of the industrial hierarchy as they actually exist, without any government intervention. A *chambre d'invention* (chamber of initiative), for example, could be made up of engineers and artists; a *chambre d'examen* (chamber of review) of physicists and mathematicians; a *chambre d'execution* (executive chamber) would have as members the principal industrial leaders, in numbers proportional to the importance of each industry.[72] There is the model of an ideal constitution in which one can find the political theory of the separation of powers fitted, so to speak, to the industrial pattern. Less ambitious was his proposal to set up a *chambre de l'industrie* (chamber of industry), made up of the leading farmers, businessmen, manufacturers, and bankers; the Minister of Finance would be chosen from the members of this council and would draw up the budget with the help of his colleagues. A council of *industriels* and scientists, conceived along the same lines, would be attached to the Ministry of the Interior, and a maritime council to the Ministry of Marine.[73] There is a still more limited reform for which Saint-Simon finally settled. Without changing the composition of the ministerial council at all, let a *commission supérieure des finances* (high commission of finance) be created, composed of the most important *industriels*. "The king can superimpose this commission on his ministerial council. He can bring this

[72] *L'Organisateur*, sixth letter, December 1819, *Oeuvres*, IV, 50 ff.

[73] *Système industriel*, 1821, *Oeuvres*, V, 106 ff.

commission together every year, order it to draw up the budget and to see to it that the ministers have properly used the appropriations made in the preceding budget and that they have not exceeded them."[74]

In proposing these reforms, Saint-Simon was neither so utopian nor so much of an innovator as he appears at first sight. He was influenced by a series of steps taken since the Consulate, if not to reorganize the guilds, which the new industrial society no longer wanted, at least to adapt to the new conditions of life all that that society was able to put up with in the way of organization. Thus, Napoleon and Louis XVIII had created a number of permanent advisory bodies—*chambres de commerce; chambres consultatives des manufactures, fabriques, arts et métiers;* a *Conseil Général du Commerce;* and a *Conseil Général des Manufactures.* These institutions, not political and governmental but economic and administrative, were the best possible reflection of the real hierarchy of industrial functions and certainly served as models for the institutions Saint-Simon called for.[75] The reforms were aimed, not at creating a new kind of government, but at abolishing as far as possible all governmental institutions, emptying them, so to speak, of all content and putting in their place the spontaneous and effective organization of industrial society. While awaiting the full realization of this program, it was necessary to set about subordinating politics to industry as fully as possible. M. de Villèle was the real initiator of industrialism when, in 1819, he called on an extraparliamentary commission, which included all the big bankers in Paris, appointed by the government, to work

[74] *Catéchisme des industriels,* 1822, *Oeuvres,* VIII, 67.
[75] [Chambers of Commerce; Advisory Councils of Manufactures, Factories, Arts, and Crafts; general councils of Commerce and of Manufactures.] See proposals similar to Saint-Simon's put forward by his contemporary F.-E. Fodéré, *Essai historique et moral sur la pauvreté des nations, la population, la medicité, les hôpitaux et les enfant trouvés* (1825), pp. 287–288, 320–321.

out a budget and to set the conditions of the loan of that year.[76] This move certainly influenced Saint-Simon, as it drew his attention to the important part played by the banks and bankers in the leadership of industrial society. In any event, the only useful constitutional reforms lay in that direction. Those based only on lawyers' arguments are useless. Why? Because, Saint-Simon tells us, the important thing is not the constitution of governmental powers, but the institution, or, what comes to the same thing, the distribution, of property. In working to industrialize the constitution, then, the real goal to pursue is to bring about a transfer of property favorable to the growth of production.

Here at last is a point on which it seems that Saint-Simon's industrial politics are clearly opposed to the politics of the liberal economists. It never occurred to them that the powers of those in charge of society would extend to interference with the institution of property. But we must note how Saint-Simon applied his principle.

He called for the unlimited reduction of military and governmental functions, which become more and more useless as the human race progresses, and, at the same time, for the unlimited reduction of the income attached to the exercise of these functions; thus wealth would be taken from those who govern without doing anything and restored to those who produce it. But did the liberal economists ever suggest anything else? Again, Saint-Simon observed that the idea of property is not simple, and that the lawyers do not define it in the same way when they are discussing movable goods as they do when they are discussing real property. If a capitalist advanced funds to an *industriel*, the latter possessed legal rights over those funds equivalent to the rights of a landed proprietor, though he had only the temporary and conditional use of the funds. It was quite different when a landed proprietor rented an

[76] *Catéchisme des industriels, Oeuvres,* VIII, 30–31.

estate to a farmer; during the time for which he had the use of the capital, the farmer would have to submit to the continual and constricting control of the idle proprietor. In such cases, to put the agricultural producer on the same footing with the industrial producer would be a transfer of ownership at the expense of the landed proprietor.[77] But were not the liberal economists in agreement with Saint-Simon in demanding such freedom for landed property?

Then there is the plan of "general public education," the working-out of which he assigned to the *chambre d'examen* in the new political system he had drawn up. Again, many economists of the liberal school were inclined to agree that the state should intervene to provide equitably for the minimum instruction considered necessary for all children. So, in the last analysis, there is nothing but Article IV of the reform scheme, which he proposed to the king in 1821 and which reads as follows: "The first item of expenditure in the budget will have as its purpose guaranteeing the subsistence of the proletarians by providing work for the able-bodied and assistance for the impotent." This double affirmation of the right to subsistence and the right to work can be considered as constituting the first germ in Saint-Simon of the future "socialism" of the Saint-Simonians. To the end of his life, however, Saint-Simon seems to have persisted in considering Adam Smith and J.-B. Say as his masters. Ought we not to believe him? Can we set an isolated sentence against his formal avowals? Actually, this is not the way to pose the problem which arises in interpreting the social doctrine of Saint-Simon. We believe that his entire doctrine, perhaps without Saint-Simon himself being aware of it, rests on a principle opposed to the principle of classical political economy. It certainly does not constitute an explicit socialism, but it includes in latent form the elements of socialism

[77] *L'Industrie, Oeuvres,* III, 84 ff.

that were to develop in the school immediately after the master's death.

As Saint-Simon conceived it, industrial society is a hierarchy of functions. Some work under the direction of others who are the "captains of industry."[78] Each member of this hierarchy is rewarded according to his rank, and each occupies the rank his ability assigns to him. But by what principle and rule is the choice of the most able made? Is it election, or competition, or co-optation that points out the leaders of the hierarchy at every level from the most insignificant to the highest? This must be understood, if we would understand as well the real character of the industrial economy as Saint-Simon saw it.

Certainly Saint-Simon did not propose to elect the managers of the economy. The only work in which he seems to make room for the elective principle in his series of reforms is the first fragment of *Opinions littéraires, philosophiques, et industrielles* (*Literary, Philosophical, and Industrial Opinions*), published only after his death. What importance should we attach to these observations? He cites the example of what happens in a joint-stock company and concludes: "The fundamental principle of an administration is that the interests of those administered must be managed so as to achieve the greatest possible prosperity for the capital of the company and to obtain the approval and support of the majority of the shareholders."[79] But, in this case, who are the associates whose support the *industriel* has to obtain? Not the workers whom he manages, but the capitalists who have lent him their capital, that is, after all, not the workers but the idle. We cannot fall back on this analogy, offered in passing and with so little rigor, to argue that the social doctrine of Saint-Simon would ultimately have evolved in a democratic direction. In the same work, Saint-Simon insists

[78] *L'Organisateur, Oeuvres,* IV, 50.
[79] *Opinions,* p. 129.

that "as the class of proletarians advances as far in the fundamentals of civilization as the class of owners, the law should admit them to full participation."[80] Does this not mean that, in the new society, they will be capable of exercising the right of suffrage? But we must note that Saint-Simon limits himself here to reproducing, almost word for word, an opinion offered by Auguste Comte in *L'Organisateur,* and that, in that passage, Comte was not at all concerned with the democratic organization of society. He intended to speak only of industrial organization as it now exists, in which the leaders *manage* without *commanding* and treat their workers, Comte tells us, as *partners,* not *subjects.* Thus, some pages farther on, Comte could conclude, without contradicting himself, that, so far as the final establishment of the new system goes, "the people have been eliminated from the question: the question will be resolved for the people, but their role will be external and passive."[81] Saint-Simon thought in exactly the same way; he was not a democrat for the "positive" reason that the democratic ideal did not conform to the facts that observation of industrial society furnishes to us.

If the workers in France and even more so in England were seduced by democratic preaching, it was the fault of the metaphysicians and lawyers, the inventors of the theory of popular sovereignty, the entirely "negative" utility of which had served to destroy the feudal theory of divine right. It was the fault, too, of the leaders of industry who were too much taken in by the prestige of the governing class. "They did not feel the superiority of their class; almost all of them wanted to escape from it to enter the noble class."[82] They remained, nevertheless, the natural leaders of the workers; and, as they possessed the necessary managerial capacity, the workers were led instinctively to carry out their instructions. It is natural, too, that

[80] *Ibid.,* pp. 95 ff.
[81] *Oeuvres,* VI, 158.
[82] *Catéchisme des industriels, Oeuvres,* VIII, 55.

they should be differently rewarded, since their tasks were different. This inequality constitutes "industrial equality" as opposed to "Turkish equality"—or Jacobin—which implies "equal admissibility to the exercise of arbitrary power."[83] As Saint-Simon defined it then, industrial society is not at all democratic. Modern socialism on the other hand is an essentially democratic doctrine. Thus, we should have to conclude that Saint-Simon's social doctrine is not a socialism unless, at the same time, it is opposed on equally essential points to the social doctrines of Adam Smith and J.-B. Say.

Adam Smith, J.-B. Say, and all their school saw things from the consumer's standpoint. They regarded the economic world as made up essentially of a public of consumers who patronize the competing producers from whom they get the largest quantity and highest quality of the goods they need at the lowest prices. One must not object that consumers are also producers; it follows from the mechanism of exchange that no one—or hardly anyone —is producer and consumer of the same commodity. A man does not consume what he produces. The goods he consumes he has almost always bought from other producers. Besides, all men are consumers; hence the interest of consumers is the interest of the whole human race. If the general interest is damaged, it is when a group of producers, favored by a monopoly, impose an artificial price on goods they supply to the mass of consumers.

We find an indication of unreserved adherence to this conception of the economy only two or three times in the writings of Saint-Simon;[84] these occur exclusively in the works he published when he was working with the liberal publicists and collaborating with Augustin Thierry. In reality, his way of conceiving economic phenomena was

[83] *Système industriel, Oeuvres,* VI, 17.
[84] See especially "Objet de l'entreprise," *L'Industrie,* II, *Oeuvres,* II, 131.

quite different; unlike the classical economists, he started, not from the consumer's standpoint, but from the producer's. He considered mankind to be composed, in very large part, of producers, joined together to work for the increase of social wealth, with each one paid according to his labor, or, more exactly, according to his "social investment": capital advanced or labor supplied. Saint-Simon kept the designation of "consumer" for those in society who are not both consumers and producers but who, without producing, consume the produce of the labor of others. The general interest is damaged when the group of consumers, defined in this way—or, if one prefers, the group of non-producers—levies a tithe on the produce of the labor of producers, that is, on the labor of the immense majority of individuals who compose the race.[85]

What, then, is the governmental or military system? It is one in which consumers exploit producers. What, on the other hand, is the industrial system? It is one in which the producers have thrown off the yoke of the consumers and have taken over the administration of industrial society for their own benefit. Finally, by what principle is the distribution of ranks worked out in this administration? As we have seen, it is neither by election nor by competition, understood as the classical economists understood it, which confers the exercise of social functions and the rewards attached to it. It seems, rather, to be what could be called a kind of administrative co-optation—competition still, but understood in a new sense. One can, indeed, conceive of two kinds of competition: one, in pursuance of which the consumer chooses his supplier, and the other in pursuance of which the supplier chooses his employees. Now, in industrial society as Saint-Simon conceived it, it is the second kind of competition that controls the distribution of ranks and rewards. Those who occupy inferior ranks in society compete with each other to make their leaders

[85] See especially *L'Industrie, Oeuvres,* VIII, 83–84.

single them out and give them the advancement they
covet. At the top of the administrative hierarchy stand the
bankers. According to Saint-Simon, an *industriel* succeeds,
not exactly to the extent to which he satisfies the needs
of consumers better than his rivals, but to the extent to
which he knows better than others how to obtain the
confidence, the "credit," of the bankers. The sums they
agree to advance to him are both the reward for his aptitudes and the means by which he renders them productive
in the interest of mankind.

In this way, in industrial society, the reconciliation of
the interest of all with the interest of each will be brought
about. But it will not be according to the same principle as
the principle in the theory of the classical economists. According to Adam Smith, the principle of the identification
of interests is the principle of commercial competition;
according to Saint-Simon, it is the principle of professional
emulation. Moreover, Saint-Simon did not think it enough
to appeal to the egoism of individuals to bring about the
harmony of interests. Here again his "positivism" was opposed to the utilitarianism of Bentham and the English
school. In his last works—in his *Système industriel*, in his
Catéchisme des industriels, and especially in his *Nouveau
christianisme*—he insisted that politics must be completed
by a morality, a religion. Charles X had mounted the
throne; the theocratic philosophers were now in the councils of government. In the liberal opposition the Protestants
and semi-Protestants were numerous: Benjamin Constant,
the Duc de Broglie, Guizot, J.-B. Say. While Victor Cousin
was not a Protestant, he popularized in France the metaphysical ideas of German Lutheranism. Between reactionary Catholicism and Protestant individualism, Saint-Simon
set himself up as an arbiter. It was on positive and industrial morality, and on that alone, that henceforward
he depended for the realization of the Christian precept,
Love one another.

No doubt Saint-Simon came to interpret this precept as

Helvetius and Bentham had done. Why do men not know how to bring about the harmony of their interests? Because they are ignorant of their true interests. "The code of Christian morality," wrote Saint-Simon, "has joined all men through their feelings, but it has dealt not at all with the question of their interests. . . . The old doctrine founded morality on belief; the new morality will have its basis in the proof that whatever is useful to the race is useful to the individual, and, reciprocally, that whatever is useful to the individual is useful to the race too."[86] But he put it still differently. He regretted that "the decadence of the old general doctrines" had left individuals incapable of disinterestedness, and "had allowed the development of the egoism that daily encroaches on society and that is eminently opposed to the formation of new doctrines. We must call on philanthropy to fight it and to bring it down."[87] He relied, then, not on considered egoism but on the "force of moral sentiment" to end the crisis thwarting mankind. "The truth in this regard—a truth established by the march of civilization—is that the passion for public welfare is much more effective in bringing about political amelioration than the egoistic passion of the classes to whom such changes must be most profitable. In a word, experience has proved that those with the greatest interest in the establishment of a new order of things are not those who work hardest to bring it about."[88] Here we are as far as possible from Helvetius and Bentham. The precondition of the harmony of interests is that each member of society not only know his own interests but that he be capable of elevating himself to a consideration of the general interest. In the theory of the classical economists, the fundamental human motivation is the desire to get rich, tempered by fear of being condemned.

[86] *Système industriel, Oeuvres,* V, 177.
[87] *Ibid.,* V, 21.
[88] *Ibid.,* VI, 120.

In Saint-Simon's theory, it is the desire to get rich, tempered by social enthusiasm.

In the history of the origins of modern socialism, we must find a place apart for Saint-Simonian socialism; it is remarkable in having grown out of liberal political economy, and in having grown out of it by an imperceptible evolution. It seems that Saint-Simon was hardly aware that his doctrine was different from that of J.-B. Say. He himself did not draw all the consequences from his principles. He wanted all social wealth to be distributed among those who had produced it, at the expense of the idle. Beyond that, he defined "industrial equality" as consisting "in that which each person draws in benefits from society in exact proportion to his social investment, that is to say, to his positive capacity and to the use which he makes of his means, among which, needless to say, his capital must be included."[89] But how can capital be considered a part of the "positive capacity" of an individual? How can we not look on the non-working capitalist, who exacts interest on his capital, as we look on one of the idle who levies a tithe on the produce of the labor of others? That this levy does not agree with the principle of "industrial equality" appears still more evident when the capital has not been created by the labor of the person who enjoys it, but has been transmitted to him by inheritance. "The industrial system," wrote Saint-Simon, "is founded on the principle of perfect equality; it is opposed to the establishment of all rights by birth and of all kinds of privilege."[90] How then could he write, without contradicting himself, "that wealth is in general a proof of capacity among the *industriels,* even when they have inherited the fortune they possess"?[91] These are problems that Saint-Simon left to his disciples. What is important is that his social doctrine already poses them, that it already constitutes a socialism

[89] *Ibid.,* VI, 17.
[90] *Catéchisme des industriels, Oeuvres,* VIII, 61.
[91] *Système industriel, Oeuvres,* V, 49.

in the sense that it sees a centralized organization of industrial labor and a planned distribution of social wealth as possible and as gradually being realized.

The word "socialism" was not uttered. When Saint-Simon died in 1825, ten more years would be needed before it became current. But the master had hardly died, indeed he was not yet dead, when his disciples, in characteristic language, were already denouncing "the spirit of individuality" and "individualism."[92] And did not Saint-Simon and his pupils use the adjective "social" in a way that raised the spectre of a corresponding noun? "The *industriels*," wrote Saint-Simon, "know well that they are the most capable of managing the financial interests of the nation, but they do not press the idea for fear of momentarily disturbing the peace; they wait patiently until opinion has come round on this subject and until a *truly social* doctrine calls them to take over the direction of affairs."[93] Enfantin, who had just become a convert to Saint-Simon's doctrine, and who was going to contribute more than anyone else to transforming it into a complete socialism, wrote barely a month after his master's death: "We shall show how it happens that production is, more and more, really managed by the producers, without bothering to ask what they will do when the administrative influence that they will one day exercise is superimposed on the governmental influence now exercised by the idle; but it will be perfectly plain that, *when the administration of production is social*, when it is completely de-

---

[92] Auguste Comte, *Lettres à Valat*, May 30, 1825, pp. 164–165: "The inevitable decay of religious doctrine has left unsupported the generous part of the human heart, and everything is reduced to the most abject individuality. . . . The spirit of individuality has penetrated into all classes." Cf. the article by Gondinet, *Producteur*, II, 162. For "individualism," see the article by Rouen, *Producteur*, II, 162; III, 389, 403. For "individualist," see the article by Rouen, *Producteur*, IV, 298.

[93] *Catéchisme des industriels, Oeuvres*, VIII, 11–12.

pendent on the will of the most capable producers, whatever administrative means they employ will do everything possible to promote production."[94]

II. *The Economic Doctrine of the Saint-Simonians*[1]

If the observations we have offered in the preceding essay are correct, it must be admitted that the essential principles of the Saint-Simonian "socialism" of 1830 were already to be found in the doctrine of Saint-Simon himself. It was to him that Bazard and Enfantin, the high priests of the "Saint-Simonian religion," owed the idea of "universal association seen as the organization of industry, a state in which the different nations scattered over the face of the earth appear only as parts of a vast workshop, laboring under a common impulse to achieve a common goal."[2] This is not to say that the generally held opinion to the contrary is not to be supported by very powerful arguments. Indeed, while Saint-Simon was alive, his doctrine was misunderstood by the readers of his manifestos and pamphlets. In vain had Saint-Simon insisted on the gulf that separated his industrialism from the current liberalism; the liberals persisted in looking on him as one of their own. Did they not have common enemies in the bureaucrats, did they not agree that their numbers should be reduced and their incomes pared down? In a general way, Saint-Simon denounced the "idle rich," but it was enough to understand by that—as he himself did every time he moved from principles to application—either landed proprietors or the holders of government securities;

[94] Letter to Thérèse Nugues, August 18, 1825.
[1] A study published in the *Revue du Mois*, VI, 39–75 (July 10, 1908).
[2] *Exposition de la doctrine, premiere année* (1st ed.), p. 107.

so again agreement seemed complete between Saint-Simon and the liberal publicists. Did he not continue to regard Adam Smith and J.-B. Say, the founders of economic liberalism, as his masters? The misunderstanding persisted until Saint-Simon's death. But when he died in 1825, it was hard for it to continue.

Saint-Simon's disciples read Sismondi's *Nouveaux principes d'économie politique*. They read the articles in the *Revue encyclopédique* in which Sismondi defended his economic heresy against J.-B. Say.[3] In 1818 Sismondi had visited England, talked with Ricardo, toured the manufacturing centers, seen the misery of the working classes, and watched one of the crises that periodically made that state of misery intolerable. He had tried to account for these crises and to explain how the invention of machines, which was prodigiously multiplying the yield of human labor, had nonetheless had the effect of rendering the existence of the great majority of workers more precarious than ever. Influenced by the writings of Robert Owen, he had developed the theory of industrial concentration. The effect of commercial competition was not, as he says, constantly to restore the balance of wealth after temporary fluctuations, thus leading ultimately to the equalization of economic conditions. The necessary effect of competition was to give the stronger the advantage over the weaker and, consequently, constantly to increase the inequality of wealth.

To succeed in a commercial and progressive society, as new machines appear, one must be in a position to change one's industrial equipment rapidly; and to be in a position to make this sacrifice of capital, one must first be rich. Hence the concentration of industry: a smaller and smaller number of larger and larger enterprises. Hence the con-

[3] *Revue encyclopédique*, XXII, 264–399 (1824). J.-B. Say's reply is in XXIII, pp. 18 ff. See in the same number, pp. 67 ff., an article signed S. (Sismondi) on William Thompson's *Inquiry*.

centration of wealth: a smaller and smaller number of richer and richer individuals facing a larger and larger number of poor. Hence the impossibility encountered by manufacturers of selling their products in the countries where they are produced. Who would absorb them? The rich? They are very rich, true, but they are very few in number; moreover, the products of the factory system are not luxury goods but goods of ordinary utility and common consumption. Will the workers buy them? They are very numerous, true, but very badly paid and in no position to buy back the produce of their own labor with their wages. Hence, finally, the need for manufacturers to seek markets abroad. But it is inevitable that each new market will soon be saturated with goods in its turn and that the glut will reappear. According to Sismondi, the economists were wrong in denying the possibility of overproduction, as they generally did, basing themselves on *a priori* arguments. The most advanced industrial nations produce too much; and, without indicating very clearly what remedy he proposed to apply, Sismondi was inclined to believe that the state would be able to intervene to limit production and to prevent the growth of productivity from outstripping the growth of demand.

At the time when Sismondi was writing, France had not yet experienced the crises from which England suffered; that pleased Saint-Simon very much. If the heads of industry were not at war with their workers, as they were in England, it was a sign, he thought, that France was destined before England to realize the industrial system founded on the peaceful creation of spontaneous feelings of solidarity between all levels of the hierarchy. But if serious conflicts had not yet broken out between French employers and their workers, was it not simply because, by 1820, French industry, exhausted by twenty years of revolution and war, had undergone only a very modest development? If it did develop, could it not be foreseen that it would have to go through the same crises as those from which English industry suffered? In 1826 the crisis came, and in the second edition of his *Nouveaux principes,* Sismondi could boast of being a prophet. So, about that time, Saint-Simon's disciples were faced with a new economic problem which they had to try to resolve in conformity with the principles set down by their master.[4] Could they follow Sismondi and admit that there will always be an excess of production? Saint-Simon had singled out production—and the most intensive production—as the sole purpose of society. When, after his death, his disciples founded a journal to propagate his ideas, they called it *Le Producteur (The Producer).* On the other hand, could they follow J.-B. Say and admit that the phenomena of overproduction revealed by Sismondi are purely illusory, and that every commodity must necessarily find a market under the system of free competition? In Saint-Simon's view, industrial society drew nearer to perfection to the degree that it was organized; when all members of society, in every industry, worked together in pursuit of a common goal, it would be perfectly organic. How was it possible, then, to admit that the balance of production and consumption could be established, without a prior understanding among the producers, by the simple action of blind competition among individuals? If the principles of Saint-Simon's economic philosophy were true, then the Saint-Simonians had to take up a position somewhere between that of Sismondi and that of J.-B. Say.

Somewhat later, Saint-Simon's disciples read the works of Fourier. That madman still had only a few disciples and a few readers. The Saint-Simonians were the first to give him some credit, until the time when the break-up of their "church" furnished the Fourierist school with some of the most intelligent and active of his converts. In Fourier they found both a social system and a system of the universe; perhaps Fourier's example was one reason

[4] See the article signed P.E. (Prosper Enfantin) on Sismondi's *Nouveaux principes* in *Le Producteur,* V, 94 ff.

why they transformed the "positive" philosophy of Saint-Simon into a metaphysical pantheism.[5] In Fourier they found a critique of competition that was not without distant analogies to the critiques of Robert Owen and Sismondi: competition resulted in the setting-up of commercial monopolies, with the merchant interposing himself between the producer and the consumer to enrich himself at the expense of both. Fourier called it "commercial feudalism," and it is highly probable that that Fourierist expression had some influence on the Saint-Simonians when they came to compare the development of industrial concentration with the developments of military feudalism around the eleventh century. Again, the Saint-Simonians found in Fourier a complete and very complicated psychology, much more complicated than the rudimentary psychology of the orthodox economists: five passive passions, four active passions, and three distributive passions, the last most important of all for anyone wanting to understand the mechanism of the economy. Of the three distributive passions, one in particular was of a kind to arrest the attention of the Saint-Simonians. The *composite*, Fourier tells us, is "a kind of blind fury"; it is that enthusiasm, made up of different passions, that seizes on individuals by the very fact that they are together, that they form a crowd. In the last analysis, it is the zeal that, in Saint-Simonian doctrine, directs the efforts of all the members of industrial society towards a common goal and transforms their rivalries into emulation. It is the "composite" that must inspire soldiers of the "industrial armies,"[6] which Fourier sends to the economic conquest of the whole world, to reclaim the seas, to make deserts fertile, and at last to bring eternal spring to the face of the

[5] On the debt of Saint-Simonianism to Fourier, see H. Bourgin, *Fourier, contribution à l'étude du socialisme français* (1905), pp. 416 ff.

[6] *Théorie des quatre mouvements*, pp. 263–267; *Théorie de l'unité universelle*, pp. 95–97.

earth. In the Saint-Simonians of 1830 we rediscover the "industrial armies" of Fourier.

Finally, and most important, Saint-Simon's disciples found in Fourier the solution to the problem raised by the debate between Sismondi and J.-B. Say in the *Revue encyclopédique*. An increase in industrial productivity must always be welcomed, said J.-B. Say, because it is impossible that a commodity, once brought to market, will not end by being distributed, by finding a consumer. An increase in production must be condemned, replied Sismondi, unless—as might and indeed did happen—it is preceded by better distribution. Fourier reversed the problem. His thesis was that the necessary precondition for an increase in production was better distribution of jobs and wealth among the workers. Under the competitive system, individual efforts were dispersed, incoherent, blind. What was needed was a systematic structure, in which everyone would take pleasure in doing a job suited to him and in which everyone would be paid accordingly, once the job was accomplished for there to be, as Fourier put it, "a quadruple product."

From the day of Saint-Simon's death, his disciples dedicated themselves to building on the principles he had enunciated as a critique of competition. Among others, there were Olinde Rodrigues, an employee of a banking house who, for two years, had kept Saint-Simon going with subsidies; Saint-Amand Bazard, famous as a conspirator and founder of secret societies, who had grown disgusted with political and revolutionary language; and, most important, Prosper Enfantin, like Olinde Rodrigues employed in a bank, who contributed more than the others to the development of the economic doctrine, until he transformed Saint-Simonianism into a metaphysical dogma and complicated it with an ecclesiastical and ritual organization.[7] They founded *Le Producteur*, a weekly publica-

[7] On the Saint-Simonian group, see S. Charlety, *Histoire du Saint-Simonisme* (1896).

tion at first, then a monthly; and the attacks on the competitive system grew more and more bitter from number to number as they became increasingly aware of the contradiction between the current formulas of classical political economy and the leading ideas of the political economy the principles of which Saint-Simon had just worked out. At first, they accepted articles by authors favoring competition as "the most powerful stimulus to perfection," limiting themselves only to adding that they could not shut their eyes "to the temporary evils which it caused."[8] They paid homage to Adam Smith, the first man to help in making the commercial and industrial point of view predominate over the political and military point of view in government.[9] But was not Adam Smith's economic philosophy based entirely on the idea of competition? Before long they began to lament that the economists, after having founded "this new science and having almost brought it from its beginnings to the positive state," had tried "to subordinate it to critical politics," and "to reduce it to the narrow confines of individualism."[10] For the moment, they blamed contemporaries, Charles Comte and Dunoyer, Saint-Simon's old friends, for the confusion. But they ended by blaming Adam Smith himself.

Adam Smith had laid the foundations of political economy as a positive science, but he was the contemporary of Voltaire, Rousseau, and the lawyers who had brought about the American and French Revolutions. He could not have been anything but an individualist; he could not have kept his work free of the influence of the "critical ideas" then in vogue. We know what value the Saint-Simonian school attached to critical ideas—a "negative

[8] *Producteur*, I, 149. Cf. the article by Artaud, I, 436. [The articles in *Le Producteur* were unsigned; the attributions given here are those in Halévy's footnotes.]

[9] Blanqui in *Producteur*, I, 344.

[10] P.-J. Rouen, "Examen d'un nouvel ouvrage de M. Dunoyer, ancien rédacteur du *Censeur européen*," *Producteur*, II, 164.

value," a "destructive value."[11] Whatever good may have been done by the corporations in the Middle Ages, it was useful in the eighteenth century to destroy whatever was exclusive and narrow about them. The true role of the theory of free competition had been to enlarge the bounds within which exchange took place and to permit men to conceive a great mercantile republic, comprising the whole race, in place of the old local, provincial, or national markets. But the error was to believe that competition was or ought to be forever the law according to which the products of human industry would be exchanged in this vast market. "Who will then be in control? No one: everyone knows so well where mankind is going that there is no need for general councils, for general rules of conduct; order is born *naturally* from disorder, union from anarchy, association from egoism. . . . That is the whole critical system."[12]

According to the apologists of competition, goods exchange naturally when their cost of production is equal; it seems to follow that the mechanism of free competition necessarily assigns to each commodity a value exactly proportionate to the labor that has gone into it. But does this theory of value, which is Ricardo's, and to which J.-B. Say's may be reduced, have a general application? One can imagine, replied Enfantin, that it applies when two producers bring the "material produce" of their industries simultaneously into the same market to exchange them. Then "it is obvious that the clash of supply and demand will determine the price of the commodities confronting each other and (when there is no privilege or monopoly) that the price must continually approach the costs of production." But what happens when the individuals facing each other are, one, a capitalist, the owner of a commodity which is the product of past labor, and the other a worker

[11] *Exposition de la doctrine*, I, 75, 127; II, 5.
[12] Prosper Enfantin, "Considérations sur l'organisation féodale et l'organisation industrielle," *Producteur*, III, 406.

"who brings for exchange only the promise of future labor"? In that situation the owner must enjoy a real privilege vis-à-vis the laborer—the right of ownership he exercises over his capital. It is in his power to pay the worker a wage far below the value of the produce of his labor. "What happens when the services of a worker are bought? He is supported so that tomorrow he will be what he was yesterday—a producer. Indeed, he is given the wherewithal to be a better producer, just as efforts are made to replenish capital by successful industrial undertakings. But must that increase go to the idle owner of the capital involved, or should it rather remain in the hands of those who know how to use it productively? To follow the comparison between capital and worker further, would it be better for the price of a worker's services to go to the master who hires him rather than to remain with the worker himself?" Ricardo was right in arguing, contrary to J.-B. Say's opinion, that rent on land is not payment for productive labor. But he was wrong in believing that the qualitative difference in land was the true cause of rent. "Rent would not exist where each landowner, cultivating his own land, lived from the produce of that land." Nor would it exist "in a community" where "all the produce was sent into common shops to be divided according to individual needs." Everything depends on the basic principle underlying the law of property; and the most important part of political economy is that which deals with the distribution of wealth. *The respective shares of the landowner, capitalist, and laborer* have an enormous influence on social welfare. The abilities of industrial entrepreneurs frequently produce nothing because they are crushed by the luxury of the idle classes, arising from the increase in interest and rents, or by the misery of the workers who wear themselves out in supporting this luxury and dissipation."[13]

[13] Enfantin, "Considérations sur la baisse progressive du loyer des objets mobiliers et immobiliers," *Producteur*, I, 214 ff.

The apologists for competition fall back on still another argument to justify it. Not content to say that the value of commodities is fixed by their cost of production, they add that that value is fixed by the lowest cost of production of commodities brought into the same market. From this they conclude that competition has beneficial effects for all consumers, in other words for the members of the society under consideration, since they can acquire more cheaply those things useful or agreeable to them. But, answered Enfantin,[14] to say that is to forget that the competition that takes place between businessmen can bring about the lowering of prices in two quite different ways. On the one hand, to be sure, they improve industrial processes and install machines of greater productivity: they succeed in "making more or better products *in the same time and with the same effort.*" In this case, all mankind benefits. But, on the other hand, they succeed in selling their products more cheaply and in beating out their competitors by lowering the wages they pay to their workers. In this case, the buyers of the product benefit, but not the workers who are its first sellers, and who will find it harder to obtain the means of subsistence with the price of their labor.

In short, competition is good when it is "in things": it is fatal when it takes place "between persons." The lowering of prices that results from it is favorable to those who are consumers without being producers. It is favorable to producers only to the extent that the lowering of prices of the goods they buy is not made up by the lowering of wages. To prove that competition is useful to the race without any qualification, one would have to prove that it necessarily stimulates the improvement of industrial processes. We see that it does no such thing. The competitive system leads, not to the division of labor and income according to capacities, but to the separation of two classes—one idle,

[14] *Producteur,* III, 385 ff.

the other working, with the idle able to take advantage of competition to the detriment of the workers. Thus the antagonism of all against all leads necessarily to the enslavement of the majority by the minority, and the liberal commercial system under which we live perpetuates certain vices that belonged to the economic structure of the feudal system. What is needed is a new social and religious structure, a "new Christianity," to finish the work begun by the Christian church—the abolition of slavery and the enfranchisement of the workers.

A revolution is needed then, in the conception of economic science. It cannot be considered as reducible to the theory of free competition, as being purely and simply, as Saint-Simon put it in 1817, the "science of liberty": we have seen that free competition is neither the best nor the only conceivable means of promoting industrial progress. If one believes the liberal economists, free competition would bring about the "division of labor" most favorable to the interests of mankind; we have seen to what a limited extent that proposition is admissible, and, to the extent to which it is admissible, we have seen that the final equilibrium is established only at the cost of crises and painful convulsions. Should not the goal of economic science be to learn how to avoid these crises? If we know the result the competitive system slowly and painfully tends to bring about, why not aim directly at the desired result? Why not look on the spontaneous and instinctive "division of labor" resulting from exchange as a special and crude form of a more general phenomenon—the "combination of efforts" towards a known goal: the exploitation of the inhabited globe? That is the true purpose of political economy.[15]

Leaving aside the auxiliary sciences, notably technology, prior knowledge of which is assumed, economic science—the "theory of industry"—is concerned with "the re-

[15] Enfantin, "Considérations sur l'organisation féodale et l'organisation industrielle," *Producteur*, III, 67.

lations that join all members of a society together in material production." These relationships have as their goal, first, "the direct increase of productive power by means of greater knowledge and a better combination of efforts"; when considered in this way, political economy tries to describe "the combined action of the *industriels* to bring about the scientific division of labor—of farmers, manufacturers, and merchants—according to their aptitudes or location." A second purpose of these economic relationships is "the division of the produce of human labor"; when it is concerned with the distribution among producers of the produce of social industry, political economy must in turn examine the relations of workers with each other, the relations of managers and workers, and the relations between producers and idle consumers, in other words, "rent, leases and interest, or, still better, *the privileges pertaining to the provision of the sites and equipment* required for production."[16] This division of the subject does not differ essentially from the distinction then generally made by economists between the theory of production and the theory of distribution of wealth. But whereas political economy as J.-B. Say conceived it tended to look on these relationships as natural and immutable, Enfantin and the Saint-Simonians defined them as social and variable. In short, the field of economic science is extended, because the method of economic science is shifted: using two terms that do not belong to the vocabulary of the school, we can say that the Saint-Simonian method in political economy is both social and historical.

First, let us say, it is a social method. Here is what we mean by that: Once having isolated a set of homogeneous facts—the particular subject of his inquiry—the economist

[16] Enfantin, "Considérations sur les progrès de l'économie politique dans ses rapports avec l'organisation sociale: premier article," *Producteur*, IV, 384–385. Cf. Saint-Amand Bazard, "De la nécessité d'une nouvelle doctrine générale," *ibid.*, III, 547.

must not assume that this set includes all social facts without exception, or that the set can be considered as completely independent of other sets of social facts. The Physiocrats did not make this mistake; they had both a political economy and a general view of politics, and made the former dependent on the latter. "They started from a general idea they had formed of the kind of social order towards which all efforts should be directed; hence they dealt with the science of wealth so as to make it harmonize with the wholly conjectural conception of natural law; they looked on political economy as philosophers."[17] Adam Smith and his successors must be blamed for having reduced political economy to the proportions of a special science, whose concern is isolated from the totality of social relations. "They wanted to lay the foundation of social organization *a posteriori*, beginning with the smallest facts, from the division of labor, even in a single individual, up to freedom of commerce among peoples. . . . They entered the subject by way of details, such as the definition of the words value, price, and production, which did not require the slightest idea of the composition or structure of societies."[18] Why should we be surprised at this? The economists of the school of Adam Smith all belonged to a critical and revolutionary epoch in human thought. It is the characteristic of critical epochs to favor the dispersion of effort and specialization of the sciences. Economic science cannot possess an organic character, nor can the society for which it would prescribe, so long as economists fail to understand the impossibility of effecting a separation between knowledge of economic phenomena and knowledge of the totality of political and juridical institutions.

The method of political economy must be historical as well. History should not be understood to mean "a collection of unrelated facts founded on a conception of hu-

[17] *Producteur*, IV, 386.
[18] *Producteur*, IV, 387–388.

manity, that is, facts arranged in chronological order or according to the geographical distribution of peoples";[19] it should be thought of, rather, as "the cumulative development of the human race," as the theory of the general progress of societies. Everyone who in the half-century before the Saint-Simonians had helped to create the positive science of economic phenomena—the Physiocrats as well as Adam Smith and his disciples—had erred in believing that the laws that observation shows us these phenomena obey are eternal laws. In this respect, their method was "metaphysical" or "ontological," suitable to the time in which they wrote. The Physiocrats believed in a natural order of societies which was the work of Providence, and they thought they could prove its existence "by considerations drawn from observing the abstract individual";[20] actually, the definition of this order was suggested by the features of the economic world in which they lived. In spite of the advances made by the critical spirit, they wrote at a time when the feudal system was still in force; that is why they gave political predominance to the landed proprietors and assigned them the major role in the "natural society" they depicted. Adam Smith wrote a little later; consequently, he was the theoretician of a society more clearly arrived in a critical state. He tried to explain all economic phenomena, and even all social phenomena, by the principle of free competition. In actuality, all social facts, and economic facts in particular, are variable, but this is not to say that they are subject to no law at all. The laws that govern them, however, are laws of "progress," of "progression," of "development,"[21] or of "evolution," to use the word that began to appear in

[19] *Producteur*, IV, 383.
[20] *Producteur*, IV, 379.
[21] *Exposition de la doctrine*, II, 72: "la loi providentielle du progrès; I, 111: "loi de progression"; I, 43, 45, II, 58: "loi de developpement."

1829 in the vocabulary of the Saint-Simonians, which they borrowed from the philosopher Ballanche.[22] Granting that all series of social phenomena are evolutionary, the problem is to determine the fixed relationships that exist between these variations. To explain scientifically a certain class of social phenomena—economic phenomena, for example—is to connect the law of variation of the series created by the succession of these phenomena to the law of variation of one or several other series. "By the study of history, taken as the cumulative development of the human race, we can arrive at an understanding of the direction in which societies move; then we can perceive the link that must join the present to the future, and sci-

[22] "The Saint-Simonian doctrine does not aim at bringing about an upheaval or a revolution; it comes to predict and accomplish a *transformation,* an *evolution;* it brings a new *education,* an ultimate *regeneration* to the world. . . . Humanity *knows* that it has undergone progressive evolutions . . . it knows the law of those crises which have continually modified it." *Exposition de la doctrine,* I, 138–158. Cf. II, 5, 88. This term, new in its scientific use, seems to have been borrowed by Bazard from Ballanche's *Essais de palingénésie sociale,* which had just appeared (see especially the third volume of his *Oeuvres,* pp. 11, 201). Ballanche is cited in *Exposition de la doctrine,* II, 34; and we know that the Saint-Simonians read a great deal of him around 1829 (see Hippolyte Carnot, "Sur le Saint-Simonisme," *Travaux de l'Academie des Sciences Morales et Politiques* [1887], p. 125). Borrowings from the *Palingénésie* are numerous in the *Système de la Méditerranée,* published by Michel Chevalier in the *Globe,* January 31, 1832, the word *palingénésie* itself being found in the essay. Now Ballanche had borrowed the word *évolution,* as he did the title of his book, from the *Palingénésie philosophique* by Charles Bonnet, in particular Part III, Chapter IV, "Préformation et évolution des êtres organisés." "Everything has been preformed from the beginning," wrote Charles Bonnet, ". . . that which we improperly call generation is only the principle of development which will render visible and palpable what hitherto has been invisible and impalpable." Bonnet's system is a development of the philosophy of Leibniz. In the last analysis, then, the word *évolution* would be Leibnizian in origin.

ence can hasten the march of humanity towards the goal to which it draws nearer and nearer."[23]

To complete the structure of economic science, then, it would be necessary to know the general law governing the evolution of society and to place the law of evolution of economic phenomena in dependence on that general law. It was from Saint-Simon that the Saint-Simonians borrowed their definition of progress: they took up the theory according to which industrial society tends steadily to win out over military society. But they completed the theory and expressed it in a new form which acquired its greater degree of doctrinal precision in a series of lectures given in 1829 by Saint-Amand Bazard and published under the title of *Exposition de la doctrine de Saint-Simon*.[24] Human associations began as a small number of members. They began to conflict with each other; antagonism was the principle of existence of these primitive societies. This antagonism had repercussions on the internal structure of each of them. A superior class lived at the expense of an inferior class reduced to slavery and "exploited" by the first: the "exploitation of man by man"—that is what the economic structure of these societies amounted to. Little by little, human groupings grew more extensive and came to include a larger number of individuals. Conflicts between these societies—each of them containing an important fraction of mankind—became rarer as the societies became less numerous. Antagonism ceased to be the basic condition of their existence, whether one considers the relationships of each of them with its neighboring societies or its internal structure; in this way little by little, in the inevitable course of history, the final destination of the human race was revealed—"the exploitation of the terrestrial globe by men in association."[25]

23 *Producteur*, IV, 380.
24 Première année, quatrième séance, first edition, pp. 77 ff.
25 *Ibid.*, I, 83. In the *Producteur*, especially in the articles by Enfantin, one can follow the progressive elaboration of the

Is this law of progress to be explained by the operation of physical and mechanical causes? Is it a particular case of the general law of evolution of the solar system, which itself is explained by the Newtonian law of molecular attraction? Such was the view Saint-Simon first took of the positive science of society; but he renounced it after 1815. Did the law have, then, to be considered as a simple "general fact," drawn by observation from discrete facts of history, and useful for predicting new facts, but an explanatory principle itself inexplicable?[26] Such was the view Saint-Simon took in the last years of his life, when he was working with Auguste Comte. Now the Saint-Simonians, the members of the "Saint-Simonian Church," inclined towards a finalist, metaphysical, and religious interpretation of progress. According to them, it was the love of order

formula. See especially I, 555: . . . "The institutions which consecrated the power of man over man were a step which societies had necessarily to take to move from barbarism to the degree of civilization we now have." III, 67: ". . . The rule of man over man was a step that societies had necessarily to take to escape from the primitive stage of barbarism which divided the people and hampered their progress." Some pages further on (III, 73), Enfantin laid down the end of society as "the exploitation of the world in which we live . . . , the most complete exploitation of the world in which we live." But the formula is anticipated in the early writings of the school. Augustin Thierry, in the *Censeur européen*, II, 128, wrote "of subjects to exploit or enemies to pillage." Cf. de Montévran, *Histoire critique et raisonnée de la situation de l'Angleterre* (1819), I, 310–311: "Ireland has been, if we may be allowed to use the word, more usefully *exploited* to the profit of Great Britain; and it becomes quite clear that . . . Ireland is only a colony of Great Britain, which will escape from the yoke at the first opportunity. . . ." The word *exploité* is underlined in the text: it was a neologism at that time.

[26] On this change of view and the corresponding distinction, in Saint-Simonian language, between the *astronomical* and the *physiological* viewpoint, see Saint-Simon's words cited by O. Rodrigues, *Producteur*, III, 105, 106. Cf. the article by Buchez, *ibid.*, IV, 68, 69, and the article by Saint-Amand Bazard, *ibid.*, IV, 118.

and unity, innate in man, immanent in nature, that explained the origin and development of society and of the science itself.

The Saint-Simonians set out to found not only a new economics, but a new philosophy of history, a new metaphysics, a new religion, and a new ecclesiastical organization. It was too much to do. One can understand why they did not have time to write a treatise on political economy according to their principles that could be set against the classical treatises of J.-B. Say and Ricardo. On two points, however, going beyond the teaching of Saint-Simon, they tried to define the law of evolution that economic phenomena obey. Their conclusions on these two points were opposed to the conclusions of the liberal economists, although they proposed only to carry further the critique of feudal institutions begun by the liberals, or, more exactly, to show how, in the inevitable course of things, two survivals of the feudal system were tending to disappear before our eyes.

The present age in the history of mankind is, the Saint-Simonians tell us, a critical period; in many respects it must resemble the last critical period through which the western world passed, the Graeco-Roman period. The revolutionaries of today, who say their aim is the restoration of liberty and equality understood as the ancient republics understood them, forget that the Graeco-Roman period was an age of dissolution of belief, of intellectual anarchy, and consequently of political and economic anarchy. The philosophers attacked the polytheism that had served as the spiritual underpinning of the great Eastern civilizations; and all classical civilization rested on the antagonism of interests, on the institution of slavery. Today critical philosophy prides itself on having discredited the Catholic religion and Christian monotheism; but a civilization founded on the principle of unlimited freedom of conscience is, by the same token, a civilization lacking any principle of order. The economic principle of free com-

petition corresponds to the philosophical principle of freedom of conscience; and the struggle of all against all perpetuates certain forms—weakened, to be sure, but still
real—of slavery, the military or feudal institution *par excellence.* "We have only to look at what goes on around
us to see that the *worker* is exploited *materially, intellectually,* and *morally* as the *slave* was once, though not so
intensely. It is perfectly clear that he can hardly provide
for himself by his labor, and that it is not up to him
whether or not he works."[27] In other words, he has, as we
shall see, neither the right to subsistence nor the right to
work. The economic institutions to which we must impute
this real enslavement of the worker of today are lending
at interest and inheritance.

Enfantin undertook a critique of interest in the *Producteur.*[28] By his own labor, a man has amassed twenty
thousand sacks of wheat; we can conceive of his living for
as long as a hundred years by consuming two hundred
sacks of wheat annually. But thanks to the institution of
lending at interest, in a country like England where interest is at three per cent, he can get a rent of six hundred
sacks, while keeping his capital of twenty thousand sacks
intact; in France, where interest is at five per cent, he can
get a rent of a thousand sacks; and in a country like southern Russia, where interest is at twenty per cent, he can get
an annual rent of four thousand sacks. Society confers on
him, then, a right not only to the use of the produce of his
past labor, but as well to the use of a portion of what is
currently produced by the labor of others. Is this just?
To answer the question, we must adopt the Saint-Simonian
standpoint to observe the course of things and to deter-

[27] *Exposition de la doctrine,* I, 105.
[28] "Considérations sur la baisse progressive du loyer des objets mobiliers et immobiliers," *Producteur,* I, 241 ff.; 555 ff.
Cf. II, 32, 124. See also an account of this theory in I. Péreire,
Leçons sur l'industrie (1832).

mine whether the natural movement of history tends to strengthen or weaken this privilege.

It is a recognized fact among economists that a steady decline in the rate of interest is proportionate to the progress of civilization. What is the cause of this decline? Is it the lessening of the productivity of capital? By no means, for the decline of interest accompanies an increase in wealth which itself is caused by the improvement of industrial processes, in other words by increasing the productivity of capital. Actually, the decline of interest stems from a more general fact which dominates all social progress, that is, the better organization of effort, the more complete association of workers. If the workers compete to get what the owners of capital consent to give them in the way of advances, the owners will be able to demand interest that is all the higher as the workers are isolated from each other and, consequently will create a still more bitter competition. But if the workers learn to combine and the bankers become, so to speak, the syndics of their association, their representatives charged with negotiating with the capitalists the conditions on which advances of funds will be made, the positions of workers and idle capitalists will be reversed; now the capitalists will compete to get the workers to use their capital. The interest on capital will drop, therefore, because of the progress brought about by the banking industry, in other words, by the organization of the association of workers; and the idle class will steadily decrease in political importance in relation to the working class. Should there be a limit to this decline in the rate of interest? What would it be? The economists regard interest on capital as made up of two parts: "one is the premium that guarantees the solvency of the borrower, the other is the share the owner actually takes from the annual produce of the labor of the borrower." When the second element entirely disappears—and there is nothing to prevent our conceiving this possibility —interest will be reduced to a simple insurance premium, and one will be able to say that credit has become free: each worker will be advanced the capital that he as a producer needs in direct proportion to the "credit" that he offers, the confidence that he inspires, and his industrial ability. Workers will cease to exist at the pleasure of the capitalists; it is the capitalists who will find themselves at the pleasure of the workers. The idle will no longer dictate the conditions of labor to the workers; the workers will dictate the conditions of ease to the idle.

In the *Producteur,* Enfantin touched on the problem of inheritance only in passing, by cursory and vague allusions.[29] It was Bazard, in the *Exposition de la doctrine,* who came to grips with the problem and established what from then on was to be the main tenet of Saint-Simonian "socialism." We live in a society, he tells us, in which all the privileges of birth have disappeared, save one, that attaching to property. The distinction between master and slave has vanished from our language; but, because property remains hereditary, in reality this distinction is perpetuated under a new name. It becomes the distinction between "bourgeois" and "proletarian." It appears to have been only after 1830 that the Saint-Simonians began to use the word "bourgeois" in this particular sense.[30] But the *Exposition de la doctrine* had already declared that inheritance of property in one class brought with it an "inheritance of misery" for another class and had used that inheritance of misery to explain "the existence in society of a class of proletarians."[31] The liberal economists refused to attack hereditary property, on the grounds that the right of property was supposedly inviolable. Now

[29] See especially the articles by Enfantin, *Producteur,* I, 566, II, 257.

[30] *Globe,* March 7, 14, 21, 1831. But before that, see *Exposition de la doctrine,* p. 254: ". . . those warmly-held conventional beliefs which too often allow an egoistic bourgeois to be taken for a dedicated citizen."

[31] *Exposition de la doctrine,* I, 105.

it is quite true that, in a sense, one cannot conceive of a society without property, a society in which every instrument of production would not be at the disposition of some particular person. The question is whether the right of property is not a variable, like all social facts, and whether it is not possible to define scientifically the law by which it varies.

Clearly the right of property varies according to the nature of the things that one regards as subject to it. At first, man could be the property of man, with no limitation, then more and more restrictions were brought to bear on the exercise of the right of property of man in man, until the time when public opinion and the law agreed in declaring that man cannot be the property of man. It is equally clear that the right of property varies according to the mode of transmission of the things subject to it. The individual is, by turns, free to bequeath his goods as he wishes, obliged to leave them to his male children and among them exclusively to his eldest son, or obliged, finally, to divide them equally among all his children, without distinction as to age or sex. Must the right always be kept within the limits of the family? Or, rather, how can we explain the fact that today transmission within the family seems necessary?

What is property? It is the right to dispose of instruments of production, and "of wealth not destined to be immediately consumed," from which an income may be derived—what the economists call "productive capital." The enjoyment of this right carries with it the obligation to fulfil a social function. It is the owner who has to allocate the instruments of production so as to make them as productive as possible. The income that the landed proprietor and the capitalist draw from their property is remuneration for this service. But why are the exercise of this function and the income attached to it hereditary? Because of a survival from feudal and military civilization, in which all functions were hereditary, and in which the income from landed property served to reward a number of governmental services rendered by the feudal lords. But why, in an age when all other social functions have ceased to be hereditary, should the function of allocating the instruments of production among workers according to their abilities alone remain hereditary? Is it because we are satisfied with the way in which it is done? Are we so blind that we do not see the scarcities and gluts that stem from the fact that the allocation of capital is badly handled? Abandoned to incompetent agents, acting in isolation without a full view of the needs of the market and chosen by the chance of birth and not by individual merit, it cannot be well done. Are we afraid to renounce this last remnant of the last organic era, this final vestige of a civilization based entirely on the principle of heredity? Is it the only fixed point, the only solid support amid universal anarchy and uncertainty? To say this is to forget that the true cause of the decay of the feudal system is not the philosophers' criticism but the slow emergence of a new organic civilization, industrial, not military, dedicated to production, not destruction. This structure will soon have acquired sufficient solidity for us to complete the revolution by deciding that property, like all other social functions, will no longer constitute a privilege of birth; rather, it will be assigned to those best qualified to exercise it in the general interest of society. "A new order is being established: it consists in transferring the right of inheritance, now limited to the household, to the state as an *association of workers.*"[32]

Depending upon whether we are considering the theory of the steady decline in the rate of interest or the theory of the coming and necessary abolition of inheritance, we see that what the Saint-Simonian school called the "social system" can and must be brought about in two different ways.

[32] *Exposition de la doctrine,* I, 115.

On the one hand, there is the natural development of industrial organization which, without state intervention, tends to socialize industry. The organization of the industrial world was at first directed towards a negative goal: the *industriels* united for the collective defense of their interests through their syndics, the bankers, against the idle class who exploited them. But this organization has the positive results both of making production more intensive and of obtaining a better distribution of the output. Production becomes more intensive because the bankers, whose function it is to allocate social capital among producers, are the most favorably placed to make the allocation according to abilities. The output is better distributed because, thanks to the centralized organization of industry, the workers—in contrast to what happened under the competitive system—set out to satisfy needs the nature and extent of which they know beforehand. Before our very eyes, a social transformation is taking place analogous to that of eight centuries ago when the allodial system was succeeded by the feudal system, when the dispersal of landed property among a host of petty free proprietors was replaced by the consolidation and organization of that property under the military leaders, the barons.[33] The essential difference between the feudalism of the Middle Ages and the new feudalism is that the former was organized for war and destruction, while the latter will be organized for peace and production. That progress, which is so favorable to the interests of the workers, will in some respects come about instinctively, but this does not mean that we must not intervene to make it more certain and direct. In the interest of the workers—in other words, of the vast majority of the human race—we can and must co-operate to foster industrial centralization—suggesting to the banks, for example, new procedures that will allow them to improve their methods

[33] *Ibid.*, I, 123.

by keeping the amount of cash required for their operations to a minimum, to institute the credit system in the
fullest sense, to "generalize confidence."[34] We ourselves
can put these techniques into operation; we can found
banks to underwrite industry and to multiply contacts between capital, scientific talent, and industrial talent.[35]
There is no need for a violent revolution to bring about
the "social system": that system is the point at which the
evolution of the present system will naturally issue. The
Saint-Simonian attitude is opposed, then, to the Fourierist
attitude. According to Charles Fourier, from financial feudalism, the ultimate scandal of the competitive system, the
contrasting system of harmony must burst forth after a
violent convulsion. The Saint-Simonians, on the other
hand, looked on industrial feudalism, the theory of which
was influenced by the Fourierist theory of financial feudalism, as the full realization of the social system. When
they set about merging credit institutions and consolidating
means of transport in France, the Péreire brothers were
showing themselves not unfaithful to the tradition of orthodox Saint-Simonianism.

But there is no reason why, by intervening, the state
should not play a part in the socialization of the industrial
system; indeed, it is impossible to see how the abolition
of inheritance could be brought about without such intervention. In any event, the Saint-Simonians were not
democrats. They did not rely on the will of the greatest
number to bring about reforms; minorities, individual leaders were needed to manage and persuade majorities.
Bankers and heads of firms are singled out by the positions they occupy and the abilities by which they qualify
for them to serve as the innovators in industrial society.

[34] Enfantin, "Des banques d'escompte," *Producteur*, II, 20.
See the two articles with this title, by Enfantin, *Producteur*,
II, 18 ff., 109 ff.
[35] P.-J. Rouen, "Société commanditaire de l'industrie," *Producteur*, I, 11 ff., 117 ff.

This is not the case with heads of state, to be sure; birth, not merit, has put them where they are; or else they are usurpers who owe their thrones to governmental and military abilities quite unrelated to the abilities needed to administer an industrial society. Yet it might happen that a head of state would by chance become accessible to Saint-Simonian teaching, that this new Constantine would allow himself to be converted by the "new Christians" and would put at their disposal the legal power the constitution of the country confers on him, as well as the real power he holds in popular confidence. Saint-Simon had already appealed to Napoleon and to Louis XVIII to put his plans of philosophical and social reorganization into effect. After the Revolution of 1830, his disciples appealed to Louis-Philippe and demanded much more of him than their master had asked of the king from the elder branch of the family.[36]

The best government, said Saint-Simon, is that which spends least. The most economical government, said his disciples, is not that which spends least; it is that which spends best. There is only one expenditure that one can say without qualification should be cut: the sum that the working classes pay to the idle classes as interest on capital.[37] By reforming the government's finances, the state can work for the limitless reduction of that expenditure, the enormity of which is too little appreciated.

To improve the situation of the workers vis-à-vis the idle, the state will not limit itself to reforming the institu-

[36] On these Saint-Simonian appeals to political power, see the series of pamphlets published in 1831 under the general title of *Réligion Saint-Simonienne*, especially those entitled "L'Armée, la concurrence"; "La concurrence"; "Organisation industrielle de l'armée"; "Ce qu'il faut pour être roi. La légalité"; "Ce que faisait Napoléon, pour exciter l'enthousiasme du peuple"; "Le choléra. Napoléon. L'ordre légal"; etc. These pamphlets first appeared as articles in the *Globe*.

[37] "Projet de discours de la couronne pour l'année 1831," *Réligion Saint-Simonienne*, p. 8.

tions of credit and mobilizing land. By imposing a tax on inheritance and eliminating collateral inheritance, it can prepare the way for the abolition of inheritance. It can go still further and substitute for this fiscal "policy of displacement" a policy of association.[38] Let the state give up making taxpayers pay for amortizing the debt; let it give up amortization. Let it give up making taxpayers pay interest on the debt; to do that, let it resort indefinitely to new loans. So the day will come when voluntary subscriptions by citizens will put the whole social capital in the hands of the state. What motive will lead the citizens to hand over all their capital to the state? They will see the state using the capital they have given to it, not for military and governmental expenses, but for the expenses of production; the state will become the general banker of the people and the leader of the nation's industry. Besides, nothing obliges the state to act so as to render the debt thus contracted in any way perpetual. "Political debate is certainly going to shift its ground. Until now, democracy has been argued about on the basis of electoral rights; the time has come when it will make inroads on property. English radicalism has come to it already; French radicalism is rapidly coming around to it. Those who proclaim that the people are sovereign and who hope that that sovereign will confer every public distinction are led irresistibly to insist that it also distribute wealth. It is said that the sovereign should name the heads of the polity; should it not follow that it should choose the heads of its industries and the managers of its factories?" The owners take fright; they dream of an "18th Brumaire"; they seek a deliverer. There is the way for a clever monarch to solve the social question without hurting a single interest and without handing society over to "anarchic" democrats. Let the property-owners entrust him with "the safekeeping of a fortune threatened from every direc-

[38] Michel Chevalier, in the *Globe*, March 30, 1832.

tion." "Nothing will be easier than, step by step, with the free consent of the owners, to convert all property into a consolidated debt in a special account, the income of which would come from the taxes for which the tax-farmer is accountable to the state in whole or in part. Further, that consolidated debt would not be perpetual; it could be gradually decreased until it could be annulled in the third generation. This would injure no one, because who in this selfish world now thinks ahead to the third generation? . . . Thus the transformation of property in Europe would be accomplished."[39]

The state, then, will justify increasing its receipts by a radical reform of its expenditures. It will take the place of the family "in matters of MORAL and *professional* education according to calling, in outfitting individuals when they come to working age, and in providing for *retirement* after *service* is completed." In production, it will increasingly take the place of industrial concerns. "Then the public services will absorb, in order to merge them gradually, many undertakings of general utility that today are left to speculation and private enterprise and that require certain operations and expenditures already involved in public administration, for example, friendly societies, savings banks, insurance and shipping companies, and companies for the building or operation of canals, bridges, and railways, for draining marshes and clearing or planting forests." Though they were radical advocates of a policy of peace, the Saint-Simonians did not call for the abolition of armies; they proposed changing their purpose. Following Fourier's idea, an *industrial army* should be established. "Then men will no longer be recruited to be taught the art of *destroying* and *killing*, but to learn how to *produce* and to *create*. . . . Then industry will emerge as *enticing* and *glorious*, and, as all the workers will tend to enlist in the regiments, the State will increasingly become

[39] "Aux hommes politiques. Michel Chevalier, apôtre," *Globe*, April 20, 1832 (the last number).

the distributor-general of *work, wages,* and *pensions* for
ALL."[40]

Such is the hypothetical "point towards which human
societies are moving," either by the natural evolution of
industrial society or by state intervention, "perhaps, indeed, without ever being able to attain it."[41] But let us
suppose that the organization of industry has been
achieved and that production has become social; how will
the distribution of the produce be made? To understand
Saint-Simonian theory on this point, we must return to
their theory of banking and imagine ourselves at the time
when the era of credit succeeds the era of cash, as the era
of cash had earlier succeeded the era of barter. Credit
has become free. It is no longer necessary to pay a tithe
to the idle to obtain their confidence and advances of their
capital; it is enough now to offer personal guarantees and
to pay an insurance premium against the accidents that
no social progress can altogether prevent and that can
entail the loss of capital that has been advanced. The
capital everyone needs is lent, then, by the bankers, pre-
siding over the industrial structure, or by the state in the
guise of a single central bank, *according to one's credit,*
or, again, "by reason of one's capacity"—the expression
used by Bazard and Enfantin in the *Producteur.*[42] The
formulation in the *Exposition*—"everyone will be endowed
according to his merit and rewarded according to his
works"—brings us close to the definitive statement, the
motto of the Saint-Simonian *Globe* after 1830: "To each
according to his capacity, to each capacity according to
its works." The rule seems clear: does it not mean that

[40] *Ibid.*
[41] *Producteur,* III, 339.
[42] Bazard, *Producteur,* III, 548 f.: ". . . l'état de choses, où
. . . les avantages de chacun seraient en raison de sa capacité."
Enfantin, *Producteur,* III, 395: ". . . les perfectionnements
du système de crédit tendent à nous rapprocher constamment
de cette époque, où les instruments de travail seront confiés
aux industriels en raison de leurs capacités."

everyone will receive, if not precisely the produce of his individual labor, at least a part of the produce of collective labor proportionate to the effectiveness of his own labor? Actually, it is obscure, and the formulation of the statement lends itself to a double interpretation.

The first interpretation, which most naturally arises from the Saint-Simonian theory of banking, is also that farthest removed from the sense in which the formula "to each according to his works" is usually understood. The banker is more or less disposed to advance his capital to one or another individual to the extent that he knows that the individual in question is more or less capable of putting that capital to work. "Today man works for himself," wrote Enfantin in the *Producteur*, "but the usefulness of his work to the welfare of his fellow men will be fully recognized only when capital and land are distributed among the *industriels* in proportion to the confidence in their effective use of it, that is, in proportion to the credit society extends to their productive faculties";[43] it is in the same sense that the *Exposition* declares that "the only right to wealth, that is, to the disposition of the instruments of production, will be the ability to put them to work."[44] Similarly, in the *Producteur*, Enfantin praised a contemporary economist, M. d'Hauterive, for having set the right of property on its true basis when he insisted that "property can belong only to the man who is at the head of his profession";[45] and this definition is clarified by the passage in the *Exposition de la doctrine* in which the future organization of industry is compared to the present organization of the army. "Since everyone is rewarded according to his function, . . . an *industriel* no more owns a firm, workers, and equipment than a colonel today owns a barracks, soldiers, and arms; yet everyone works enthusiastically because the man who *produces* can

[43] *Producteur*, I, 556.
[44] *Exposition de la doctrine*, I, 115. Cf. I, 160.
[45] *Producteur*, II, 257.

love glory and can have a sense of honor as well as the man who destroys."[46] In other words, the formula "to each according to his capacity" implies not the right to enjoyment of the produce, but the right to use tools, the right to work, or, more precisely, the right to carry out the task at which each individual is most adept: "the only right conferred upon the owner is the management, use, and exploitation of the property."[47]

But is the Saint-Simonian formula made up of two parts for nothing? It does not come to the same thing to say that everyone must be "endowed according to his merit," and that he must be "rewarded according to his works." Nor does it come to the same thing to say "to each according to his capacities" and "to each capacity according to its works." We have not cited the full passage in which the industrial functions of the head of a firm are compared to the military functions of a colonel; here is the complete text, which complicates the Saint-Simonian theory of distribution of wealth with a new element. "Since everyone is rewarded according to his function, what today is called income is no more than a stipend or a pension. An *industriel* no more owns a firm, workers, and equipment than a colonel today owns a barracks, soldiers, and arms." Now clearly a colonel does not "own" the barracks in which his regiment is billeted in the same sense that he owns the "stipend" that rewards the exercise of his function; basing ourselves on the analogy of the military industry, let us try to elucidate the double character of the right of property in Saint-Simonian theory.

The purpose of the military industry is to produce national power and security by the use of certain implements of defense and destruction—firearms and swords. A good organization of military labor will be one in which each individual is given the implements he is most adept at handling. To the colonel will be assigned the management,

[46] *Exposition de la doctrine*, I, 134.
[47] *Ibid.*, I, 116.

the "ownership" of the barracks, and all that it includes. The ordinary soldier will be, so to speak, the sub-delegate of society in the ownership of a bed, a gun, and military equipment—the co-owner, subordinate to the colonel, of a part of the capital. But, to live, the colonel and the ordinary soldier must consume a certain quantity of wealth; they must be housed and clothed. Now while the consumption fund can be considered in certain respects part of productive capital, since it is necessary to consume in order to produce, it is proper, in considering the problem of distribution, to distinguish between the problem of how the division of functions (and so of implements) will be made and the different problem of how consumption goods will be divided according to the needs of each agent. Do those needs differ according to function? If so, it is important to explain why, because this is not a point that emerges from the principles enunciated thus far. But the Saint-Simonians wanted it that way. Enfantin, in the *Producteur*, would not grant that the possession of capital carried with it the right to exact a premium on the labor of others, nor would he grant that such possession justified hereditary transmission of capital to an individual who had done nothing by his own labor to earn it. But he recognized the individual's right freely to consume the value created by his own labor.

It is very likely that there was always some confusion, in the minds of the Saint-Simonians, between the two rules; that is probably why it is hard to find a justification of the second in their writings. "The differences of position between producers in the social unit," wrote Olinde Rodrigues, "bring differences of habit as to needs and give rise to a necessarily variable line of demarcation between the needs of workers placed unequally in the industrial hierarchy."[48] Since every function creates its own needs, it follows that the satisfaction of these needs would

[48] "Considérations générales sur l'industrie," *Producteur*, I, 194.

become a necessary condition of fulfilling the function. But why admit that inequality of functions necessarily creates inequality of needs? Does that hypothesis not run counter to the spirit of a doctrine that foresaw the suppression of all antagonisms and the realization of a universal association in which everyone will be equally happy in fulfilling functions that are not unequal but different? Further on in the very essay that we have just cited, Rodrigues tries to soften the theory according to which diversity of functions brings with it inequality of needs. He explains that individuals in subordinate positions in industrial society must not be considered excluded forever from the higher pleasures allotted to the heads of industry. In a progressive society in which, according to the Saint-Simonian formula, "all are called and all are chosen," pleasures are steadily diffused from the top to the bottom of the social scale. We must not say that the leaders of society are the only ones to experience certain higher pleasures; they are only the first, until the perfecting of industry, by increasing production of the goods necessary to securing these pleasures, permits those who are led to enjoy them in their turn. "When new needs, growing out of the progress of all the human faculties, are introduced into society, they are first felt by the leaders, situated, so to speak, in the van of general development; in time, they descend successively to the lowest ranks of the working class who, until then, had looked on them as artificial needs and on the goods that satisfied them as luxuries or extravagances."[49]

On the other hand, should the inequality of income among different agents in the industrial hierarchy be explained by the love inferiors in a well-ordered society develop for their superiors, which constitutes a voluntary homage on their part? "There is in the human heart," wrote Isaac Péreire in 1832, "a feeling that leads an in-

[49] *Ibid.*, I, 195.

dividual to offer the better of two objects to the man who has won his love, his admiration, and his respect."[50] But is not that love reciprocal? Must the leader not return his love to the led? And must this reciprocity of affections not be translated into material form by equality of reward? The Saint-Simonian apostles felt this so strongly that, in organizing their Church, they themselves, the future spiritual leaders of the reformed society, refused to claim the higher rewards to which their theory of distribution entitled them. One of them declared that, until the time when payment according to works is organized, "the only reward we recognize is the place we hold in the hierarchy, the place we occupy in the heart of our supreme father. Beyond that, I recognize no difference between any of the children of the family, between any of the Saint-Simonian agents, but that which is visible on this platform, a slight difference in dress reflecting the functions to be fulfilled. As to monetary reward, the apostles receive none; their needs are very strictly provided for, and what is left of our budget will go to serve the needs of propagating our faith."[51]

In the same vein, Isaac Péreire declared: "It is not a question of setting up a mathematical proportion between services and reward, although there is a tendency to bring them closer and closer to such a proportion without ever hoping to attain it completely. . . . At present, the difference of ranks among us is marked especially by the *love* and *respect* the superior evokes by his labours from those who are placed below him in the hierarchy." But why should the principle that obtains "at present" in the Saint-Simonian hierarchy cease to be true in the future society that their Church was intended to bring about more swiftly? Once again, why the second of the two rules for the distribution of wealth, according to the Saint-

[50] *Leçons sur l'industrie,* second lesson, p. 34.
[51] Stéphane Flachat, *Enseignement des ouvriers,* p. 7.

Simonians? To each according to his capacity: that is the first rule; in other words, everyone has a right to the work marked out for him by his nature. In a society that respects this rule, every job would become, as Fourier put it, "attractive," and so would in itself constitute the immediate reward of each worker. Why then add: "to each capacity according to its works"? "Reward according to works," wrote Père Enfantin, "makes one *love* what one *must do*."[52]

Why? For an excellent reason, but the sentimental mysticism into which the Saint-Simonians plunged in 1830 perhaps prevented their setting it out with the clarity we could wish. It is this: we cannot conceive an association so perfect that antagonism will not still play a part. In this and any society, the problem of political organization is not to eliminate but to use a principle of antagonism that is, as it were, rooted in the nature of things. The second Saint-Simonian rule for the distribution of wealth, the rule they apply to the distribution, not of productive capital among those who are going to work, but of the consumption fund among those who have just worked, is a modified form—or, if one prefers, a weaker form—of that other maxim: "To each according to his strength." Little by little, the industrial economy of the Saint-Simonians separated itself from political economy as the liberal school understood it, based on the idea of free competition. The Saint-Simonians forced a profound transformation on the idea of competition; they did not, however, eliminate it. In the *Producteur*, they distinguished expressly between two forms of competition. Competition seemed to them injurious when it was "between persons"—when it turned man's powers against those who are, or should be, his associates, when it was used for the exploitation of man. But they considered it good when it was "in things"—when it turned man's powers against external nature and ended in creating rivalry among men

[52] "Lettre du père Enfantin," *Réligion Saint-Simonienne*, p. 8.

as to the best means of exploiting the terrestrial globe. In the *Exposition de la doctrine* and in the *Globe,* they did not dare to vindicate so explicitly this idea of competition, which lies at the base of economic individualism. They denounced those who "in principle propose the absence of all general faith, of all direction, of all choice from above, failing to see that in this way they are, to all intents and purposes, rewarding the cleverest and strongest."[53] But the second Saint-Simonian rule for the distribution of wealth amounts to rewarding the "cleverest and strongest"; and whether they were aware of it or not, the Saint-Simonians made it very clear. "Saint-Simon," they tell us, "ushered in the new era in which *virtue* no more than *value* will be measured by the strength of a sabre blow or by skill in aiming a cannon; but there will still be value in strength and virtue in its use. But it has long been maintained in the doctrine that it will no longer be the science and the power that destroy—the science and the power of Caesar—but the science and the power that create, produce, and conserve—the science of Monge, Lavoisier, Bichat, and Cabanis, the power of Watt or Montgolfier."[54] In short, reward according to works is only the transposition—or, if one prefers, the industrial transfiguration—of the right of the strongest. In the society the Saint-Simonians wanted to bring into being, the best paid will always be the "cleverest and strongest," on condition that that intelligence and strength be used to produce and not to destroy, to exploit nature and not one's fellow man.

* * *

There is no need to tell the story of the Saint-Simonian school after 1830: public attention suddenly attracted to the little society; the preachings in Paris, in the provinces, and abroad; the crisis of mystical madness and the

[53] *De la religion Saint-Simonienne: Aux élèves de l'École Polytechnique,* p. 41.
[54] *Ibid.,* p. 68. Cf. *Exposition de la doctrine,* pp. 218, 222.

break-up of the "Church"; then the influence of the school surviving the break-up of the Church, with the Saint-Simonians giving nascent socialism its terminology and emerging French industry its organization. We have accomplished our task if we have correctly defined the principles of the industrial economy according to Saint-Simon and the Saint-Simonians. Saint-Simon's disciples can be forgiven for having so often fallen over into the extravagances of religious prophecy; they were in fact prophets.

To look no further than their economic theories, the Saint-Simonians proved to be prophets in their criticism of the idea of competition. The theorists of the classical school were perhaps right in making that idea basic in political economy; but they were certainly wrong in holding that it is a simple idea; it is indeed complex, and obscure so long as its complexity has not been analyzed. Are we talking about the competition of capitalists in offering their capital? It is beneficial since it tends to cheapen capital and so makes capital available to those who know how to use it. Are we talking about the competition of the heads of firms in offering the products of their industries to consumers? It is beneficial to the extent that it encourages them to lower prices by using better machines and so lessening human fatigue; but it is evil to the extent that it encourages them to lower prices by cutting wages and to undervalue the produce of labor by undervaluing the producers. Or, finally, are we talking about the competition of workers among themselves? It is useful to the extent that it serves as a stimulus to production, harmful to the extent that the resulting increase in production goes to augment not the wealth of the workers but the profits and the interest of the head of the firm and the capitalist. Reduced to its essentials, economic competition presupposes rules; it is not the same thing as the struggle for survival that assures the victory of the strong by the brutal extermination of the weak; it precludes violence; it even precludes fraud. And just as it is lawful in its very nature, its law of evolution is to be subject to rules that grow steadily more numerous and more precise. That is what the Saint-Simonians saw; that is why they could see that the "unlimited competition" of European industry of their time was a transitory system, destined before long to be transformed by the operation of forces already in existence.

Consequently, they foresaw what we shall call the growing syndicalization of industry. In France, as the founders of great railway and navigation companies and banks, they themselves contributed to it. The German cartel and the American trust bear out their theories. In current language, the head of an American trust is called a "captain of industry"; the expression probably comes from Carlyle, and Carlyle himself borrowed it from the terminology of Bazard and Enfantin. The Saint-Simonians also foresaw what we shall call the increasing state control of industry. Once industry is concentrated in large units, how can the state, the natural instrument of social centralization, avoid stepping in to control or to take over entirely the great syndicalized enterprises in the name of society? At the University of Berlin, Adolf Wagner taught what he called "the law of the extension of state intervention": he had borrowed the formulation of this law from his master Rodbertus, himself a disciple of the Saint-Simonians. When M. Paul Leroy-Beaulieu, so devoted to liberal orthodoxy, also advanced the law of the steady growth of the public domain in his *Essai sur la répartition des richesses* (*Essay on the Distribution of Wealth*), who knows but that he had been unconsciously influenced by Saint-Simonian doctrine by way of Michel Chevalier?

On only one point concerning the organization of the new world of industry did the Saint-Simonians show themselves less good as prophets. They foresaw the concentration but not the democratization of industrial production. They predicted state intervention, transforming private enterprises into public services; they were not concerned about whether the constitution of that state would be autocratic or democratic. They heralded the employers' association, but not the trade union. But cannot the democratization of Saint-Simonian theory develop in conformity with the very principles on which the theory is founded? In Saint-Simonian theory, the alliance or association organized by producers against the idle rests essentially on the institution of banking. But "in our disorganized society" can we be certain that the bankers will carry out the beneficial mission assigned them by the theory with the necessary conscientiousness? The author of the *Exposition de la doctrine*, having posed the question, confesses that "the bankers often set themselves up between the workers and the idle to exploit both at the expense of the whole of society." What is the remedy against this degeneracy of the system? Always the same. To prevent the bankers, once they have defended the workers against the idle, from themselves becoming idle vis-à-vis the workers, the workers must once more unite against these new capitalists. The Saint-Simonian prescription still holds: the alliance of producers against consumers, or, more precisely, the alliance of those who are both consumers and producers against those in whom the consumer predominates over the producer.

A new industrial world is emerging. Economic competition remains, but it is subjected to rules that grow more complex every day. The employers' association and the trade union are at war; wages rise, or should rise, after every invention of a new technique, and the invention of a new technique follows each rise in wages; this competition, not between isolated individuals but between large groups, is tending to become the very law of industrial progress. But the fact that the heads of industry have come together has not eliminated all competition between them; it has rather tended to regulate it; from now on, among associated *industriels*, competition will no longer affect the price but the quality of products. The trade union will no longer necessarily prevent the businessman from choosing his employees and preferring the best to the worst; it will aim only at preventing him from hiring labor at cut rates, by setting the conditions of labor. Finally, the state intervenes to regulate the struggle, guaranteeing to everyone the enjoyment of certain basic rights to a minimum of leisure, health, education, and assistance. We hope that the two essays we have devoted to the economic ideas of the Saint-Simonians will ·contribute to rehabilitating those thinkers, well known but little read, whose imaginations foresaw these transformations of industrial society. Saint-Simonian "socialism" is not a communism; the formula "to each according to his works" proves that, in their doctrine, rivalry remains the fundamental stimulus to production. The Saint-Simonians looked on society as, following them, we tend to look on it, as an association, not for the abolition of competition, but for its organization.

Conclusion

In the introduction he wrote with C. Bouglé in 1924 for a new edition of the Doctrine de Saint-Simon, première année, *Élie Halévy incorporated a number of fragments of the preceding article. In conclusion, he added the following remarks about the influence of Saint-Simonianism:*

To what extent have the Saint-Simonian prophecies been realized? Looking at the state of the civilized world a century later, one is tempted, at first sight, to conclude that they have failed. The old Christian religion has not given way to the "new Christianity." The era of wars has not come to an end; far from it. We have just witnessed a bloody convulsion far more horrible than that from which Europe was emerging when Saint-Simon was constructing his system. How far we are still from the time when

99

the human race will be truly united, in the interest of all workers, for the peaceful exploitation of the earth! Yet there are many men, who call and believe themselves Christians in the same sense in which one could be Christian in the year 1000, who are more or less consciously converted in practice to an industrialism deriving from Saint-Simon. In spite of wars, through wars, a cosmopolitan world of production and exchange is being built, confusedly, like a city in the clouds. The actions of employers' associations and trade unions are focussed beyond national frontiers. Men dream of projects and inventions that, by shrinking the dimensions of the globe, will reduce the quarrels of great nations to the level of petty local disputes. We are engaged in a long crisis in which nationalisms are defending themselves with increasing violence against the encroachments of others; but in which perhaps in fact they are defending themselves—the more violently because they feel more threatened—against a cosmopolitanism that encroaches on all of them. No, Saint-Simonianism has not yet failed. It has left its traces everywhere, all around us. Hardly a party or an ideology has not borrowed something from the doctrine, or at least from the phraseology, of the Saint-Simonians, the true heralds of an entire century.

Just think. The future world of which the Saint-Simonians dreamed is a world in which the antithesis of liberty and oppression will have no meaning, a world in which obedience will not be servitude, because it will be willing submission to the injunctions of positive science. Still, ostentatiously declaring war on the metaphysical dogma of liberty, they offered themselves to the public as the sole means of restoring the order overthrown by the French Revolution through a new philosophy. As a result, they naturally attracted a certain number of minds with an instinctive aversion to modern individualist society, minds that sought a doctrine to justify this distaste by arguments that were not those of the old theology and the old politics. The German Rodbertus and the Englishman Thomas Carlyle were both disciples of Saint-Simon —the first perhaps unconsciously and without our being able to say through whom precisely Saint-Simonian influence was brought to bear on him; the second consciously: we know the date and the circumstances of his conversion. And both were precursors of Bismarck, who, like Carlyle and Rodbertus, ignored the cosmopolitan aspects of the original Saint-Simonianism; he was content to follow it in adapting modern industry to the forms of the traditional religious and national state. One need not go outside France: the greatest of Saint-Simon's disciples, or, better, collaborators, was Auguste Comte. The positivist school was merely a dissident sect of the Saint-Simonian Church, the only one to prosper; and it prospered on the very ruins of the main Church. Were the conservative parties completely unjustified in using the doctrine of Auguste Comte for their own ends? Disciples of Comte, men like Brunetière and Charles Maurras are, without knowing it, disciples of Saint-Simon. They stand on the extreme right of Saint-Simonian positivism.

Let us go in another direction. The Saint-Simonians foresaw the concentration but not the democratization of industrial production; but cannot the democratization of Saint-Simonian theory develop in conformity with the very principles on which the theory is founded? In Saint-Simonian theory, the alliance or association organized by producers against the idle rests essentially on the institution of banking. But in our still poorly organized society can we be certain that the bankers will carry out the beneficial mission assigned to them by the theory with the necessary conscientiousness? To prevent the bankers, once they have defended the workers against the idle, from themselves becoming idle vis-à-vis the workers, is it not fitting that the workers once more unite against these new capitalists? This democratization of Saint-Simonian socialism came about rapidly, especially in Paris. Buonarroti,

Buchez, and Louis Blanc discovered that the French Revolution had not been exclusively critical and destructive, that Jean-Jacques Rousseau and Robespierre had indeed wanted to build a new order on the ruins of the old order undermined by Voltaire, and that the doctrine of popular sovereignty made it possible to overcome the morality of anarchic competition. Louis Blanc was responsible for the Revolution of 1848, seen as a democratic and social revolution. Ferdinand Lassalle, the founder of the German workers' party, was a disciple of Louis Blanc. And Louis Blanc was a child of Saint-Simon.

That is not all. The history of Saint-Simonianism shows more than a democratic left. It has its revolutionary far left too. How, indeed, is the Saint-Simonian law of progress formulated? Why is an organic society condemned to perish, to be replaced by another? Because it is destroyed by an internal contradiction, by the "antagonism" of clashing forces. These social forces are "classes," freemen and slaves, lords and serfs, "bourgeois" and "proletarians." The complete vocabulary that would soon become that of the revolutionary socialists was already in use by the first Saint-Simonians. They should have said, and almost did say, that "the history of mankind is the history of the class struggle." They were deliberately opposed to all violence; probably that is why they were so anxious to enlighten us as to the goal towards which humanity is necessarily moving; then reason, controlling our actions, would allow us to move ahead without useless revolutions. But why did that matter? Were Marx and his followers completely unfaithful to the spirit of the Saint-Simonian philosophy of history when they pushed a bit beyond Bazard and Enfantin on the road of historical fatalism? Science taught them that the transition from one state of society to a higher state was always accompanied by violence. What was true in the past would continue to be true in the future. Where antagonism exists, can a collision be avoided? Why not accept it, why not welcome it, if real progress could be bought only at that price? When Lenin moved into the Kremlin and put the three volumes of *Das Kapital* on his desk, the Saint-Simonian far left took over, in him, the palace of the Tsars and claimed to bring about, by violence, "the universal association of workers."

Having said this, we readily admit that to attribute so large a role and so widespread an influence to Saint-Simonianism is, in a way, to point to failure as well as to fertility. To compare Saint-Simonianism to another great contemporary doctrine of equally great prestige, one can say that, once a Hegelian "left" and "right" came into being, Hegelianism died. The far right of Saint-Simonianism, the direction of which we have just indicated, could discover, through Saint-Simon and Auguste Comte, only the doctrine of Joseph de Maistre and de Bonald, and could demand only a return to the theological and feudal system the Saint-Simonians had declared outworn. On the other hand, while consciously or unconsciously repeating Saint-Simonian formulas, the far left revived the destructive Jacobinism the Saint-Simonians detested. The Saint-Simonians believed that the revolutionary crisis taking place as they wrote would be the last and that thereafter Europe was going to proceed—under their direction and without a new crisis—towards a final state of organization. But antagonisms and crises have reappeared, so they have failed.

Probably so. But the nature of these new antagonisms must be clearly understood. They do not resemble the antagonisms that arose between individuals under the system of free competition as the disciples of Adam Smith and Say defined it. A new industrial world is emerging; it still reveals "struggle," "competition," and "antagonism," but in new forms that are really Saint-Simonian. Now that the "liberals" are no more than an intermediate or "center" party, the conflict is between a Caesarist *étatisme* and a democratic *étatisme*, between a corporatism with capitalistic and Christian tendencies and a syndicalism with emancipationist tendencies. Does this not mean that modern socialism is a doctrine with a double aspect, as the Saint-Simonians warned us it would be? It is a doctrine of emancipation, which aims at abolishing the last traces of slavery remaining in industrialism, and it is a doctrine of organization, which, to protect the freedom of the weak against the strong, needs a restored and strengthened social power. Though overoptimism led the Saint-Simonians to err in proclaiming the imminent end of all war and all revolution, at least they defined with remarkable insight the new forms the system of production would take in the modern world; and, without desiring them, they predicted the forms social antagonisms would take in the new world that was growing up around them. That is why we are brought back again and again to the authors of that forgotten classic reprinted here, to see in them the prophets of the modern world.

THE POLICY OF SOCIAL PEACE
IN ENGLAND

The Whitley Councils[1]

The war had not been long under way before the English were already preoccupied with the solution of what we in France call *les problèmes de l'après-guerre* and what in England have come habitually to be called the problems of "reconstruction." The word "reconstruction" can be understood in two senses, one narrow, the other broad. In the narrow sense, it means undoing the confusion caused by the war and restoring things to their prewar state. Thus defined, measures of "reconstruction" are essentially transitory; the problem is, while avoiding turmoil and dissension as much as possible, to get through the months of crisis that will inevitably follow the re-establishment of peace. In the broad sense, "reconstruction" means something else: the building of a new social edifice, conceived according to a plan better than all the plans conceived before the war. The ordeal of war showed us the gaps in our social structure; on the other hand, we have learned that, to a greater degree than we had hoped, we can appeal to the co-operation of classes; and we have at last gained a growing confidence in the efficacy of state intervention. We are thus led to think of "reconstruction" not as a collection of temporary expedients, but as a permanent system, not as a mere

[1] A study published in the *Revue d'économie politique*, XXXIII, 385–431 (July–August 1919).

"restoration" of the past, but as a way of organizing progress.

In this spirit, in March 1916, a Committee of Reconstruction was set up under the chairmanship of the Prime
Minister; it was soon divided into several subcommittees.
One of these subcommittees, presided over by Mr. J. H.
Whitley, Chairman of Committees of the House of Commons, was assigned the task of seeking the right means
to a permanent improvement in the relations between
employers and employed. It was, therefore, as we can
see, a question of reconstruction in the broad sense. The
problems that must necessarily arise during the period of
transition immediately following the re-establishment of
peace would certainly be dealt with: demobilization, re-
instatement of munitions workers in civilian industry,
completion of apprenticeships interrupted by the war, and
the occupational rehabilitation of war invalids. But the
ambitions of the government in setting up the subcommittee were longer-range and loftier. They hoped to
found permanent institutions, to build a new system of
industrial relations for the future. Profiting from the lessons the country had learned in practicing *union sacrée*[2]
(sacred union) during the war, they wanted to find a
cure for the malaise that, before the war, had every year
weighed more heavily on industry and, in consequence,
on all of English politics.

A British statesman can consider his country finally
cured of the disease of political revolution and rioting.
But if the English people have little taste for pure politics
and stubbornly resist revolutionary phraseology, they are
very much concerned about questions that touch their
immediate material interests: political economy interests
them as much as doctrinal politics leaves them indiffer-
ent. The refusal to work—the strike or the threat to strike

[2] [*Union sacrée* was the phrase used in President Poincaré's
war message of August 4, 1914, to indicate the unity with
which France would confront the enemy.]

—is the surest weapon available to the worker to intimidate his employer and to obtain from him the concessions he wants. If twentieth-century England does not know rioting, it is the classical home of the strike. Strikes are a chronic disease, the symptoms of which seem to grow worse and worse. They are an ever-recurring cause of impoverishment for the nation, a veritable scandal for the statesman. How can strikes be eliminated?

The first procedure to come to mind is repression pure and simple. Not exactly repression by armed force; English statesmen resort to that only rarely, and the idea is highly repugnant to them. But the trade unions in England are powerful organizations which accumulate large reserve funds. It is not impossible rigorously to apply existing laws to workers who in the course of every strike inevitably commit excesses and to make the unions pay heavy fines. During the reactionary period that followed the Conservative victory in 1895, this method was used, and used successfully. For four or five years, to keep their unions from being wrecked, English workers did not dare to strike. The victory of the employers was, however, only temporary. While they gave up the fight for the time being, the unions were preparing their revenge. They organized the Labour Party, to whose efforts more than to any other cause we must attribute the swamping of the Conservative Party in the general election of 1906. Some months later, at the demand of the Labour Party, Parliament passed a Trade Disputes Act which, on the one hand, construed the right to strike more broadly and, on the other hand, expressly forbade holding trade unions financially responsible for criminal acts committed by their members during a strike.

Throughout the United Kingdom, the strike movement at once took on a new intensity; it was a time when syndicalist doctrines, which originated in France, were spreading throughout the West. Legal repression having come to grief, other ways had to be found to stop it. Could not the evil be prevented by organized conciliation?

A quarter of a century before, the cotton workers in Lancashire had concluded a pact with their employers which, as the Brooklands Agreement, remains famous in the history of English trade unionism. It is still in force today; it remains and seems likely for a long time to remain the charter of the cotton industry.[3] Signed in 1893 and revised and completed in 1905, the Brooklands Agreement defined the principles by which wages must vary directly with the profits on capital and the rules according to which those profits were to be calculated; it provided for the periodic review by experts of the application of these principles and rules; and it set up a series of graded committees for the amicable settlement of disputes that might arise between employers and workingmen, without recourse to strikes. Would it not be possible to do what had been done successfully for one of the great industries of the kingdom for all industries and to organize the whole world of labor peacefully?

In 1894, a year after the Brooklands pact was signed, a society was founded, under the name of Industrial Union, which worked for the attainment of this ideal. The death of the promoter and lack of funds brought the project to an end. We find the idea taken up again in 1900 by one Mr. John Lockie, of Stonehouse in Devonshire. With a fund of £50,000, he proposed to create a National Federation of Employers' Associations and Trade Unions. This federation would give employers and workers the opportunity to meet on an equal footing, to bring about a rapid and amicable settlement of disputes and strikes, to ease relations between capital and labor, to establish them on a perfectly harmonious and just foundation, and to

[3] On the Brooklands Agreement, see S. and B. Webb, *Industrial Democracy* (1898), pp. 198 ff. [Halévy was mistaken about the Agreement continuing in force. It was denounced by the union in January 1913.]

create and cement the feeling of a community of interests between employer and employed. As patrons of the federation that he proposed, Mr. John Lockie found some aristocrats, some members of parliament, some businessmen—and not a single workingman. The idea seems to have collapsed almost at once.[4]

We must come down to 1911 to see it reborn and finally acquire some semblance of life. In October, following advice given by one of the kings of the cotton industry, Sir Charles Macara, who had been involved in the drafting of the Brooklands Agreement, the government set up an Industrial Council, composed of thirteen employers and thirteen workers. Nominated by the Board of Trade, the Industrial Council had as its chairman Sir George Askwith, the Comptroller-General of the Labour Department, with the new title of Chief Industrial Commissioner. He was to, and did effectively, exercise the functions of an arbitrator whenever a dispute broke out in one or another trade that could not be resolved by the interested parties left to their own resources. The Board of Trade, it should be said, was careful to explain that there was no question at all of introducing an element of legal obligation into the agreements arrived at between employers and workingmen; it was only a matter of bringing more zeal and new methods to the application of the Conciliation Act that Parliament had passed in 1896, which excluded any notion of compulsory arbitration. When, however, in 1912 the Industrial Council was invited by the government to open a broad inquiry to find out to what extent and in what way they could "guarantee" or "enforce the execution of industrial agreements arrived at by representatives of employers and the em-

4 We have been able to gather material on the Industrial Union of 1894 and on the National Federation of 1900 in the archives of the parliamentary committee of the Trades Union Congress, thanks to the kindness of Mr. Fred Bramley, assistant secretary of the committee.

ployed in a given industry and region,"[5] the trade unionists rightly took offense. Certainly some notion of compulsory arbitration and penal sanctions lay concealed behind this inquiry. In 1912, at Newport, and in 1913, at Manchester, the Trades Union Congress expressly declared itself opposed to this policy in principle.

The Industrial Council is a thing of the past. Eight years have gone by since it was founded, and we have not succeeded in uncovering any traces of it; many men, even in industrial and trade union circles, have forgotten that it ever existed. But the concerns which had led to its founding long ago have begun to haunt men's minds again since the war and because of the war, at the same time that wartime institutions were making the idea of peaceful collaboration between employers and the working classes appear less utopian.

Raw materials and manpower were in short supply, but the needs of the military state were urgent. Now the chief consumer of the nation, the state set itself up as the final arbiter of production and distribution. To make its task easier, all the heads of firms in each industry were encouraged to combine; on the other hand, where their trade-union organizations were still incomplete, workers were urged to make them more nearly universal. The state forced associations of employers and workers to become agents of its authority. It would consult them before acting. Once its decisions were taken, it was up to them to transmit its orders and to enjoin all employers and workers to carry them out.

Take the textile industries. Two boards of control were

[5] *The Minutes of Evidence taken before the Industrial Council in connection with their inquiry into industrial agreements* (Cd. 6953), [*Parliamentary Papers,* 1913, XXVIII.] give an excellent picture of the English trade union world on the eve of the Great War. We shall use them on a number of occasions in the course of this essay.

set up, on which the state, the employers' association, and the trade unions were represented, to administer the cotton and woolen industries.[6] Let us take wool as an example. The board of control was composed of thirty-three members, eleven representing the War Ministry, eleven the employers, and eleven the organized workers. The president and the secretary were named by the Ministry. The deputy-chairman was elected by the board. After the raw wool had been bought, sorted, washed, and combed, thanks to the government, and once the army's needs were satisfied and the government had decided what quantity would be set aside for civilian consumption, it was the board that advised the Ministry on giving out its orders, that rationed the wool reserved for civilian consumption among the various firms, and that regulated conditions of labor. The woolen unions, poorly organized until then, received a new stimulus from the fact that they had become allies of the employers and the state in running one of the largest industries in the kingdom. These arrangements worked to the satisfaction of all the interested parties. There was not a single serious quarrel between employers and workers. The consumer was satisfied. Did it not seem that that policy of social peace to which the Industrial Union of 1894, the National Federation of 1900, and the Industrial Council of 1911 had all aspired was miraculously realized in the face of national peril?

Or take munitions. While manpower in the factories became scarcer and scarcer, because more and more able-bodied men were needed in the army, more and more intensive production was wanted. To get it, it was necessary to break all the rules the trade unions had imposed on employers over the past century with a view to limiting production. How could this be done without provoking innumerable strikes? The trade unions were appealed to,

[6] [See H. D. Henderson, *The Cotton Control Board* (1922) and, on wool, E. M. H. Lloyd, *Experiments in State Control at the War Office and the Ministry of Food* (1924).]

and in agreement with their leaders a comprehensive pact was signed, destined somehow or other to be respected for the rest of the war. Every change of shop rules, subject to final approval by the union, was to be made only for the duration of the war. The substitution of female for male labor and of unqualified labor for qualified was never to entail a cut in wages. The workers were always to be given advance notice of every such change, which would not be put into effect without consulting their representatives. In return, there would be no stoppage of work. Any quarrel that could not be settled by the directly interested parties would be arbitrated by the Board of Trade, which would be represented either by the Committee on Production, or by a single arbitrator agreed to by the parties, or by a Court of Arbitration on which an equal number of employers and workers would sit.[7] So, after having fought the idea of unionism for a century, the state and the employers, radically changing their outlook, found themselves looking on trade unions as a principle of social order; they expected that the workers, who had organized originally to defend their class interests, would learn to submit to the discipline of their unions in the interests of the whole community.

Is it surprising that the success of these wartime institutions spawned a multitude of more or less utopian plans to bring about social peace by means of the joint association in which employers and workers in the same industry would co-operate? The Garton Foundation is a philanthropic institution that had as its original purpose the study of pacifism and the organization of international arbitration. Now that, contrary to the hopes of its founders, war raged throughout Europe, the philanthropists of the Garton Foundation set themselves to study the social question within the country. In October 1916 they published a long anonymous report "on the industrial situation after

[7] [See G. D. H. Cole, *Trade Unionism and Munitions* (1923).]

the war."[8] They suggested the formation in each firm of a joint committee on which management and labor would be duly represented. At the head of each of the large industries of the United Kingdom, they suggested a joint board of control, a national industrial council, on which representatives of the employers' association and the trade union would sit side by side in equal numbers. These councils would have as their function increasing production, conciliating class interests, and on occasion—"but [adds the report] this would necessitate careful watching" —getting the Board of Trade to give legal sanction to their decisions. On these subjects, the Garton Foundation seems to have been influenced by a London building contractor, Mr. Malcolm Sparkes, a Quaker and an out-and-out pacifist who would soon be condemned to prison for refusing military service; we shall return to him soon. Mr. Ernest J. P. Benn, a businessman who had left business for politics and public service, developed similar ideas in a small book published in the same year.[9] He called for the compulsory association of all producers, workers as well as employers. He sketched a plan for a sort of parliamentarianism of the English industrial world: collaboration of workers with employers in the management of large-scale industry and direct participation of the organized producers in the nation's government.

Thus, in the second year of the war, the imagination of the system-makers, dormant at first, came to life. But we must not think that everyone concurred in these plans for social peace and brotherhood.

The doctrinaire socialists would not hear of an alliance between capitalists and workers; they wanted the expropriation of the capitalists. They did not want to share the management of factories between the two; they wanted a full take-over of power by the workers. They in-

[8] *Memorandum on the Industrial Situation after the War.*

[9] *Trade as a Science.* Mr. Benn returned to the same ideas in 1917 in a new work entitled *Trade Tomorrow.*

sisted that the state intervene from outside to lay down the conditions that the employers would have to grant to the wage-earners. Every member of an industrial society had a claim to certain basic conditions of life—a "national minimum," to use the expression invented by Mr. and Mrs. Sidney Webb; if the existing industrial system was incapable of granting it to them, then that system should disappear.

The Trade Boards Act of 1909 was the first labor law that enshrined that principle in England. In certain industries in which the workers, lacking the power to unionize, had been intolerably exploited, trade boards had been set up, composed of civil servants, representatives of employers, and representatives of the working class. On the advice of these boards, the state fixed the schedule of minimum wages. It was up to Parliament to extend the benefits of the law to other industries where the circumstances might seem parallel to those of the four industries to which the legislation of 1909 had applied. The application of the principle of the minimum wage to the coal miners in 1912 was, then, an important innovation, for no one could say that the miners were badly organized or left defenseless against exploitation by employers. In the munitions factories, in 1915 and 1916, the principle of a legal minimum wage came into general use.[10] The Trades Union Congress came out for the generalization of this principle in 1916. It called for the closed shop, the compulsory eight hour day, and a compulsory minimum wage of thirty shillings.

The syndicalists were up in arms too. They were still socialists, but socialists who approached the problem of

[10] For a view of all the measures which had tended for a decade to the fixing of wages, see the brochure entitled *State Regulation of Wages*, which has just been published by the Ministry of Reconstruction (*Reconstruction Problems*, No. 19). [See also Dorothy M. Sells, *British Wages Boards: a Study in Industrial Democracy* (1939).]

industrial reorganization from another direction than the democratic socialists. The workers saw the presidents and secretaries of their giant organizations mixing with ministers and the heads of the civil service and signing treaties of peace, almost treaties of alliance, with the leaders of industry. They were offended; they felt themselves deserted and perhaps betrayed. During the whole summer of 1916—in the English provinces and particularly among the engineers on the Clyde—true workers' rebellions broke out, not only against the state and the employers, but also —one is tempted to say especially—against the union administrations. In each factory the workers elected shop stewards whom they no longer considered minor officials in the union hierarchy; thereafter, they looked on them as their agents, charged with running the union in their name and with giving peremptory orders to the union leaders themselves.[11]

It was the struggle, which had repeatedly cropped up in the world of labor for a half-century, between the "anarchists" and the "authoritarians," between the "federalists" and the "centralizers." The shop stewards organized themselves into autonomous groups and insisted on remodeling the whole system of English unions on the basis of works committees. By direct action in each firm they hoped to bring about the expropriation of the capitalists. They found revolutionary writers to transform their aspirations into doctrine. Other writers, more moderate, also made advances to them. One such was Mr. G. D. H. Cole, the young theorist of Guild Socialism. In the working-class movement of today, Mr. Cole has taken the role that Mr. and Mrs. Webb played at the end of the nineteenth century. He is the "Fabian," the opportunist of revolutionary syndicalism, as Mr. and Mrs. Webb have been the opportunists of democratic socialism. He relies on the trade unions, having become the owners of their respec-

[11] [See G. D. H. Cole, *Workshop Organization* (1923).]

tive industries, to bring about the socialization of the nation's capital; but he continues to want the unions kept under the control of Parliament and the ministries. In the men of the shop stewards' movement he sees the direct heirs of the revolutionary syndicalism of ten years ago. He makes advances to them too. In order to make the unions more aggressive and active, he wants them to be reorganized, as far as possible, according to the wishes of the shop stewards, on the basis of "works committees."[12]

In the subcommittee that the minister had charged with studying the relations of employers and workers, every effort was made to have all points of view taken into consideration. There were four representatives of large-scale industry, who were anxious to do whatever was necessary to "tame" the syndicalist militants; three workers, two of whom were moderate and conciliatory, whereas the third, Robert Smillie, was well known for his intransigent revolutionary views; and two economists, sympathetic to socialism. Two other members, Miss A. Susan Lawrence and Mr. J. J. Mallon, were noted for the dedication with which they had fought against the abuses of sweated labor: their philosophy was that of the trade boards and the legal protection of workers. Miss Mona Wilson, a National Health Insurance Commissioner since 1912, shared their views. The choice of secretaries was characteristic. One was a civil servant, Mr. H. J. Wilson, who had been registrar of the Industrial Council of 1911 and who, with Sir George Askwith, had arbitrated many trade disputes. The other, Mr. Greenwood, was a young university lecturer; he had been especially concerned with worker education and came close to sharing the ideas of Mr. Cole and the Guild Socialists.

How could a compromise between such disparate opin-

12 For an account of G. D. H. Cole's views, see in particular his *Self-Government in Industry* (1918). There is a good account of the shop stewards' movement in an excellent work by the same author, *An Introduction to Trade Unionism*, pp. 53 ff.

ions be arrived at? How could they avoid what usually happens in England with a committee: the issuance of several reports, each expressing diverging views? By his diplomacy, Mr. J. H. Whitley, the chairman of the committee, was able to bring about this miracle. The reports the two secretaries drew up were such that the members of the committee, without a single exception, could sign them.[13]

The first report—an interim report—proposed the formation of Joint Standing Industrial Councils, composed of equal numbers of representatives of the employers' organization and of the trade union. Certain questions that would become urgent as soon as peace was re-established were submitted for immediate consideration by these councils, once they were formed: the problem of demobilization, the problem of re-establishing prewar union practices. But at the same time they were given permanent functions, namely, "securing . . . the largest possible measure of co-operation between employers and employed." They were given an agenda of eleven points, which we shall reduce to four essentials: first, amicable negotiations concerning wage rates, the mode of payment of wages, the working day, and general conditions of employment; second, using the workers' practical knowledge and experience to improve industrial techniques; third, the examination of questions indirectly affecting the progress

[13] [*Interim Report of the Subcommittee on Relations between Employers and Employed* (Cd. 8606), *Parliamentary Papers*, 1917–18, XVIII; Committee on Employers and Employed, *Second Report on Joint Standing Industrial Councils* (Cd. 9002), *P.P.*, 1918, X; *Supplementary Report on Works Committees* (Cd. 9001), *P.P.*, 1918, XIV; *Report on Conciliation and Arbitration* (Cd. 9099), *P.P.*, 1918, VII; *Final Report* (Cd. 9153), *P.P.*, 1918, VIII. The reports were reprinted by the Ministry of Labour under the general title of *Industrial Reports*. They are conveniently grouped with other relevant documents in *The Industrial Council Plan in Great Britain* (Bureau of Industrial Research, Washington, D. C., 1919).]

of industry, such as technical education and scientific research; and fourth, industrial legislation. It was a program that conformed to the wishes of at least the more intelligent leaders of industry and of at least the more moderate trade union leaders.

The report asked, moreover, that each national industrial council—set up to look after the interests of a given industry throughout the kingdom—not be considered complete in itself. It should be complemented by district councils, the whole kingdom having been divided into a number of districts for each industry, each district having its council. It was to be further complemented by works committees, one to a factory. This was a concession to the syndicalists, a way of reconciling, more or less, the leaders of the big unions and the rebels of the shop stewards' movement.

A second report, some months later, went further into detail. It pointed out the impossibility of adopting the same form of organization for all industries. It proposed a classification into three groups. Group A comprised those industries in which organization among employers and workers was sufficiently developed so that they could at once establish councils along the lines laid down by the committee's program. Group B included industries in which organization was insufficient and for which they proposed a second type of council, in which the representatives of the employers and workers would be assisted, as advisers and guides, by one or two representatives of the Ministry. Finally, Group C covered those industries that were thoroughly disorganized. To organize industries in this third group, the report recommended a considerable extension of trade boards legislation. This was a concession to the socialists, who would have been antagonized by a too single-minded advocacy of a program of joint councils. Where workers' and employers' organizations were strong enough to bargain on an equal footing, the state withdrew. But it reserved the right to ascertain if the workers' organization really had the necessary strength. If not, it would intervene to restore the balance.

It was a program of compromise and eclecticism, in which concessions were made to the views of all sides, and in which no one's ideas were followed through completely. The application would show if this complexity and these contradictions were a guarantee of adaptability or a sign of weakness.

※ ※ ※

Public opinion at first received the Whitley Committee's reports leniently. The eight committees appointed by the government in 1917 to inquire into the causes of renewed labor agitation recommended adopting the conclusions of the Whitley Report; they stressed the useful role that district councils and works committees would play.[14] Through the great Federation of British Industries, which since 1917 has brought the heads of all the firms of the United Kingdom together into one research and pressure group the employers came out clearly in favor of the plan; the Federation urged the establishment of a national industrial council for each industry, making reservations only about district councils and works committees.[15] The socialist organizations—the Fabian Society and the National Guilds League[16]—criticized the plan; but their criticisms were not severe, and the Trades Union Congress and the Labour Party Conference, while expressing serious reservations, avoided complete denunciation. Groups were

[14] [The Commission of Enquiry into Industrial Unrest was divided into eight groups, each assigned to a different part of the country. Their reports, Cd. 8662–8669, are in *Parliamentary Papers*, 1917–18, XV.]

[15] Federation of British Industries, *Industrial Councils: Recommendations on the Whitley Report . . .* , August 3, 1917.

[16] Margaret L. Postgate [Margaret Cole], *The Whitley Reports and Their Application* (Fabian Research Department, Memorandum No. 6, August 1918). National Guilds League, *National Guilds or Whitley Councils?*

formed under philanthropic auspices to spread the idea of the reconciliation of classes through the Whitley Council system; there were the Industrial Reconstruction Council, headed by Mr. Ernest J. P. Benn, and the Industrial League, whose president, Mr. G. H. Roberts, a member of the Labour Party, until last November was Minister of Labour. The government felt encouraged by this new war-born spirit to follow up the committee's report. A pressing appeal was addressed to employers' and workers' organizations. A special service was set up in the Ministry of Labour to supervise the operation of the new councils. While insisting that the Whitley Councils should remain free institutions, the Ministry made a civil servant available to each of them to function as a "liaison officer"— to use the official phrase—with the Ministry.

Two years have gone by since the publication of the committee's first report. What has been accomplished? Some thirty councils have been set up. What is their numerical importance and influence? What trade unions have remained deaf to the appeals of the government and the philanthropists? On the other hand, what unions have adopted the conclusions of the Whitley Reports and why?

We can dismiss at the outset the host of little unions that seem to have set up industrial councils only to give themselves an air of importance. The militants were amused to see in the list of Whitley Councils, councils for electrical contracting, vehicle-building, wallpaper, asbestos, and bobbins and shuttles. When they were faced with an industrial council for coir mats and matting, they were hard put to it to say what the coir was from which the mats were made. They asked why the painters and decorators wanted to have their own council separate from that of the building trade. All these unions serve to lengthen the list without noticeably enlarging the effective forces of the joint industrial councils. But some are more serious; and in examining them we believe we can find the reasons that have led the workers and the employers to agree to adopt the new form of organization in a number of well-defined cases.

I. Since 1905 union membership has grown enormously. Between 1905 and 1914 the number of workers represented in the annual Trades Union Congress had risen from about two million to about four million; from 1914 to 1918, the increase exceeded half a million. Such growth in numbers must necessarily result in the growth of union organization, particularly as regards the relations between employers and workers. At that point the state intervened to propose joint industrial councils to the union militants. Why not accept the proposals of the Ministry of Labour and its liaison officer to get together with the employers? Without the Whitley Report, they would have tried to set up a conciliation board. After the Whitley Report, they set up joint industrial councils to answer the same needs and to carry out the same functions.

Consequently it is possible to define precisely what one can call the new institution's field of development. The old unions whose organization had long since been perfected —the miners, the railwaymen, the Lancashire cotton workers, the engineers—are not interested in the new councils. It has been different with the unions caught by the war in the full crisis of expansion—expansion due in some instances to the war—which are moving towards, without having arrived at, organizing their relations with employers as successfully as other unions; they are ripe for joint industrial councils. Two examples will make this perfectly clear. There are two textile districts in England, the woolen district and the cotton district. Wool has its Whitley Council; cotton will not have one. Let us see why.

The cotton workers have been the pioneers of English unionism. In 1915 the number of organized workers in the factories and weaving shops of Lancashire was estimated at 250,000. These are the workers who pride themselves on having drawn up the Brooklands Agreement in 1893, the model that for twenty-five years has inspired all the plans for social pacification, including the Whitley Report. The cotton workers have no need for an industrial council. They have not and will not set one up.

The history of the neighboring district where wool is manufactured is quite different. In the West Riding of Yorkshire, during the years that preceded the war, employers and workers sought to consolidate their respective organizations; the most intelligent of the organized workers wanted to see employers' organizations strengthened, just as the most intelligent of the employers wanted stronger labor organizations. But for the moment these hopes remained unsatisfied: the cotton trade remained an ideal the West Riding could not attain. In Yorkshire, hardly a quarter of the workers employed in manufacturing woolens belonged to unions; thirty to thirty-five little trade organizations wrecked all the efforts of the General Union of Weavers and Textile Workers to concentrate labor strength. Then came the war. The government set up the board of control and ushered in a system of general unionization. As an official report put it, "it recognized groups and ignored individuals." When, with the return of peace, the time came to dismantle this organization, the employers and workers in the woolen industry, unlike those in Lancashire, could not fall back on a previously existing organization. Was not the simplest thing to use the framework proposed by the Ministry of Labour? At first organizing an ordinary "reconstruction" committee, in the narrow sense of the word, was considered, to regulate the woolen industry during the period of crisis that had to precede the full re-establishment of peace. But in the end it became a permanent industrial council—the most noteworthy of the existing councils, representing nearly 250,000 workers—which was inaugurated last January by the mayor of Bradford.

Another difficulty in the trade union world stood in the way of agreements between employers and workers. This time it was not so much the insufficiency as a defect of organization. The Whitley Report proposed a remedy. Workers in one industry often belong to several craft unions, and these craft unions in turn are able to straddle several industries. By going out on strike, a single craft union can force workers who belong to other unions to stop work against their will; on the other hand, by refusing to strike, it can paralyze the power of the others to strike. For many years, a whole section of the world of labor has hoped to reform union organization to bring all the workers in the same industry, whatever their specialty, together into a single union—to reconstitute unions on the basis of the industry, not the craft. But this policy comes up against obstinate resistance from the old craft unions. For a quarter of a century it has been complicated by the appearance of unions of general workers, unskilled laborers, who are hard to absorb into the same organization with skilled workers. In the single union, would the high dues of the old union of skilled workers be lowered to the level of the dues that until then were paid by the general workers? To do so would deprive the skilled workers of all the advantages they had received from their high dues in the form of friendly society benefits. Or, alternatively, would the dues of the unskilled workers be raised to the level of the dues formerly paid by the skilled workers? They could not pay them. In some cases the device of the industrial council seems to offer a solution to this difficult problem. Without being absorbed into a single union, several unions can send representatives to a single council. The difficulties that hinder the formation of an "industrial union" are avoided, while the workers gain certain advantages from the formation of the councils that they would have got by setting up a single union. Is this why the unions of general workers most often seem to be favorable to the conclusions of the Whitley Report?

II. The rivalry of the trade boards has also contributed to a considerable degree to the creation of industrial councils.

On this point the Whitley Committee achieved complete success. A new Trade Boards Act was passed in 1918 along the lines of the conclusions of the Committee's report.[17] Now a simple decision of the Ministry is enough to impose a trade board on any industry whatsoever; the wages paid in that industry need not be, as the law of 1909 put it, "exceptionally" low; the new law says "unduly" instead of "exceptionally," leaving it up to the Ministry of Labour to determine the moment at which wages fall below the level of what is "due" the worker.[18] The law has been quickly applied. Last October, thirteen trade boards supervised half a million workers. Eleven new boards, supervising 357,000 workers, had been set up by the end of April, and one can foresee a time when the wages of two million workers of both sexes will be regulated by trade boards. We should add that the functions of the trade boards are beginning to be extended. Under the new law, they can send a department "recommendations" that deal not only with wages but more generally with "industrial conditions."

Thus the Ministry of Labour is creating a sort of rivalry between the growing number of trade boards with extended functions and the industrial councils that are beginning to be formed. The employers distrust the trade boards, on which their representatives are named by the government instead of being elected by themselves, and in which all questions are settled by the casting votes of

17 8 and 9 Geo. V, c. 32.

18 [Under the 1918 act (8 and 9 Geo. V, c. 32), the minister was authorized to set up a trade board if he was "of opinion that no adequate machinery exists for the effective regulation of wages throughout the trade and that, accordingly, having regard to the rates of wages prevailing in the trade or any part of the trade, it is expedient that the principal Act should apply to that trade."]

a few civil servants. The trade unions are less hostile, but still not completely favorable; the setting-up of a trade board is an indication in a particular industry of their impotence when it comes to getting satisfaction for their demands by direct negotiation; for them, too, there is something humiliating about it. At times, therefore, an employers' association and a trade union will agree to set up a Whitley Council to escape from the authority of a trade board. We have been told that two well-established trade boards, one of which goes back to 1909—for paper-box making and tin-box making—are presently undergoing this transformation. Other organizations of this kind have clearly been established with the same intention.

The industrial council for hosiery is an example. Before the war, this was a very poorly organized industry. There was no understanding among employers. On the workers' side, there was certainly a union, the Leicester and Leicestershire Amalgamated Hosiery Union. But it tried in vain to muster its forces. To some degree it succeeded in Leicester itself. But elsewhere factories were in small towns where one or two manufacturers laid down the law and, by a variety of intimidations, shattered the unions as soon as they succeeded in organizing. There was, then, no possibility of collective bargaining between employers and workers, and the workers began to demand the establishment of a trade board. During the years that followed, an industry that worked largely for the Ministry of War had to familiarize itself, on the one hand, with union practices and, on the other hand, with state control. When the government set about putting the conclusions of the Whitley Report into practice, the hosiers, both workers and employers, had to choose between the establishment of a trade board by the state or the establishment of an industrial council by themselves. They chose the second alternative. A Joint Industrial Council for the Hosiery Trade held its first meeting on October 10, 1918.

Another example is to be found in those industrial councils of the second degree, so to speak, thirty-one in number, that were set up as Interim Industrial Reconstruction Committees. They are the work, not of the Ministry of Labour, but of a new ministry, the Ministry of Reconstruction, formed in 1917. Let us look briefly at their history.

It will be remembered that the second report of the Whitley Committee, published in October 1917, distinguished between two groups of industries. In group A, employer and trade union organization was sufficiently developed so that they could be considered to represent, respectively, the great majority of employers and workers. In Group B, the organization of the two classes, while having acquired considerable importance, was less impressive. For these two groups, two types of councils were proposed: the difference between the two types lay chiefly in the fact that one or two representatives of the government would be assigned to the governing committee in the councils of Group B. In June 1918 the Ministry of Reconstruction and the Ministry of Labour declared publicly that they had not succeeded in establishing a well defined boundary between the two groups and that, consequently, they were giving up the proposed distinction. The truth was that the industries of Group A refused to take advantage of the facilities the government put at their disposal for forming industrial councils, and that, with a few exceptions, all the industrial councils that were being organized fell into Group B.

But were all those industries insufficiently organized to be classified even in Group B to be forced to submit to the authority of a trade board? Since the Ministry of Labour did not allow them to set up industrial councils under its patronage, the new Ministry of Reconstruction would come to their aid. Mr. Ernest J. P. Benn went to work. He liked to think of himself as the spiritual father of the industrial councils and found public opinion too ready to forget the services he has rendered in writing and speaking for the cause of social peace. He got permission to establish, with the help of the Ministry of Reconstruction, organizations called Interim Industrial Reconstruction Committees, which, following the original plan of the Whitley Report, once more set up a second level of industrial councils. The word "Interim" meant that, like everything involved with the Ministry of Reconstruction, these committees were provisional. They would last while the Ministry lasted, as long as the period of transition between war and peace had not come to an end. They would also last as long as the organization of employers and workers was not sufficiently perfected to justify their transformation into industrial councils, properly so called. Running through the list of reconstruction committees, I have certainly found many kinds of workers: confectioners, glovemakers, optical instrument makers, lead and zinc workers. Without going into detail, we can see that it is a source from which, in time, the system of industrial councils can be recruited. I say without going into detail, because, if we were to do so, it would be necessary to tell the story, more amusing than instructive, of the war between the two ministries. Talk to a civil servant at the Ministry of Reconstruction and he complains: "Our reconstruction committees are simply industrial councils that have not yet reached their majority. Why does the Ministry of Labour ignore what we are doing? Why don't they help us? We are doing their work for them." Go to the Ministry of Labour, and you will be told: "Reconstruction committees? What are they? Mr. Benn's industrial councils!" It seems that the civil servants in Montagu House do not want to hear about this counterfeiting of *their* councils and *their* trade boards.

III. As an employer, the state has always obstinately resisted the trade-union demands of its workers and employees. Reluctantly and tardily, it recognized their right to form unions and consented to listen to their grievances through their union representatives. Until 1914 it never admitted the principle of collective bargaining in either its factories or its offices. Here, too, the war had its revolutionary effect. In every department arbitration boards have been set up to oversee all questions relating to salaries. The composition of these arbitration boards is far from satisfactory to the employees. Each of the boards is composed of three members: a representative of the employer (in this case the Ministry), a representative of the employees, and an "impartial" chairman, whose impartiality the interested parties regard as far from offering all the necessary guarantees.[19] But now that the state is urging industry to set up Whitley Councils, it would be remarkable if, in the state services and there alone, it was forbidden to set up permanent conciliation councils for dealing with discipline, promotion, and remuneration. The employees of the state are asking that it organize its own services, as it is working to organize industry.

The government is not giving in without hesitation: at the time of writing, the question is not yet settled. The government began by capitulating so far as its strictly industrial establishments were concerned—arsenals, for example. Joint councils were set up in these establishments; these councils are of two kinds. In one, the heads of a department and the representatives of the workers employed under it sit opposite each other, without distinction as to specialty. In the other, representatives of a given

[19] [In March 1915 the government rejected a claim by the Joint Committee of Postal and Telegraph Associations, referring it to a single arbitrator, thereby admitting the principle of arbitration for the first time; the award was made in September 1916. A Conciliation and Arbitration Board for Government Employees was set up, which made its first award in May 1917. This board was abolished in 1922. Since 1925 one form or another of arbitral court has existed for this purpose. See E. N. Gladden, *Civil Service Staff Relationships* (1943), pp. 105 ff. See also L. D. White, *Whitley Councils in the British Civil Service* (1933). Departmental arbitration boards are not discussed.]

union meet with the representatives of all the departments under which members of that union are employed. The first deals with questions of discipline, organization of labor, sanitary conditions in the shops, and technical education. The other discusses questions of wages. In this case, then, a victory has been won. But, in making this first concession last February, the state expressly reserved the question of whether or not it would apply the same procedure to the administrative services proper, among which it included the post office.

We must not fail to recognize the validity of the arguments the government invoked to justify its hesitation and resistance. In the case of government workers it is difficult to draw the distinction between employers and employees. Should the higher civil servants, the heads of departments, be considered employees in the same sense as the most lowly of their assistants or their office boys? What community of outlook or interest could there ever be between men belonging to such widely separated classes? On the other hand, who will represent the employers? Should the heads of departments be required to represent the power of the state as employer as against those who occupy less exalted positions in the administrative hierarchy? Is it not clear that higher civil servants are not employers in the real sense of the word? If they accept an arrangement, they do not have the necessary powers to bind the state, the Treasury, Parliament, or the taxpayers. But, while these difficulties are real, public opinion will not admit that they are insoluble and demands that they be resolved in the way most favorable to the employees. The interdepartmental committee charged with studying the application of the Whitley Report to the state services went to work; it drew up a report which Mr. Austen Chamberlain, the Chancellor of the Exchequer, and Sir Robert Horne, the Minister of Labour, submitted on April 8 to a meeting of all the staff professional associations.

The report still contains many reservations. It points

out that the public services are in a special situation and that they cannot be confused with private enterprises. The Whitley Councils are not to be allowed to discuss questions of general interest such as, for example, revision of the postal rates or problems of customs policy; for answers to these questions, the government is responsible to Parliament, not to its officials. Moreover, the councils are not to be allowed to approve or condemn a ministerial decision by which a particular civil servant is retired or promoted. Given the questions, both general and specific, that the government would like to remove from the competence of the councils, one asks what their powers amount to. It seems that they are limited to proposing rules concerning discipline in the services, advancement, working hours, and pay.

The report envisages a national council for all the public services, whose members will not number more than fifty. The staff unions will name half of the council. The state will name the other half, which will include, besides the heads of departments, representatives from the Treasury and the Ministry of Labour. A departmental committee is proposed for each department. When the departments are not concentrated in London, as is the case with customs, the post office, etc., there will be district or local office committees. Further, within the departmental committees, sectional committees are proposed. At the meeting of April 8 the union representatives were pleased that the principle of organization had at last been recognized by the state; on the other hand, they protested against the restrictions with which that recognition continued to be hedged about; they denounced the Treasury's claim to what they considered a tyrannical control; and the government agreed to appoint a joint committee of thirty members to revise the proposal. There the question remains, but there is no doubt that it will be resolved in a way more or less in line with the wishes of the staff associations.

A few days after this conference, when for the first time the government fully recognized the right of its employees to set up Whitley Councils, the Minister of Labour, speaking in the House of Commons, felt able to affirm the complete success of the new policy of social peace. "There are now," he declared, "thirty-one councils in existence, covering 2,000,000 work people, and at the present time drafting committees are at work in twenty-two other committees covering another million people."[20] The sentence was constructed to give the impression that step by step industrial councils would come to govern the whole world of industry. It was a completely illusory impression. Let us look at the rate at which the number of industrial councils has grown. Nearly twenty during the second half of 1918, but only eleven in the following four months; the movement is already slowing down. How long will it take to establish the twenty-two new councils, whose formation was announced? Of these councils, how many will fail? We know that the most important of the trade unions, on the basis of numbers of members, refuse to form councils. One of the councils, and not the least important—the Bread and Baking Council—can already be considered moribund; the employers have refused to agree to certain concessions that their representatives in the council had offered to the workers; and, if our information is correct, the Furniture Council threatens similarly to disappear. The number given by Sir Robert Horne must be considered a maximum which will not be surpassed and which perhaps will not be reached. Now, out of sixteen million workers, are three million very many? According to the most optimistic estimates, less than a fifth of the British working class will be organized into Whitley Councils.

Again, we must remember why some groups of workers have supported the policy of the Whitley Report. If the

20 [Sir Robert Horne, April 29, 1919, *Parliamentary Debates*, vol. 115, 54.]

preceding analysis is correct, they have done so to the extent that this policy exactly reflects the ruling tendencies in the English trade-union world for the past quarter of a century. The organized workers want their wages and, in general, all their working conditions regulated by collective bargaining and permanently protected by joint committees of employers and workers. The Whitley Report, then, is not without real importance in the social history of England. It marks the moment when management as a whole and the state itself, after long years of opposition, specifically concurred in the principle of this working-class policy. This has brought with it the consequences we must expect. Less well organized associations have seized the opportunity to raise themselves under state patronage to a higher level of organization, which had already been reached, to take a few examples, by the miners, the cotton workers, and the engineers. But the Whitley Report was pursuing another goal. More or less confusedly, it tried to create a new industrial system, to give new functions to these councils, functions different from those that the various conciliation boards in different industries had assumed in the past. From the preceding analysis, it really seems that the goal of these ambitions has not been reached and that it has perhaps not even been understood by the workers who have formed Whitley Councils. Let us examine this more closely.

※　※　※

The first Whitley Council to register as such was the Pottery Council, in January 1918; only four months later the Building Trade Council appeared on the Ministry of Labour's list. This second council was, however, the first to be actually organized; it is the real prototype of all the councils that have been founded under government auspices in the last eighteen months. We must be aware of the concerns that prompted this council's promoters in order subsequently to measure, in describing the present

132

state of things, the gap that separates reality from that ideal.

On March 8, 1916, Mr. Malcolm Sparkes, whose name we have already encountered, made his plan public for the first time in a letter addressed to the Amalgamated Society of Carpenters and Joiners. He won over opinion in the London district in a week, in the national organization in a month. Three months later, in London, twelve building trades unions accepted the plan. Meanwhile, with the assistance of the Garton Foundation, Mr. Sparkes published his scheme in a pamphlet and got help in his propaganda from a small pacifist society, the Fellowship of Reconciliation. Mr. Sparkes is a Quaker. He belongs to a sect that has always shown an equal aversion to war and revolution, and that has always sought the reconciliation of nations and classes.

An article published in December in the *Venturer*, the organ of that society, would have attracted the attention of Mr. Whitley, and Mr. Sparkes's friends like to think that he exercised a decisive influence on the drawing-up of the Whitley Report. Meanwhile, without waiting for the committee to finish its work, the building workers, in February 1917, established the first national joint council, that of painters and decorators. In June the building employers' association adopted Mr. Sparkes' ideas. In May 1918 the Industrial Council for the Building Industry, or the Building Trade Parliament, was solemnly inaugurated. What form did it take? On two counts it marks a bold innovation.

In the first place the Building Trade Parliament expressly abstains from intervening in disputes between capital and labor. The employers and workers in building had set up a conciliation board to arbitrate their differences. The board remains distinct from the council; and if the same individuals happen to be named as members of both, it is not in the same capacity. As members of the board, they exercise judicial functions. As members of the council, the Building Trade Parliament, they exercise legislative functions. Mr. Sparkes declares that the aim of the council is "constructive and nothing but constructive": it is to get employers and workers to co-operate, and, to that end, to avoid the areas in which there might be a clash of interests between the two classes. It is to lead to the elaboration of an industrial code that it will be up to the state one day to convert into a system of legally binding obligations. But it can begin by establishing a voluntary code, that is, an industrial code that, in order to be respected, requires only the consent of the members of the industry.

In the second place the Building Council is composed of two equal groups: employers on one side and workers on the other. But, so as to underline the aim pursued by the founder of the new institution—the breaking down of barriers between classes—it is specified that voting will be, not by classes, but by individuals. Every employer and every worker will have a voice, and—all their ballots being mixed in the same ballot box—decisions will be taken by majority. As a result, they will avoid the danger of meetings in which no decision can ever be reached because the two parties are overwhelmingly opposed to each other. According to Mr. Sparkes, it is the progressive employers who, voting with the workers, will be the real arbiters of the assembly. One hears an echo of the libertarian philosophy of Mr. Bertrand Russell when Mr. Sparkes boasts of appealing through the form of the council "to the creative impulses of man *qua* man."[21]

The Building Trade Parliament exists; its statutes are

[21] On the industrial council in building and the ends which its promoters were pursuing, Malcolm Sparkes, *A Memorandum on Industrial Self-government* [1917], and Thomas Foster, *Masters and Men, a New Co-partnership* [1918]. [The last quotation is not to be found in Sparkes's pamphlet; the Foster pamphlet is in neither the British Museum nor the library of the Trades Union Congress; so this quotation is a translation from Halévy's translation.]

deposited with the Ministry of Labour. This is the answer the founders of the council can give those who might be tempted to reproach them with having built castles in the air. But the critics persist; they want to know under what conditions it exists. On the eve of the war, the building industry was in a deep crisis. The workers, still very badly organized, were beginning to think about an industrial union in which their strength would be concentrated. Meanwhile, through sabotage and strikes, they were preparing for battle. The employers on their side were organizing for resistance and had just answered the strike by a national lockout when the war came, and everything was suspended. The workers were absorbed into the army. Building stopped. While the industry lay dormant, the heads of firms and union leaders listened sympathetically to the philanthropists who came bringing their plan for an institution that could, if they were to be believed, bring the era of goodwill among men and eliminate poverty, unemployment, and crises. They ratified the statutes of the new institution, or, better, of the future institution; for, at the time of writing, the Building Parliament has still to be put to the test of reality. When work begins again, and when the employers have to deal with the mass of workers themselves and not only with their leaders, we shall see if it is able to meet the test successfully.

Trade unions were founded and have grown to protect wages and working conditions. How can their members be suddenly required to enter into organizations of a new type in which they will be forbidden to exercise the functions to which they have been accustomed by long practice? How, really, is it possible to maintain the rigid distinction Mr. Sparkes would establish between the functions of the conciliation board and those of the industrial council? A dispute can arise between employers and workmen because, after concluding an agreement, the workers complain that the provisions of the agreement have not been

135

carried out. Then it is a mere question of fact to be settled, and, if necessary, the council could be permitted to delegate investigation of this question to a subordinate board. But, more often and in the most serious cases, the workers are simply asking for more favorable working conditions and a revision of current rates of pay. It then becomes a question of modifying the industrial code, the drawing-up of which, according to Mr. Sparkes's formula, falls to the Industrial Parliament. Whether we like it or not, it must go there. In actuality, not one of the thirty industrial councils that have been set up, which we agree can be considered to have been modeled on the Building Trade Parliament, has escaped the burden of discussing questions of wages. Without exception, all of them are charged with, among other things, "regular consideration of wages, piecework prices, and conditions with a view to establishing and maintaining equitable conditions throughout the industry." And as soon as that becomes one of their duties, it inevitably becomes their principal task. It was to carry out that task that the trade unions were originally founded; it is in the power neither of Mr. Sparkes nor of the Whitley Committee to interrupt that natural development.

Let us go on to the second point. Employers and workers confront each other in the industrial council. Whether one likes it or not, they belong to two distinct classes; the word "class" has been adopted in the modern world to designate precisely the two hostile groups to which they belong. When they have just formed a council, can employers be ordered to forget that they are employers and workers that they are workers, to consider themselves indifferently "as men *qua* men"? The proof that the idea is chimerical is that, again on this point, not one of the thirty councils has followed the pattern established by the Building Parliament. In all of them without exception, it is laid down that employers and workers will vote separately; a majority of both sides must agree for a decision of the council to be valid. Actually, if it were otherwise, if some fifty employers and workers sitting around the table in some industrial council were enough to make the class struggle disappear into thin air, one could approach the solution of the social problem with a light heart. But the class struggle is the very essence of every trade union and of every institution in which the trade union is represented. An organization that pretends to ignore it is a sociological monster.

In fact, when employers and workers come together in an industrial council, there is a misunderstanding between them. Not to understand its nature is to live in a dream world.

To the extent that they hope to draw some advantage from the Whitley Councils, the workers do not at all consider the councils to have been formed for a purpose utterly different from that for which unions were originally founded. They think that they have already got a number of advantages by trade union activity; they hope to pursue trade union activity in the council. They have got higher wages and shorter working hours; now, continuing along their victorious road, they would like to gain some participation by their class in the operation of industrial firms—what is called joint control. It is because they hope to use the Whitley Councils to gain joint control that socialists and syndicalists sometimes decide against outright condemnation of the new organizations.

Participation of the working class in the management of industry is not a complete innovation in the history of British trade unionism. All the victories won by the trade unions for half a century constitute infringements of the employers' authority and so are a beginning of control by the trade unions over industrial enterprise.

Do we see in the profits on capital—the truly industrial factor on which Ricardo, as well as Karl Marx, concentrated all his attention—the premium taken by the employer from the worker whose labor he has been able to render more productive without proportionally increasing the remuneration of that labor? If so, we must say that all the union practices the English worker has been increasingly able to force the employer to respect to better his economic circumstances imply a real beginning of joint control. It is not yet a system of "industrial democracy," but a mixed system in which the aristocratic element falls back steadily before the invasions of the democratic element. In some firms where labor organization has been perfected, one has the impression at times of an almost totally realized industrial democracy—the employer has lost the right to hire the workers whom he wants to do a certain job, being obliged to submit either to the choice of the union or to rules fixed by the union, and he has practically lost the right to lay off a worker without the consent of the other organized workers.

Or, on the other hand, do we see in these profits the commercial factor—the premium taken by the capitalist not from the producer whom he has hired and whom he pays for his labor at a low price, but from the consumer whom he succeeds in forcing to pay more than the cost of production of his products? Here again the recovery of profit by the working class has started, and that cannot be done without a kind of control over the commercial management of the enterprise. At first, in certain industries, the workers asked for the establishment of a "sliding scale," by which wages vary regularly with the selling price of the product. It is a practice whose principle is certainly arguable, and to which we shall return shortly. But once the principle is admitted, the workers very quickly come to wonder if the profit on capital necessarily varies directly with the selling price of the product, and whether the union should not try to find out about profits in order to base its demands on that knowledge. They want their auditors to get together with the employers' auditors and, after a detailed examination of the commercial situation of the industry, to furnish the conciliation board with all the necessary elements for the systematic fixing of wages. It seems that on this point the Lancashire cotton workers have begun to get satisfaction; the battle had been joined in the coal industry before the question of nationalization of the mines abruptly threw all other problems into the background.

The real battlefield between the two rival classes today is in the industries in which union organization has reached its highest point of perfection. Already subject to strict controls as employers, the heads of industry would like to keep their freedom of action as merchants. This is one of the paradoxical aspects of the struggle. Just when some theorists and philanthropists are seeking to use the joint industrial councils to promote the participation of the working class in the management of industry, the employers are seeking to use the same councils to save, and perhaps to strengthen, their threatened authority.

The workers talk about participation in the management of the business. The employers reply by talking about participation in profits and, in the most favorable cases, concede only a bastard form of joint control to the workers. For example, they will make each worker a petty stockholder in the business for which he works. From then on, is not the worker a co-proprietor of the business? Is he not called upon each year, at the stockholders' meeting, to audit the accounts and elect the officers? But we know very well how illusory this control is, and how the appearance of control is intended to create the narrowest possible bond between the interests of the worker and the interests of the employer who hires him. Hence the suspicion of such plans of profit-sharing among all the doctrinaires of working-class parties.

Half a century ago the English recommended and practiced the policy of universal cheapness: cheap products and cheap labor. Subsequently, through their unions, the

THE ERA OF TYRANNIES

workers organized a sort of protectionism of labor; they aimed to get more for their labor, while everything else remained cheap. The employers have opposed protectionism to protectionism: they give raises to the workers, if the workers are willing to permit them to increase their profits proportionally and, if necessary, to increase the price of the finished product. To the socialists who call on the workers of the world to unite against international capitalism, the employers reply by proposing that employers and workers in the same industry unite against the employers and workers in other industries, that employers and workers in one nation unite against the employers and workers of the rest of the world.

In the last analysis, this protectionist logic is at the bottom of all the arrangements concluded by employers with their workers in which wages vary with the selling price of the products. It has triumphed in a still more open form in Birmingham where Chamberlain, after having become the tribune of a sort of socialist radicalism, ended by becoming the leader of British neo-protectionism. There organizations of a new kind have appeared, called "Alliances," which have as their object—we quote the statutes of one of them—"the improvement of selling prices and the regulation of wages upon the basis of such selling prices . . . thereby securing better profits to the manufacturers and better wages to the work people." The employers agree to hire only workers, and the workers agree to work only for employers, who are members of the alliance. A wages board, made up of an equal number of employers and workers, is charged with periodically fixing the selling prices of the product and the wages regulated by those prices.[22] These alliances, as much as the utopian

[22] S. and B. Webb, *Industrial Democracy*, pp. 577 ff. [For a recent discussion of this and other aspects of industrial relations in these years, see E. H. Phelps-Brown, *The Growth of British Industrial Relations, a Study from the Standpoint of 1906–14* (1960).]

industrial parliament of Mr. Malcolm Sparkes, underlay the Whitley Councils.

It is a fact that one of the Whitley Councils, the Joint Industrial Council for the Metallic Bedstead Industry, is only the transformation of one of the most notorious alliances; the artificially high prices of metal beds have provoked strong protests in England for many years. It is a fact that, in two or three of the newly formed Councils—in particular the first to be entered on the Ministry of Labour's list, the Pottery Council—one stated goal of the new organizations was "to assist . . . in the maintenance of such selling prices as will afford a reasonable remuneration to both employers and employed." It is a fact that a protectionist motive has manifestly prompted the formation of several of the Councils. Thanks to the war, the tin mines of Cornwall, largely abandoned in 1914, experienced a revival of an artificial prosperity; if the employers and workers in these mines formed a council, it was to bring pressure to bear on the government to protect their newly threatened existence by means of customs duties against foreign competition. The inaugural celebration of the Pottery Council gave rise to a typical demonstration. Mr. G. H. Roberts, a member of the Labour Party who was then Minister of Labour, came to preside over the celebration, and, in a studied speech, encouraged the new council to become an organ of protectionist demands. "If an industry, united in determination, makes itself heard, then it does not matter if its demands are heterodox, or if they conflict with the fiscal policy of the party in power, for no government can ignore them. So long as it is united, an industry can ask whatever it wants. The members of an industry are the best judges of the interests of that industry."[23]

23 [This is a translation of Halévy's translation, the source of which I have been unable to find. The account in *The Times*, January 13, 1918, summarizes Roberts' speech in this way: "No matter if the concession asked for by an industry were

There is a working-class, or rather a socialist, theory about worker participation in the management of businesses. There is an employers' theory about the agreement of employers and workers to raise wages and prices simultaneously. We could wish that the two theories had been clearly defined in the Whitley Report, so that we might know for which one the members of the committee had opted, and into which of these two courses the Ministry of Labour wanted to steer the councils that were being formed. But the committee and the Ministry seem to have understood that, in order to preserve a precarious agreement, it was wise to avoid all precision in such matters.

If the goal of the Whitley Committee was to lead English industry towards a system of joint control, or, more exactly, if the intention of the organizers of the Whitley Councils was to use the new institution to that end, then all effort should have been directed towards setting up works committees. In broad terms, the national and district councils could easily define certain conditions of labor, the general acceptance of which would limit competition among individual firms. But to the extent that these firms still remain competing commercial enterprises, worker control remains necessary within each of them to protect the worker. While a number of national councils have been created, covering more than a sixth of the British proletariat, and while these councils have set up a number of district councils, it seems that nothing, or almost nothing, has been done to set up works committees at the bottom.

In March 1918 the Ministry of Labour published an interesting report on the functioning of works committees, which were already established in a number of firms before the Whitley Committee published its report.[24] These

heterodox or conflicted with the views of the party in power, no government could resist the voice of industry on fiscal and similar questions expressed through these national councils."]

[24] Ministry of Labour, *Industrial Reports*, No. 2 (1918).

committees were generally concerned with working conditions and factory discipline; they never touched the question of controlling commercial operations. They were created on the initiative of the employer who, in making a friendly appeal for the assistance of his workers, sometimes seems to have wanted to escape from the meddling of the industrial union. Since then, no statistics have been published to tell us how many works committees have been set up after the publication of the report. In the course of our research, we have gathered some isolated specimens, whose appearance does not seem to have been brought about by the efforts of the Whitley Committee. The active assistance of the big unions cannot be counted on for the development of these works committees; their officers, committed to centralization, are hostile to anything that compromises their authority in any way. Distrusted by employers and unions alike, the works committees have made only modest progress. As a result, the idea of a system of joint control has suffered.

The phrase "joint control" is not even used in the Whitley Reports. For a moment the men who drafted the reports were interested in looking into the different methods industrial leaders could devise to tie the workers to their interests. But it was only for a moment, and they decided not to make room in their report for a review of these systems. Might not employers and workers in a given industry conspire to raise prices artificially? The draftsmen drove this embarrassing thought from their minds. "We have . . . assumed that the Councils, in their work of promoting the interests of their own industries, will have regard for the National interest." If, nevertheless, they neglected it, would it not be in the state's power to intervene to protect the interests of the community? "The State," they assure us, "never parts with its inherent overriding power," but, they hasten to add, "such power may be least needed when least obtruded." As to the various mechanisms that have been devised to allow workers to share in profits, they did not think it wise to recommend their adoption. "We are convinced . . . that a permanent improvement in the relations between employers and employed must be founded upon something other than a cash basis. What is wanted is that the work people should have a greater opportunity of participating in the discussions about and adjustment of those parts of industry by which they are most affected." How is this imprecise language to be interpreted? It seems that they shrank from tracing the outlines of a social order, that they sought only the most likely means to bring employers and workers together and to get them to converse amicably, and that the subjects for discussion were chosen so as to avoid all subjects of possible quarrels.

If employers and workers accede to the suggestions of the government and go no further, the danger is that, in effect, there will be nothing but discussion and that, after a few months or years, they will grow weary of purely academic institutions. Take the case of one joint industrial council whose statutes I have studied. According to these statutes, the council must hold four meetings a year, one meeting every three months. The first will deal with wages; the second, with ways to improve the industry, either by using better machines or by better organization of labor; the third, with problems of foreign trade; and the fourth, with general and technical education of the workers. I can certainly see the importance of the questions that will be dealt with during the first meeting: I ask only if a conciliation board would not be adequate for discussing questions of wages. On the other hand, what can we say about the other three meetings? The active trade unionists are few in number; they are jealously watched by the workers who have elected them; they are poorly paid; and they are already overworked. What will this increase in work or the additional traveling expenses accomplish but to make them neglect their essential activity, the protection of wages and working conditions? I do not foresee an active revolt against the industrial council so much as a growing skepticism until the time when the institution, insofar as it differs from a simple conciliation board, becomes obsolete.

* * *

The Armistice has been signed; the war is over. The government has come to grips with those economic difficulties, long foreseen, against which it had urged the setting up of industrial councils. But in November 1918 hardly twenty industrial councils had been formed. It was, moreover, clear to everyone that the great majority of workers would not allow themselves to be brought in. The question was not what program should be adopted to resolve the difficulties of the day with the help of the joint industrial councils. A decision had to be made without waiting for the organization of these councils.

The soldiers demanded and got a rapid demobilization. They streamed back to the factories. But raw materials were still scarce and expensive, and work began only slowly. The unemployed grew in number; giving them unemployment benefits was a way to prolong the crisis as well as a way to ease it. The workers, as always, had their remedy: to absorb this surplus of labor, cut down the productivity of labor already employed, and, to do that, cut down the length of the working day without a corresponding reduction in wages. I remember that, when I was fifteen, the demand for the eight hour day seemed one of the most striking utopias of revolutionary socialism; the great war of 1914 made a reality of that utopia. The workers got not only the eight hour day, but the forty-eight or forty-seven hour week. They began to demand a forty-four or forty hour week and the six hour day. The same phenomena of union anarchy that had appeared in 1916 and 1917 cropped up again in the first months of 1919; on the basis of such extreme demands, local strikes

145

took place without the consent of the union leaders, sometimes even in spite of their formal disavowal.

At the head of the discontented workers stood the members of the powerful "Triple Alliance": the miners, railwaymen, and transport workers. According to the pact that joined these three unions, it was understood that no one of them would strike without the consent of the other two, but that, once a strike had been called within the terms laid down in the pact, each union would be helped by the other two in every way, including sympathetic strikes. If it had not been for the war, a strike of all three would have taken place in the autumn of 1914. Now, the national war having ended, the class war immediately began again. The miners, railwaymen, and transport workers—more than a million members in all—never considered the possibility of forming Whitley Councils. To get satisfaction for their demands, they counted on the power conferred on them by their numbers, their organization, and their formidable strategic position. The railway workers were asking for neither the eight hour day—they had just got it—nor the nationalization of the railways—in England that was virtually an accomplished fact. They wanted a general revision of wage rates. The transport workers were asking for the forty-four hour week and a wage rise of a fifth. The miners were demanding the six hour day, a thirty per cent rise in their wages, and nationalization of the mines. The government had started negotiating with the three big unions, but, their intransigence making any such dealings difficult, the government proposed a commission of inquiry. On February 12, after hurried debates, the National Conference of the Miners' Federation, sitting at Southport, noting the refusal the government had returned to their demands, decided to call for an immediate vote of the union membership on the question of whether or not a strike was called for. The union leaders were asking the miners to strike.

Mr. Lloyd George had returned from Paris on February

8 to attend the opening of Parliament, which took place on the same day that the Miners' Federation announced their intention to strike. He extended his stay, abandoning the work of the peace conference for the time being, and decided to resort to a new procedure to try to clear up the crisis. On the seventeenth he publicly announced his intention to call a National Industrial Conference in London on Thursday the twenty-seventh, to allow the government to consult with the employers and workers about the general situation. All the joint industrial councils and all the interim industrial reconstruction committees were invited to send their chairmen, vice-chairmen and two other members. "In industries where such councils or committees do not exist, the invitations [were] addressed direct to organizations most fully representing the employers and work people respectively."[25] In short, the policy of the Whitley Report was taken up again, although on a new plan not laid down in the report. It was hoped that a principle of order and social peace would be found in the unions. The local strikes, which were breaking out daily, were, in the last analysis, the work of undisciplined minorities. Was not the Triple Alliance, which seemed so menacing, itself only a minority whose arrogance would perhaps end by alienating public opinion? To appeal to the mass of organized workers to stop this revolutionary movement was clever policy, perhaps. To be sure, the government intended only a brief consultation limited to current questions. But some observers thought they saw in the assembly called for February 27 the outlines of a future Labour Parliament which, sitting more or less permanently, would, through its advice, enlighten and guide the government on the one hand and the world of labor on the other.

On Monday, February 24, the decisive week opened with the introduction in the House of Commons of a bill

[25] [*The Times,* February 18, 1919.]

instituting a royal commission of inquiry on the situation in the mining industry. Passage of the bill by the House was not in doubt; the problem was to draw labor opposition. One after another, the twenty-five mineworkers who sat in Parliament demanded that the miners' claims be granted without a preliminary inquiry. Mr. Adamson, a leader of the Labour Party and himself a mineworker, gave Parliament the results of the vote taken by the miners: 612,000 were for a strike, against a little over 100,000 opposed. The strike would begin on March 15, unless the miners had got satisfaction in the meantime. Now, the Prime Minister had just said that it was impossible to expect the commission to hand down its first report before the end of the month. It was known, moreover, that the railwaymen and the transport workers were prepared to make common cause with the miners. In a few days the three strikes would paralyze the whole system of production and national distribution: it would be, in fact, a general strike.

Debate resumed in the House of Commons on Tuesday the twenty-fifth. Mr. Lloyd George was still in his place. The workers' resistance was as obstinate as ever. Mr. Brace, the Welsh miner, introduced an amendment according to which the commission would have to hand down its report on questions of hours and wages on March 12. Mr. Lloyd George then intervened in the debate: he had spoken with the man whom he had already named as chairman of the commission and had agreed with him that the report would be handed down on the compromise date of March 20. Mr. Brace courteously accepted this gesture and withdrew his amendment. The bill was passed. It was now up to the labor organizations to say if they would accept the compromise.

On Wednesday, February 26, while the Ministry was introducing a bill in Parliament under which the state would acquire the right to nationalize railways and canals by simple order-in-council with a minimum of administrative delay, the miners were conferring on the attitude to be taken towards the royal commission. The debates were long and strenuous; as time was passing, they ended by adjourning the discussion to the following day. The outcome was still uncertain, then, when on Thursday morning Sir Robert Horne, the Minister of Labour, opened the proceedings of the National Industrial Conference at Central Hall, Westminster, before three hundred representatives of the employers and five hundred representatives of the working classes.

Sir Robert Horne was a Scottish advocate, a Tory, and new to Parliament; public opinion was amazed to see him quickly promoted in the last ministerial reshuffle to a post for which nothing seemed to indicate him. Imposing and serious, he presented his case with a reticence and timidity that at times went beyond what was acceptable, even for a Briton. He did not claim "any special qualifications for the office." He felt "overwhelmed from day to day with the sense of his own inadequacy." He excused his having accepted the Ministry of Labour by explaining that "ever since the beginning of the war, whenever he had been asked to undertake any task, he had always tried to do it." His program was very circumspect. Were hours of labor at issue? Only in the exceptional case in which it could be proved that some workers worked too long and were unable to obtain a reduction of the working day from their employers by negotiation, was it the duty of the state to intervene. But, given the great diversity of circumstances, the desirable solution of the problem was that employers and workers in each industry should get together to avoid state intervention. Was it a question of wages? No principle forbade the state to fix a minimum wage. The English state had set up and would continue to set up trade boards wherever workers' organizations were not strong enough to protect the rights of the workers. But the seriousness of the dangers that resulted from any state intervention in these matters should not be underestimated.

"The great positive reform to which one looked with the most hope for the prevention of industrial disputes in the future was the scheme which Mr. Whitley's committee submitted to the country not long ago. . . . When . . . they had given the operatives in any industry a responsible share in determining the conditions under which the industry was to work and the rates of pay which could be afforded, they would have advanced a long way to preventing disputes in the future. . . ."[26]

The end that the Minister sought was very clear. For the state, it was a matter of bringing together the two rival parties—employers and workers; the state stood to one side and abandoned to them the responsibility of resolving all the problems posed by the crisis.

The speech was badly received. The questions that followed from the workers were bitter and insistent. Had so many people been inconvenienced to hear a minister confess his incompetence and the state itself confess its incapacity? Mr. J. H. Thomas, of the railwaymen, spoke in the name of the Triple Alliance. He asked why not a word was said by the Minister of what, for the moment, constituted the essence of socialist demands: the taking over by the state of the mines, the railways, and all means of transport. The Prime Minister was present. Wisely he had refused to make the opening speech; he wanted to listen before talking. He attentively followed the debates, which his own speech would bring to an end. Suddenly he was called out.

It was the miners who requested his presence. Having taken, if we are correctly informed, the advice of Mr. Sidney Webb, they had decided that they would wait for the handing down of the report of the royal commission. But they would do so on one condition, the principle of which had been suggested to them by Mr. Sidney Webb. They insisted that half the members of the commission be ap-

26 [*The Times,* February 28, 1919.]

pointed by the Crown on nomination by the miners' union: three trade unionists, three socialist theorists. They had their list ready. If Mr. Lloyd George refused, there would be a strike. They gave him ten minutes to accept, and Mr. Lloyd George accepted. "He was furious," our socialist informant told us delightedly. With that over, and having avoided the peril of a general strike—at a cost—he went back into the hall.

The conference was presented with two draft resolutions. One came from Sir Allan Smith, the president of the Engineering Employers' Federation. Sir Allan asked for the appointment of an industrial committee of twenty employers and twenty workers, plus a certain number of representatives of the civil service, to undertake an inquiry, the conclusions of which would later be submitted to the conference, into "the causes of the present unrest and the steps necessary to safeguard and promote the best interests of employers, work people, and the State."

To this program of reconstruction in the narrow sense, Mr. Arthur Henderson, the clever politician who for two years had maneuvered with such skill and success on the borders of parliamentarianism and revolution, opposed a more ambitious program of reconstruction in the broad sense. If the draft resolution that he submitted to the meeting was adopted, a joint committee, composed of equal numbers of employers and workers, would examine (1) questions of hours, wages, and general conditions of employment; (2) the question of unemployment; and (3) the best method of promoting co-operation between capital and labor. The committee would have to hand down its report on April 5 at the latest. Mr. Lloyd George arose and declared that, aside from a modification or two in detail, he supported Mr. Henderson's proposal. He was eloquent and persuasive. The proposal was put to a vote, and the chairman declared it passed by a large majority. There were protests. Did the members of the conference have the power to vote and ought they not first to refer the matter back to their respective organizations? How large was that majority, and what did it mean? Was it known how many workers and how many employers made it up? All the Whitley Councils had been called together, but they did not represent more than a handful of workers; was not their attendance enough to falsify the majority? These vehement protests were disregarded. The result that Mr. Lloyd George wanted to obtain was achieved. The danger of a general strike was averted, and employers and workingmen were going to deliberate together on the future of British industry.

Six weeks went by: the National Industrial Conference met again to discuss the report of the joint committee which had been set up on February 27. Circumstances had changed, and Mr. Lloyd George had clearly won. The coal commission had granted the workers considerable advantages as to salaries and schedules, and nationalization of the mines had been promised in principle. The transport workers got everything they had asked for. Negotiations were still going on with the railwaymen, but there was no doubt that, under the direction of their secretary, J. H. Thomas, a conciliator and opportunist *par excellence,* the negotiations would result in a peaceful settlement. I attended this second session of the Industrial Conference. What courtesy, what cordiality, what good humor! Mr. Lloyd George had thought it useless this time to make the trip to London; Sir Robert Horne presided alone, without a great man to help him. He supported the conclusions of the report, which he praised as stamped with "Scotch caution." There was laughter, because he was a Scot. But Sir Allan Smith, seated beside him, was a Scot too; so were Sir Thomas Munro, chairman of the committee, Mr. Arthur Henderson, and still another man to whom everyone pointed, but whose name I do not know.[27] "All

27 [It was probably Mr. William Shaw of the Scottish Trades Union Congress.]

Scotch!" cried Sir Robert Horne, and the laughter re-doubled. "Scotch and water!" cried a worker; if you wish to understand the joke, translate it as "There is a lot of water in your Scotch whisky."[28] The laughter broke out again. In this very quiet congress, it was the only protest the revolutionary party could utter.

Let us examine the report whose terms were approved unanimously by the members of the joint committee.[29] It had been drawn up exactly two years after the first report of the Whitley Committee. Let us measure the progress.

Firstly, concerning hours and wages, the report is in favor of a legal week of forty-eight hours and varying minimum wages applicable to all the industries of the kingdom. Sir Robert Horne had shown what difficulties he foresaw in adopting these two reforms. He had made it clear that he counted on the Whitley Councils to rid the state of this double responsibility. The whole world of labor—employers and workers—is in agreement to throw it back on the state.

Secondly, concerning "the best method of promoting co-operation between capital and labor," the committee is far from attributing to the Whitley Councils the importance that one might expect. They urge employers and workers to organize and to do everything in their power to develop the machinery of conciliation boards. To the Whitley Councils they more particularly reserve discussion of questions concerning unemployment. It is not easy to see why such questions would not fall within the competence of the conciliation boards for the same reason as

[28] [The account in *The Times*, April 5, 1919, quotes the anonymous heckler as saying, "Put a little water in it," which could suggest another source and another interpretation. But Halévy's recollection seems more circumstantial.]

[29] [*Report of Provisional Joint Committee presented to Meeting of Industrial Conference* . . . (Cd. 139), *Parliamentary Papers*, 1919, XXIV.]

questions of wages and working hours do: are they not closely linked? But a place had to be found for the joint industrial councils; could a long report on the remedies for the industrial crisis be drawn up and not even mention that entirely new institution, the pride of Sir Robert Horne's own ministry?

Thirdly, the committee recommends the establishment of a National Industrial Council, a consultative assembly, which will meet at least twice a year and which will be made up of four hundred members, half elected by the employers' association, half by the trade unions. On the one hand, it will form an arbitral tribunal, a conciliation board of last resort: when conciliation boards have not succeeded in settling a dispute between employers and workers in a particular industry, the National Council will be able to intervene in the dispute and try to resolve the problem, taking the general interests of the country into account. On the other hand, it will take into consideration all legislative proposals that touch on industrial production: all labor legislation will be prepared after consultation with the National Council. We should note that the new institution is in no way based on the organization of the Whitley Councils. The representatives who are going to sit in the National Council will be directly elected, either by the employers' associations or by the trade unions. As to the joint industrial councils which the government had invited to be represented in the conference of that year, the conference itself, in drawing up the statutes of the National Council, ignored them. The world of labor obviously considers the Whitley Councils a failure.

The fate of these councils will have been truly strange. Those who had first urged their adoption wanted at the base of each industry a works committee in every firm; higher up, a district committee for each industry and each region; higher still, a national council for each industry and for the whole nation. No one's imagination seems to have risen so high as to dream that it would be possible to create a single superior national council for all the industries of the country. Now, in reality, things turned out quite differently, following a road, so to speak, running in the opposite direction. The idea of works committees has failed miserably; the national councils that have been founded have been slow to form a few district councils; the national councils are already more numerous, although they are far from covering a majority of the British proletariat. And now at the summit, this National Industrial Council seems about to be established, with the support of all the employers and almost all the workers, a council that was not mentioned in the reports of the Whitley Committee. We believe this National Council to be viable and capable of rendering appreciable services. We shall be asked why, when we have shown so much skepticism about the Whitley Councils. Has not the same inspiration given rise to both? Yes and no. The idea of the National Industrial Council is at once similar to and different from the idea of the Whitley Councils; that is what we want to explain in a few concluding words.

From the end of the nineteenth century, conciliation boards were spontaneously set up by employers and workers; their number and importance will probably grow steadily. The purpose of these conciliation boards is the settlement through negotiation of the disputes that constantly divide employers and workers. There is no contradiction between the existence of a conciliation board and the principle of the class struggle; one would be disposed to say, rather, that the principle of the class struggle is the vital principle of every conciliation board. A board presupposes the existence of two conflicting classes whose interests need to be adjusted. But why rush into the violent and ruinous method of the strike to adjust them? Is it not wiser to bargain first and to consider the strike only as a last desperate resort? Because two nations have ended a war, they do not in consequence come together into a single nation; they simply prefer diplomatic means to bel-

155

ligerent means. If the Whitley Councils are only conciliation boards under another name, they are certain to survive and to be useful. But what good is a new name to
designate something old?

In fact, the Whitley Council sought to innovate and to
create a kind of mixed institution, half worker, half employer, from which the idea of the class struggle would
be absent. Members of a Whitley Council are expected,
during meetings, to forget that some of them are employers and that others are workers, and to work together
for the progress of industrial technique in a spirit of brotherhood. The workers taking part will inevitably be the
active trade unionists whose function, as such, is to protect the workers' interests against the employers' interests,
taking it for granted that these interests conflict. From the
moment they enter a Whitley Council, they are expected
to consider the interests of all producers—industrial leaders
and ordinary wage-earners—as they appear to be bound up
with each other. This abrupt reversal of outlook seems to
us inconceivable; if it is necessary to have it in order to
have a Whitley Council function normally, we can say
that the Whitley Councils are not viable. Those that do
not die a violent death are condemned to waste away.
The question, then, is reduced to whether the National
Industrial Council is inspired by the same principle as the
conciliation boards, whose vitality is great, or by the Whitley Councils, whose future seems doubtful.

We believe that, in its essence, the National Industrial
Council, far from denying the idea of the class struggle, is
organized to permit that struggle to go on, since it must
go on, in forms as legal and, so to speak, as "peaceable"
as they can be. It is an absolutely obvious fact, the basic
fact of political life today: employers and workers are in
conflict. Must we willingly blind ourselves, shutting our
eyes to an annoying reality, and, with the inventors of the
Whitley Councils, deny this very real conflict of interests
and passions? That is not the English way. Or, accepting

the idea of struggle, should we talk of crushing working-class insurrection in blood or of resolving the social question by the dictatorship of the proletariat? That is continental language, not British. The English method and language are the method and language of parliamentarianism.

England has known religious war. How did she escape from that chaos? Not by suppressing all dissent, but by granting tolerance to all sects. She accepted religious war, and religious war lost its horror. England has known civil war. Since then the two factions have, so to speak, grown accustomed to each other, have adjusted to each other: subject to commonly accepted rules of courtesy, civil war has become the clash of parties, and civil war, losing its horror like religious war, has been the normal mode of English political life. Now the time for class war has come, for England as for the whole western world. What an honor it would be for English wisdom if the same methods from which she has profited on so many occasions could again be brought to bear. In the National Industrial Council, two rival classes will vent their quarrels, but they will do so according to the traditional forms of the Parliament of Westminster, religiously respecting the decisions of an impartial chairman and complying with the sometimes childish minutiae of an ancient protocol. Do not call it utopia: utopia is the Whitley Council and the dream of a fusion of classes. The hypothesis we propose is very different; it has nothing utopian about it. If it comes true, we shall see the class struggle, acclimatized on English soil, adapting itself to the traditional party system. After so many political triumphs in the last two centuries, it is possible that England will bring about this new triumph.

June 4, 1919

THE PROBLEM OF WORKER CONTROL[1]

This talk is the first of a series. Following me, others will speak to you about the problem of worker control as it appears in Germany, Italy, and France. In listening to us, you are being asked to undertake a real exercise in comparative sociology. The very diversity of testimony will help you to see things in totality.

Before beginning, I must say, in all modesty, that I know my limitations. I am a specialist in the general history of England. There are, then, few subjects in English history on which I cannot enlighten you; but, on the other hand, there is not one of them that specialists cannot deal with more capably than I. If, for example, you had asked me to give you an account of the recent history of the Church and Dissent in England, and if I knew that, among my listeners, there was a theologian, a minister, or a priest, I should urge him to fill in the gaps in my knowledge. So today, if there are professional economists and representatives of employers or of the Confédération Générale du Travail among you, I shall be happy to have whatever observations and criticisms they may care to make, and I shall expect to profit greatly from them.

That said by way of precaution, on the other hand, here are my qualifications. Two years ago I undertook a particularly detailed study of a group of joint councils, the Whitley Councils, which have been organized by employers and workers under state auspices, and which, some people hoped, were to mark the beginning of worker con-

[1] Lecture given March 7, 1921, to the Comité National d'Études Politiques et Sociales.

159

trol in industry. On that occasion, I again came into touch with socialist circles. I am growing older, and the socialists whom I used to know belonged to the older generation of the Fabian socialists and of Mr. and Mrs. Sidney Webb. Because of my researches, I made contact with the young men who call themselves Guild Socialists and who are, so to speak, moderate syndicalists. I have also made friends with a number of trade-union leaders. Finally, I spent three weeks or a month in Wales, in that coal-mining region that the English look on, not without exaggeration, as the home of British Bolshevism.

The problem of worker control became important in English working-class and socialist circles only recently; a very few years ago, no one would have dreamed of posing it. That is what I should like to show at the outset.

Let us begin with the doctrine of Mr. and Mrs. Webb, as it was set out in 1897 in their great work *Industrial Democracy*. It was they who formulated the ideas of doctrinal socialism current in England at the end of the nineteenth century. But we must not be misled by those words "industrial democracy." Today our French syndicalists like to borrow the term. Actually, when the Webbs speak of industrial democracy, they are not thinking about a democratic organization of producers in the factory itself, or of the factory as a producer's republic. They are talking about something quite different—about industrial democracy as a system in which industries are subject to the government of a democratic state.

As I understand its spirit, their doctrine is the glorification, the religion, of the state—democratic, I think, but bureaucratic too. They were influenced by the success attained in Germany by Bismarckian ideas and by the world-wide prestige of the Bismarckian state. It should be added that, in England itself, they are fighting the old liberalism of Manchester and Gladstone. There is something wilfully provoking in their eloquent insistence on *étatisme*.

Ten or twelve years went by. A new generation arose, in revolt against the Webbs. They did not break with socialism, but they brought a new formulation to it; it is this Guild Socialism that I was speaking of a moment ago. If you want to put proper names to this movement of ideas, I shall mention G. D. H. Cole and S. G. Hobson.[2] Their point of view is diametrically opposed to that of the Webbs.

Mr. and Mrs. Webb defined their point of view by a happy formula when they declared: "Our goal, as socialists, is the elimination of capitalism, but not of the wage system. Far from wanting to abolish the wage system, we want to universalize it. We want all men, instead of being divided into wage-earners and profiteers, to be equally, if not with the same rank, paid functionaries of the State." The Guild Socialists reply: "If we confine ourselves to eliminating capitalism to universalize the wage system, we will simply have replaced one slavery by another. What we want is the abolition of the wage system. Once the great industrial services are taken over for the community —the railways or mines, for example—nothing will be accomplished if the miners or the railwaymen are left as employees of the State. In these great public services, we want the associated [miners and] railwaymen to take over the operation of the mines and the railways, as a limited partnership, so to speak; to deal on an equal footing with the State; and to remain completely free, as a republic of producers, to organize production and the division of profits in their own way."[3] You can see the vast

2 Among other works, one can consult the following in particular: A. R. Orage, ed., *National Guilds, an Enquiry into the Wage-system and the Way Out* (1914). S. G. Hobson, *National Guilds and the State* (1920), and *Problems of a New World* (1921). G. D. H. Cole, *Self-government in Industry* (1918), and *Guild Socialism Restated* (1920).

3 [I have been able to trace neither quotation. The Webbs' remarks may well have been made in private conversation; the sentiment, in any event, is parallel to a statement by Sidney

difference of points of view. In the time of the Webbs, in the last years of the nineteenth century, the goal pursued by socialists was a takeover by the state. Since 1910 the main concern has changed completely. They have learned to distrust the state, and the goal they now pursue is the establishment of direct control of industrial enterprises by the working class.

I shall not enter into detail concerning Guild Socialism. I shall not tell you how it is to be distinguished from pure syndicalism by the fact that it still assigns a number of functions to the democratic state. As to its descent and its sources, I shall only remind you that in some respects it comes from Ruskin and William Morris. From their school the Guild Socialists have derived their concern with reviving a liking for work and a corporative zeal and enthusiasm in the minds of the producers: the word guild is borrowed from the vocabulary of Ruskin. But, on the other hand, it is more certain still that the Guild Socialists have been influenced by French syndicalism; the point of departure for all that literature must be sought in the little pamphlet by M. Georges Sorel, dating from 1898, on *L'avenir socialiste des syndicats* (*The Socialist Future of Trade Unions*).

Leaving aside the history of the doctrines, which does not concern us today, let us try to see how and why these ideas have gained ground among the mass of workingmen. They began to spread during the four or five years before the war. After having sent a large contingent to Parliament —more than fifty working-class members—the workers realized that these labor members were not giving them everything that they had expected of them. They passed social legislation, to be sure, but these laws did not raise wages in proportion to the rise in the cost of living, which

Webb in *Socialism: True and False*, Fabian Tract No. 51, pp. 17–18 in the sixth reprint, 1921. The Guild Socialist view is so much a commonplace in their literature that I suspect Halévy constructed a "typical" reply.]

had begun to go up very rapidly since the beginning of the century. On the other hand, they felt that labor members were too closely tied to the bourgeois Liberal Party and even that social legislation often resulted in the creation of a bureaucracy in which the labor members and trade union secretaries found it easy to settle down. Hence a shift of opinion favorable to direct action and strikes, in preference to parliamentary methods.

The war had hardly begun when the syndicalist and anti-state movement took on still more violence and intensity. The labor members who were criticized before the war for being too closely tied to the ruling class were still more sharply criticized after the declaration of war when, in the name of *union sacrée,* they became partners of the government in organizing the defense of the realm. In particular, it was they who organized munitions work on a new footing. Industrial production went on thereafter under state control. All the industry of the country came into the public sector, and the secretaries of the big unions worked with civil servants and leading industrialists at the head of this centralized structure. Now while this centralized structure guaranteed the workers many material and monetary advantages, on the other hand it deprived them of all sorts of liberties. It eliminated a number of hitherto respected trade union practices that, it was said, slowed down production. Finally, and especially, by an express agreement, it suppressed the right to strike.

At that juncture, a violent agitation developed in the provinces, especially in the Glasgow area, not only against the state but against the leaders of the big unions. In the workshops of this region, there were certain subordinate union officials called shop stewards, delegates from the workshops who had formerly had as their only functions getting rules obeyed and collecting dues for the central union. The shop stewards rebelled against the central union, got themselves elected by the workers in each shop, and demanded the reconstitution of all unions on a federative, not a centralized, basis.

In place of craft unions, in which workers in a single trade would be federated throughout the country without direct contact with each other, each firm or each workshop would now have one local union, bringing together all the workers without regard to specialty. They would give their shop stewards a mandate to fight the employers within the firm itself and to chip away at the employers' authority until the time when that authority would finally pass into the hands of the working class. Towards the end of the war, the shop stewards' movement became a matter of very great concern to the government and the trade-union leaders. Everywhere it was causing strikes which were often difficult to suppress.

We come now to the years 1917 and 1918. Mr. Lloyd George was anxious to present the electorate with a big program of postwar reforms, promising the masses that the end of the war was going to launch a new era of social peace and justice in the history of the world. At a stroke, Parliament voted not only universal suffrage as we have it in France, but complete universal suffrage, for women as well as men; it also passed a sweeping law which made education compulsory between the ages of thirteen and eighteen.[4] Was it not also necessary to do something to satisfy the syndicalist or semi-syndicalist agitation then stirring up the working class? A large extra-parliamentary body, the Reconstruction Committee, had been appointed to consider the reorganization and reconstruction of England after the peace. A subcommittee, presided over by Mr. J. H. Whitley, had as its mission

[4] [Actually, only women over thirty were given the vote in 1918; in 1928 the "flapper franchise" gave the vote to women between twenty-one and thirty. The education act required part-time attendance at "continuation schools" by "young persons" between the ages of thirteen and eighteen.]

164

finding out what the state could do to improve relations between employers and employed.

This subcommittee was made up of extremely disparate elements, intentionally disparate: some were employers, some workers; some were economists of extremely diverse tendencies; the working-class members of the committee were themselves divided between moderates and extremists. But, following the government's suggestion, the chairman succeeded in getting everyone to agree to a sort of common program, necessarily vague in order to be accepted and able both to reassure the most conservative and to encourage the hopes that the syndicalist theorists had conceived. In 1918, as a result of the work of this subcommittee, a program was promulgated under which all the industries of the kingdom that wished to do so were authorized to set up joint standing industrial councils of employers and workers. Three levels of these organizations were foreseen.

At the top, for each industry, there would be a joint committee which would be called national. Below that, a division by region or district was proposed; heading each district would be another joint committee, half employer and half trade-unionist. Finally, at the bottom, in each workshop and firm, joint committees were to be formed to which the subcommittee's report gave the name of works committees. It was an expression borrowed literally from the terminology of the shop stewards: "works committee" was the term used by the shop stewards to designate the little groups that they set about forming in rebellion against the big union organizations which were too centralized for their liking.

What duties did they propose to give to these joint councils? For the sake of clarity, it is advisable to reduce the eleven-point program drawn up by the rapporteurs of the Whitley Committee to three essential points. In the first place, the joint councils would consider questions of working conditions: wages, hours, sanitation in the shops.

In the second place, they would consider everything that had to do with technical progress in the industry. In the third place, they would be concerned with questions of labor legislation, stating desires agreed upon by employers and workers which could influence the government when it came to make laws on these matters.

The second point, which implies that workers and employers should co-operate in promoting technical progress in the industry, is the one that led some workers to believe that it was a means of beginning worker control in industry, not complete worker control, but joint control by workers and employers.

In 1918, a number of these councils began to appear. If one keeps to the official statistics, the movement appears to have succeeded admirably. At present about sixty councils exist, covering, the Ministry of Labour tells us, more than three million workers. The statistics are perhaps unreliable; I have no intention, however, of discussing them. The question that I want to pose is how much these Whitley Councils have really done towards introducing joint control into British industry.

In the article that I published on this question two years ago in the *Revue d'économie politique,* I tried to show that the Whitley Councils had not introduced any really new element into the structure of industrial society. In a number of industries in which the workers were particularly well organized, conciliation boards had already been organized spontaneously; divided between employers and workers, these boards pursued a double aim: first, the negotiation of contracts between employers and workers, and, second, overseeing the execution of those contracts, once they were concluded. I tried to show that the Whitley Councils had done no more than imitate these institutions and, under state auspices, having finally gained the goodwill of the employers, created joint councils and conciliation boards in a number of industries in which the workers, less well organized, had not yet set them up.

I do not have time to go into the detail of the proofs I gave in that article, so I shall limit myself to giving you two which seem to me decisive.

The first proof. I have said that these joint councils were organized on three levels: national councils at the top; district councils in the middle; and committees for each factory and for each particular firm at the bottom. The syndicalists were especially interested in setting up works committees for the reasons I have just indicated. They thought that a central union headquarters—representing not all the personnel of a firm but all the workers with a certain specialty, however diverse the firms in which they were employed—could do little towards recapturing the direction of the firms themselves from the employers. But if all the workers in each firm were brought together, without distinction as to specialty, to deal with the employers, they would be able to accomplish the take-over which they wanted so much.

Now, what happened? As a matter of fact, if we refer to the statistics furnished by the Ministry of Labour, we note that a large number of national councils, with central offices, have been set up for all England, or for England and Scotland together; that district councils are less numerous; but that when we come down to works committees, we find only a small number spread over the whole kingdom. Not only are they few in number, but—a still more serious fact—the small number of works committees that have been set up have not been organized in a revolutionary spirit; they have been founded, rather, by philanthropic employers to break up the solidarity of the union and to create a special community of interest between themselves and the workers in their factories, as opposed to the solidarity that united, or could unite, their workers to unionized workers in other firms.

I have studied the reports published by the Ministry of Labour. Better than that, a large firm which I visited in

Wales has for two years done me the honor of sending me regularly the minutes of a large works committee which functions under its patronage. It is a firm that covers several villages and includes among its employees all the inhabitants of several towns. There is really nothing revolutionary in these periodic conversations, the minutes of which I receive. I sometimes get the impression that I am attending a meeting of a municipal council; they talk about means of transport, about electric or gas lighting, and about working conditions—the reworking of time-schedules and the raising of wages. There is never anything that even remotely resembles working-class participation in the management of the firm.

Second proof. If the Whitley Councils were really supposed to give the organized workers something more for discussing working conditions with employers than they had already got through their conciliation boards, what should have happened? All the big labor organizations that had already set up conciliation boards would have rushed to form Whitley Councils to get these new advantages. Is this what happened? Not at all.

Let us accept the official figures, although, like all official figures, they are of necessity unreliable: it is difficult to know on what data the estimates of the number of workers employed in an industry are based. But let us accept a figure of three and a half million workers. We must not forget that the workers represented in the annual Trades Union Congress alone number more than eight million. Only a minority of the English labor movement, then, is represented in the Whitley Councils. Furthermore this number of three and a half millions will not be exceeded; it is a maximum; a large number of unions let the government know that they would have nothing to do with Whitley Councils. What unions are they? Precisely those that were best organized, that could already through their conciliation boards deal with employers on an equal footing on all conditions of labor. Thus, the powerful organization of cotton workers has refused to set up Whitley Councils; there are no Whitley Councils among the railwaymen; none among the miners, of whom there are more than a million in England and Scotland; they are no more evident in the metal trades, in machinery, or in shipbuilding. You can see how exceptional they are.

The trade unions that wanted to form Whitley Councils were those not yet organized which sought government support to accomplish what they had not been able to accomplish by themselves and what the miners and cotton workers, for example, had already accomplished.

Again, the employees of the state had not, until then, succeeded in getting their associations recognized. When the state took the initiative in inviting the employers and workers of the country to form joint councils, it was hoist on its own petard. How could it refuse to its own employees what it offered to all other workers in the kingdom? As a matter of fact, among the unions that have formed Whitley Councils there are seven hundred thousand employees of the state and of municipalities. This is an important fact. The formation of Whitley Councils has symbolized the recognition of trade unions by the state in England. But so far as the functions of these joint councils go, there is nothing new to be noted. The state has simply resigned itself to accepting at last what most of the big businessmen had accepted earlier. In all this business I see no beginning at all of what I have earlier called worker control.

I must anticipate an objection, however. I will be told that the mere fact that workers are grouped into unions to form joint councils and to dictate conditions of labor to the employers, if they can, already constitutes worker control. If you like, perhaps so. I wonder, though, whether we should not distinguish between two very different functions in the organization of an industry.

First, there is the function of the manager who, placed in charge of the firm, serves the needs of the customers, perhaps even increasing or stimulating them, and who puts production at the service of consumption by improving technical equipment and by the skillful use of labor. The second function consists in protecting the interests of the worker against the employer within the factory. To be sure, it is a good thing to serve the consumer by production that is as abundant and as cheap as possible. But the interests of the producer himself must not be sacrificed to the interests of the consumer. Now, since the worker is entitled to a minimum in wages, leisure, and sanitation, I quite agree that one can use the term "worker control" for the function that the union exercises when it "controls" the conditions of labor in the factory and prevents the producers from being sacrificed to the passion for production. But that is not what the Guild Socialists are talking about when they demand the "control of industry" for organized workers. They are asking that the elected heads of the unions be put in charge of production to serve the interests of the consumer. So we move from the exercise of one function to the exercise of another. This passage the Whitley Councils have not made.

All the Whitley Councils that have been set up are for dealing with conditions of labor, for getting the employers, through friendly discussions, to take account of the interests of the working class in the operation of the industry. It cannot be said that any one of them has begun to bring about the invasion of management by the working class.

"Granted," it will be said, "that the Whitley Councils have not allowed the working class to take the forward step the Guild Socialists wanted to see it take and to pass from control over conditions of labor to worker control properly so called, which would consist in the unions' taking over the management of industrial production. But you have just shown how, alongside the unions that have set up Whitley Councils, there are others, numerous and powerful, who have refused to enter into the new organization. Have not these unions, whose power is so great, not tried to acquire something of the worker control that nowadays so much concerns the doctrinaires and the agitators?"

I cannot deny it seems to be the case. The concern with worker control could not but make itself felt in big unions as powerfully organized for battle as those in the railways and the mines. Leaving the Whitley Councils aside, let us see what the mineworkers have tried to do, with much publicity but little success, to solve the problem of worker control.

I ask you to go back with me to the end of the war, to the months immediately following the Armistice. Apart from the rest of the English trade-union world, three big unions, numbering more than a million organized workers —the transport workers, the railwaymen, and the miners— had formed what is called the Triple Alliance to oppose the employers and the state and to enforce respect for their demands. In the early months of 1919, the miners, the railwaymen, and the transport workers presented their demands together. It was difficult for Mr. Lloyd George to satisfy everyone without going beyond what a reasonable government could grant without causing a revolution.

He had the cunning to satisfy the railwaymen and the transport workers, leaving the miners isolated. They had three demands. One concerned wages: they asked for a rise in wages of six shillings per ton; they also asked for a reduction in hours of labor from eight to seven and six a day. Finally, they demanded nationalization of the mines.

When they asked for nationalization of the mines, they were asking for it in the new sense of calling for the establishment of worker control over operations inside the nationalized mines. Here is a chance to understand, through a dramatic example, the speed with which English working-class ideas had evolved on this point. In 1912, the very year in which the English miners had got the law granting them a minimum wage, the Labour Party introduced into the House of Commons a bill for nationalizing the mines. On analysis, it is a strange bill; there is no question of worker control; the only goals pursued by those who drew it up were the take-over by the state, the conditions of purchase, and, finally, state operation.

All that had changed in 1919. Now what the workers demanded, along with and beyond nationalization, was the establishment of worker control.

To satisfy the workers without, however, immediately committing himself, Mr. Lloyd George got the question referred to a royal commission. At first and hurriedly, this royal commission would deal with the question of wages and working hours, on which the miners demanded full and immediate satisfaction. Then, taking their time, they would approach the great problem of nationalization and worker control.

The first question—wages and working hours—was dealt with as the workers had wanted on the last day of March. Then, from April until June, the commission met in a second session to study the bigger problem in depth. I shall not go into detail about the work of this commission;[5] but I believe you will be interested in the attitudes of the different members on the question of worker control. There, in brief, you will find a picture of English opinion on this critical question, among the working classes as well as among the employers.

The commission was composed of twelve members; of these, six were employers and six were workers or socialist theorists, such as Mr. Sidney Webb, for example. Over these twelve members was an impartial chairman, Mr. Justice Sankey. Here are their conclusions.

Of the six employers, five declared themselves clearly opposed to nationalization; they went no further than ask-

[5] See Coal Industry Commission, vols. I and II, Reports and Minutes of Evidence; vol. III, Appendices, Charts, and Indexes (Cmd. 359, 360, 361) [Parliamentary Papers, 1919, XI–XIII].

ing that Whitley Councils be set up at all levels of the mining industry. They certainly did not wish to establish worker control: they considered the setting up of Whitley Councils in the collieries as being the most harmless of all conceivable solutions.

One of the six representatives of the employers, Sir Arthur Duckham, separated himself from his colleagues, however, and proposed a different plan. He asked that the legislature bring the mining industry out of its chaotic state. Indeed, I was struck in the spring of 1919, when I visited Wales, by a fact that was new to me: the coal-mining industry in England is highly fragmented. Even today it often happens that men of small means, ordinary shopkeepers in Cardiff or Swansea, get together in twos or threes to bore into the side of a Welsh mountain and to chance striking it rich. Sir Arthur Duckham asked that the state intervene to amalgamate the mines into a limited number of great regional companies which would have a kind of statutory existence. In the district coal board which would preside over the management of each of these regional companies, some places would be kept for representatives of the workers: of the seven members who would make up each board, two, according to Sir Arthur Duckham's plan, would be workers.

The six working-class and socialist members, on their side, demanded nationalization with worker control. At the head of the industry would be a National Mining Council, half the members of which would be named by the government, and half by the miners' unions. Below this council, the collieries would be grouped into a number of districts; the miners' plan envisaged fourteen of them; at the head of each of these groups would be still another joint council, half of it made up of representatives of the unions and half named by the government. Finally, in each colliery, there would be a works committee, here called a pit council. Half the pit council would still be made up of workers; and the management of the mine would be in the hands of the pit council.[6]

Mr. Justice Sankey, the chairman of the commission, settled the question in favor of the workers: he came out in favor of nationalization of the mines with worker control. Without going into the details of the Sankey plan, it is enough to say that, in general, the difference between the Sankey plan and that of the miners is that the Sankey plan, instead of allowing a dual government and union representation in the two higher degrees—in the National Mining Council and in the district councils—allowed a tripartite representation—one part representing the miners, another part the technical and commercial sides of the industry, and a third part, the consumers. Finally, at the base as the miners had demanded, there were to be local mining councils. But these pit committees would have the protection of the safety and health of the miners as their only object: the actual operation of the mine would not be among their functions.

The mineworkers lined up behind the Sankey plan, which was consequently carried by a vote of seven to six. I was in England at the time. Among the public and in the press, the dominant impression was that nationalization of the railways and mines was coming rapidly: that of the railways was taken as done, that of the coal mines seemed inevitable. Such was the more or less apparent apathy among the business classes. Such was the enthusiasm among the working class.

In a few months Mr. Lloyd George was able to master the situation and to let this grand plan of nationalization with worker control fall into oblivion. I do not have time to tell you with what dexterity he was able to prove to the English public that, while of course, he was committed in advance to the conclusions of the royal commission which he had himself appointed in February, he nonethe-

[6] [See below, p. 190 n. 3.]

less did not consider himself bound by the Sankey report. He proposed a plan that resembled Sir Arthur Duckham's —no nationalization, but large mining corporations, and, in each of these big companies, joint conciliation boards, whose powers remained vague.

Meanwhile, he let the workers' agitation develop, anxious to see how far it would go and how dangerous it would be. At the beginning of September the miners appealed to the Trades Union Congress, then meeting in Glasgow, and demanded that it take a stand on the question of nationalization of the mines. But the miners realized at once that they were up against the inertia of their comrades, and that the mass of the working classes were not disposed to strike—a general sympathetic strike was what was needed—to get nationalization and control for the miners.

The Glasgow Congress referred the question to a special congress whose members would be specially chosen to consider it. The special congress met in December and ended in a new adjournment. It decided that a new special congress should be called after the opening of the parliamentary session: the attitude of Parliament and the government would be clearer then.

Parliament resumed in February, and Mr. Lloyd George declared not only that he had always been opposed to any kind of nationalization, but also that he was abandoning his August plan, since it had not gained the approval of the working class. The House of Commons backed him up by an overwhelming majority. Then the second special congress, back to the wall, flatly refused by a large majority to strike in support of the miners' demands. It was especially serious that the secretary of the railwaymen's union, J. H. Thomas, a member of the Triple Alliance that had been set up to allow the railwaymen, miners, and transport workers to concert their demands, spoke forcefully against a strike. The miners were left to their own devices. They asked themselves if they were going to strike to win nationalization and worker control. They decided not. They completely changed the orientation of their demands.

Instead of calling for nationalization and worker control—questions that clearly did not interest the mass of workers—they began to demand a rise in wages. In September they threatened a strike if they were not satisfied on this score. The government ended by giving in almost completely to their demands.

At this very moment, there is a critical question as to what will happen when, in two or three weeks, the mining industry will be decontrolled, that is, when state control of English collieries will be eliminated and they revert to free enterprise. Now, at this critical moment, what issue stirs the working men?

Is it participation in industrial management? Is it worker control? Not at all. According to private information I have received, I see that there is much discussion of what representation will be given to the workers on the conciliation boards, once the mines revert to free enterprise. Will the workers elect their representatives on these boards directly? Or will the unions send their representatives to sit on them? But, however the question is resolved, the boards that will be set up will be the same old conciliation boards, having as their only object the protection of working conditions and not the management of the mines. The only question that interests the mass of workers in the English collieries at present is how they will be paid once the mines have gone back to free enterprise.

Before the war, in 1912, a law was passed which established a minimum wage in the coal mines, but which did not grant a minimum wage for the entire United Kingdom. The country was divided into a number of regions; in each region a joint committee fixed a minimum wage which thereupon had the force of law.

The war came. The mines were unified under state control. Once there was equalization of profits, there was no reason for not equalizing wages. Since 1917 the miners have drawn uniform pay throughout England. But when free enterprise returns, there will no longer be equalization of profits. It is clear, then, that in the districts where extraction is most difficult, employers will not be able to pay their workers wages as high as those in more fortunate districts. Otherwise, they would fail: they would have failed already had it not been for equalization of profits. The employers are asking, therefore, that wages vary according to district. The workers insist that the system of a single minimum wage be maintained.

If I go into details that at first sight seem to have nothing to do with my subject, it is to show that the same conclusion to which we just came in examining the Whitley Councils is again forced on us when we look at the recent history of the miners' union and its demands. Leaving the doctrinaires aside, what interests the workers deeply is not industrial management but wages, or, in more general terms, the conditions of labor. A few months were enough to make the miners' trade-union leaders give in to the force of circumstances and to fall back, so to speak, from the first to the second.

Let me sum up. In studying the Whitley Councils two years ago, I concluded that this institution faced a doubtful future, because of the deep misunderstanding that divided workers and employers when they entered into the councils.

On the workers' side, or, to speak more exactly, on the socialist side, the conviction had spread that bit by bit they were going to establish the right of workers to oversee the management of industries and in the long run, by that means, to take part in management. Some unionists have called it "encroaching control."

One of the first councils entered on the official list of Whitley Councils, the first, in fact, to be set up and the one that is generally considered to have served as a model for the whole movement, was the Building Trade Council. It was founded on the initiative of Mr. Malcolm Sparkes, an eccentric employer, a Quaker, and an out-and-out pacifist, who believes neither in war between nations nor in war between classes. In getting equal numbers of employers and workers to sit side by side in a joint committee, he wanted to have workers initiated into the technical and commercial management of industry and employers to learn to consider themselves collaborators with their employees. He worked out and submitted for the approval of the council a sweeping plan of reform for the building industry. Building would become a huge closed corporation, entirely working-class, which would pay a fixed return on invested capital, assure a fixed income to workers, and succeed besides in reducing slack periods and unemployment to a minimum. It would be the realization, obtained amicably from the employers, of a veritable "guild," much like the dream of the Guild Socialists.

As I speak, the whole system constructed by Mr. Malcolm Sparkes is coming to grief. Submitted for the approval of the Building Trade Council, it has been purely and simply returned to the subcommittee that had worked it out. There is nothing surprising about this failure; what is remarkable is that for two years Mr. Sparkes was able to get the contractors, not to accept it, but simply to discuss and examine it.[7] The aims of the many

[7] On the strange history of this movement, which deserves a monograph, see especially the following pamphlets: Thomas Foster, *Masters and Men, a New Co-partnership* [1918]; Malcolm Sparkes, *A Memorandum on Industrial Self-government.* . . . [1917]; *The Industrial Council for the Building Industry.* . . . [Garton Foundation, 1920]. On the commercial efforts of the Building Guild, see *The Building Guild, Its Principles, Objects, and Structure* (Co-operative Press Agency, Manchester). [Sparkes's *Memorandum* is fairly readily obtainable. The Foster pamphlet and the Garton Foundation publication appear in the *English Catalogue,* but are in neither the British Museum nor the T. U. C. library. An inquiry of the

employers who had encouraged the Whitley Council experiment had little in common with the utopia of Mr. Malcolm Sparkes.

In England—and I believe that it is still more true in Germany—some capitalists are wondering whether it would not be in the employers' interest to create a community of interests in each industry between employers and workers in that industry by setting up a kind of corporative system. The employers would guarantee the workers what they are more concerned about than anything else—security. They would promise to establish a fund to insure them against the perils of unemployment. They would offer them a system of profit-sharing. In return, once the workers were directly interested in the prosperity of the enterprise, the employers would ask their help in getting assistance from the state, protection against foreign competition, and higher prices by way of customs reform. Sir Allan Smith, the great man of engineering and shipbuilding, advocates an organization of the industry that does not seem to us to differ much from what we have just set down in principle.

Now, between these two conceptions—one working-class, the other emanating from the employers—the difference is obvious. One looks to the gradual expropriation of the employers and the elimination of profit. The other wants to interest the working class in the growth of capitalist profits. Two years ago I said that one day or another, the misunderstanding would become clear, and then the defeat of the Whitley Councils would be complete. But today I will go further. I predict the decline of that whole great propaganda movement for worker control among the working class, perhaps because it does not correspond to the deep needs of the proletariat in large-scale industry.

Co-operative Union, Manchester, has failed to turn up the pamphlet from the Co-operative Press Agency.]

What working men want is not to share the chances of gain and, with them, the risks of loss inseparable from the management of a large enterprise. They are eager for security; they want a stable wage and guarantees against unemployment. They have set up trade unions to protect their working conditions in the factories against pressure from the employers; they have assigned no other duties to their trade-union representatives.

And these representatives know it very well. "The new functions they want to give to the trade-union leaders," I was told by a very highly placed trade unionist, "are outside their sphere. The function of a trade-union leader is to protect the interests of the workers against the employers. He is the workers' advocate; you could go as far as to say that he does not have the right to look too closely in each case into whether the workers are right or wrong. He is their chief spokesman. To want him, beyond that, to become an associate of the employer in the management of his business is to ask more than he can give. It is asking him to go outside his role, and the workers would never forgive him. One day or another, he would inevitably have to explain to the workers that their demands were unreasonable, and he would stop being what he is by his very nature, the advocate of the working class. See how hard it is for the trade unionists whom the cooperatives put in charge of their factories: because of the situation they hold, they are forced to talk to their workers in the language of employers. They could not be more unpopular!"

There is a vast difference between the social function of a leader of industry, which is to make production as intensive as possible, and the social function of a trade-union leader, which is to prevent that intensification of production from working to the detriment of the physical and moral welfare of the worker. To associate the trade-union leader with the management of industry is to ask him to play two roles at once: it is to commit an error in sociology. I do not deny that room could be found for a number of union representatives in the administrative councils of large enterprises. But, in order to avoid any disappointment, it should be clearly understood that they are not there to speed up production; they are there only to plead the cause of the working class against those who want to increase production at any cost. They play the part of a brake, not a motor.

I have finished, and in concluding, I want only to draw your attention to the two distinct elements in the observations I have just made.

In the first place, there is a statement of a fact that does not, it seems to me, allow of any discussion. The fact is that opinion in the English working-class movement, after having seemed so eager for the establishment of worker control two years ago, has subsided to a remarkable degree. In the spring of 1919 it was difficult to resist the impression that England was on the edge of a social revolution, not violent like the Russian, but nevertheless sweeping, which was going to transform industrial organization from the top to the bottom. A year later I found only apathy with regard to these matters; the only questions that then held the attention of trade-union leaders were the improvement of conditions of labor and the raising of wages.

Secondly, there is the interpretation of this fact. Is the failure of Guild Socialism something ephemeral, something that can be ignored by whoever is not completely given over to momentary impressions? Or is it, rather, a significant fact, arising from deep causes. I incline to the latter hypothesis. I believe that the syndicalists, with their program of controlling industry by means of professional associations, are committing what I have just called an error in sociology, so far as the real functions of a union are concerned. But I do not claim infallibility, and it is on this second point that I should like to have the benefit of your criticisms.

THE PRESENT STATE OF THE
SOCIAL QUESTION IN ENGLAND[1]

After the Armistice, in the flush of victory finally won, and while waiting for the peace treaty that would disarm Germany forever, England surrendered to the hope that a new era was opening for the whole human race, and for English democracy in particular. The dazzling statesman, who for six years—or should one say for fourteen years?— had presided over the nation's destinies, promised to do everything in his power to make England a land "fit for heroes to live in," to abolish poverty, and to solve the social question through the collaboration of classes once at odds but now reconciled. He believed that he could do a great deal. In that respect, the lessons of the war seemed encouraging.

In the midst of the war, thanks to the miracle which we in France have called *union sacrée*, Parliament had unanimously passed an electoral reform law and an education law, the radicalism of which would have provoked possibly invincible resistance before 1914. With the consent of all parties, the state had assumed a host of functions that some years earlier the most determined collectivist would not have dared to claim.

When peace came, the state was monopolizing the nation's commerce; it decided what exports and imports could be allowed; it restricted civilian consumption; it operated all the coal mines; it ran all the railways and the entire merchant fleet; it manufactured munitions and con-

[1] A study published in the *Revue politique et parlementaire,* Vol. 112, pp. 5–29 (July 1922).

trolled all the industries that affected the conduct of the war in any degree. Was this admirable work of organization by which victory had been won to be abruptly broken off? Because there was peace, was that a reason to return to the old anarchy? The workers did not think so, nor did the intellectuals. And the Prime Minister, whose intelligent sensibility is always so prompt to follow the moods of public opinion, seemed himself for several months to have intended in all sincerity to prolong into peacetime, for the good of the working class, that formidable *étatisme* of war on which victory had just conferred so much prestige.

In 1919 the government introduced a bill to deal with the growing crisis in housing. It imposed on local authorities the obligation of submitting to the central government within three months plans for the erection, at the taxpayers' expense, of the number of houses needed for the working classes; these plans would have the force of law as soon as they were approved by the Ministry; the Ministry would have the right to refuse its approval and to return them to the local authorities for revision only when they judged them "inadequate," in other words, too timid.

Another bill was introduced to set up a Ministry of Ways and Communications. The scope of this ministry would include railways, tramways, canals and waterways, roads, bridges, ferries, harbors, docks, piers, and the supply of electricity. All the powers in these matters, which under the wartime regime already belonged to the government, would pass at once and for a period of two years to the new ministry. But the new minister would acquire many other powers under the bill. By simple order-in-council he would be able to purchase "by agreement or compulsorily" and to operate all or part of any means of communication whatever, railway or tramway, canal, port or dock. Over such an order Parliament would have only the negative right of a veto for a period of thirty days. The mention made of electricity in the original bill was quickly eliminated; but that is not to say that the *étatistes* were beating a retreat. A special bill proposed the creation of the Electricity Commissioners, ordinary bureaucrats under the Board of Trade, some irremovable, some removable, who would have the power to create electricity districts and district electricity boards throughout the country. These local bodies, on which representatives of the trade unions would sit but in which the elective principle would play only a small part, would have the right to acquire generating stations or to construct new ones. The production of light and electric power would tend to become a public service. To become a public service throughout the kingdom, all that was needed was the steady backing of the Board of Trade.

The coal mines were not dealt with in the provisions of these *étatiste* bills. For many years, however, the miners had asked for nationalization of the mines, in addition to wage rises and a shorter working day. At the beginning of 1919 they put forward the same demands, threatening to paralyze all the industry of the kingdom by a general coal strike if they were not listened to. They were. A royal commission of inquiry was appointed. Presided over by Mr. Justice Sankey, it was composed, not counting the chairman, of twelve members: six representing big capitalist organizations and six defenders of working-class interests. When the question of nationalization came to a vote, they divided equally. But the chairman threw the balance in favor of the working-class position. The government had let it be clearly understood that it would adopt the conclusions of the Sankey Commission. For several weeks during the summer of 1919 it appeared that the nationalization of the railways and the mines was virtually accomplished.

For many years Mr. and Mrs. Webb had worked tirelessly to socialize and to "bureaucratize" England. To attain that goal they had turned out innumerable propagandist pamphlets for the Fabian Society; written their great, intentionally tendentious works of social history; and founded the London School of Economics and Political Science to serve as an administrative academy for the socialist state they dreamed of giving their native land. It is probable that their hatred of Germany during the war had not been very great; but they had avoided compromising themselves in the company of raving pacifists. They kept quiet; foreign policy did not fall within their competence. And they took advantage of the war to bring their ideas to triumph; as a member of the Sankey Commission, Mr. Webb could claim that it had been done with complete success. Equally significant was Lord Haldane's testimony before that commission. For the greater part of the war, he had been the victim of a kind of ostracism. He was accused of having misled the English about the real inclinations of the Germans because of his germanophilia, and, at best, of having played a highly equivocal double game between London and Berlin. The fact that he was invited to testify before the royal commission on mines proved that he was returning to favor. It was recognized that he was the one man in the War Office who had done something to prepare the English army to intervene on the continent; he had been able to do so precisely because of his germanophilia, that admiration for German and Prussian methods for which he had been so criticized. Full of his administrative experience and his Hegelian *étatisme,* he explained the steps necessary to make the state capable of industrial initiative and to communicate to all the public services something of the spirit of collective honor and the patriotic zeal that produces the poetry and moral grandeur of war service. From the date at which his testimony appeared as a pamphlet published through the efforts of two young socialists, it gets all the impact of a manifesto.[2]

[2] Viscount Haldane of Cloan, *The Problem of Nationalization,* with an introduction by R. H. Tawney and Harold J. Laski, London, 1921.

But surely the war was not, following the secret desire of the Webbs and Lord Haldane, to have as its only result the triumph of Prussian militarism and bureaucracy in the nations that had just won out over Prussia? In innumerable proclamations, the victors had spoken the language of liberty too loudly for such a thing to be possible, and socialist circles had for a long time been shot through with very different ideas to which the war had given new force.

Already for ten years some socialists, heirs of the old Ruskinian tradition, had been in rebellion against what was dry, prosaic, and wilfully materialistic in the bureaucratic collectivism of the Webbs. Would a society in which all industry was run as we see the post office and the telegraphs being run be the new heaven and the new earth that so many prophets had promised to the working class? Men like Mr. A. J. Penty dreamed of a non-bureaucratic corporative regime which would bring something of the poetry of the Christian Middle Ages into modern society. Others, Mr. G. D. H. Cole among the most prominent, had learned the lesson of revolutionary syndicalism in Paris; they were asking if, after having promised the workers the abolition of the wage system, it was not a hoax only to transform them and their former employers with them into employees of the state. Between them, they had elaborated that new doctrine, Guild Socialism, which, without going so far as to insist with the pure syndicalists on the complete elimination of the political state, demanded that each industry, once transformed into a social service, be brought under the direct control of the workers in that industry, organized corporatively.

The war came. All the workers who had not been sent into the army had undergone a harsh regime of quasi-military discipline in the factories. High wages for them, their wives, and their children; but the suspension of all the union rules that in peacetime allowed them to take it easy; what is more, if they wanted to express their discontent, the right to strike was suspended with the consent of the trade-union leaders. They had rebelled, both against the government that employed them and against the trade-union leaders whom they suspected of conspiring with the government at their expense. They had claimed the right to control the operation of each factory for the workers grouped into local unions in each factory under directly elected leaders.

This agitation was already a serious problem for the government when it became still more serious in the summer of 1917, following the Russian Revolution. How could overworked and exasperated men not have been moved by the news that the Russian workers, formed into factory soviets, had in a few weeks radically transformed a great state of more than a hundred million persons? Faithful to a tradition of opportunism which in England has always been consecrated by success, the cabinet came to terms with these new demands. A committee, generally called the Whitley Committee from the name of its chairman, had been asked to study ways of permanently bettering relations between employers and employed; it speeded up its work, and in a series of reports appearing in 1917 and 1918 it recommended the establishment of joint committees of employers and workers at every level of industrial production to consider questions that interested them both. We have told elsewhere the details of the history of these Whitley Councils. As they were assigned, in vague terms, the duty of studying measures to be taken to assure the technical progress of industry, an optimist could think them a first step towards Guild Socialism or, again, to use the language of worried conservatives, towards "sovietization" of the factories.

The government hastened to follow up the recommendations of the Whitley Committee. The committee had asked for the strengthening and generalization of trade boards—named by the government, made up of employers, workers, and a certain number of outside experts, and charged with fixing wages in industries where workers were exceptionally badly organized or exceptionally poorly paid. They got satisfaction in the passage of a new Trade Boards Act at the end of 1918, even before the war was over. The government, moreover, encouraged the formation of Whitley Councils wherever employers and workers wanted them, even in the public services. Finally, a National Industrial Conference was convened in which representatives of the employers and of the working class sat on an equal footing. The conference, of which Mr. Cole, the theorist of Guild Socialism, was the secretary, came out in favor of the compulsory eight hour day and the legal minimum wage. It urged that a National Industrial Council, a consultative assembly of four hundred members, half elected by the employers' associations, half by the trade unions, meet twice a year. So many victories for the new idea of "worker control," so alien to the old bureaucratic collectivism! But nowhere was the progress of this new idea more obvious than in the discussions in the royal commission on mines.

When the mineworkers and the trade union or socialist congresses asked for nationalization of the mines before the war, they limited themselves to nationalization pure and simple, without bothering themselves about the part the workers would play in the operation of the mining industry. By 1919 everything had changed, and the six working-class or socialist members of the Sankey Commission voted in favor of a complete plan of worker control. At the top, they proposed a Mining Council of ten members, under the chairmanship of the Minister of Mines: five named by the minister, of whom two would represent consumers, and five named by the miners' union. At a lower level came district mining councils of ten members, of whom five were elected by the miners' union. At the bottom, in each mine, was to be a pit committee of ten members, of whom five were elected by the miners.[3]

This plan did not get a majority of votes in the commission, but the miners rallied to the proposal of the chairman, Sir John Sankey, and gave it a majority. This plan too contained a complete system of union control, more complicated than the workers' system. At the bottom, in each mine, was a local mining council of ten members: the manager, the under-manager, the commercial manager; four members elected by the workers; three members elected by the council immediately above the local council in the hierarchy, that is the district council. This local council would have as its only function giving workers "an effective voice in all questions where their own safety and health are concerned." Above the local councils there were to be fourteen district mining councils of fourteen members. The chairman and vice-chairman would be nominated by the minister. Four members would be elected by the workers of the district, and eight by the national council, which stood above the district councils in the hierarchy. Of these eight members, four were to be designated as representing the consumers, two as representing the technicians, and two as representing the commercial side of the mining operation. Finally, at the top, would stand a National Mining Council, elected by the district councils in the proportion of one member for every five million tons produced. Elected for three years, the members of the council would themselves elect a standing committee of eighteen members, of whom six

[3] [Halévy is apparently referring to the draft bill presented to the commission by the Miners' Federation; it was a reworking of the draft bill prepared by the union in 1913, with the principle of worker control added. The Mining Council was to number twenty members, rather than the ten mentioned by Halévy. The miners' proposal was discussed at length in the commission, but no vote was actually taken on it; it was, rather, "supported" by the working-class and socialist members of the commission.]

would represent the workers, six the consumers, and six the commercial and technical sides of the industry. Such was the system that was to have served as the basis of a government bill if Mr. Lloyd George kept his promise.

But he did not keep it. Bureaucratic collectivism and Guild Socialism were very far from reinforcing each other to bring about the realization of a system in which, beginning with the mines and the railways, the political state and the trade union would divide the management of industry between them; on the contrary, as it happened, they canceled each other out. With the help of the government, capitalism played them off against each other and very cleverly used the Guild Socialism of Mr. Cole to escape the bureaucratic collectivism of the Webbs. We should like to relate briefly how it seems to have succeeded, at least temporarily.

Let us look at the mines first. On the royal commission, six advocates of capitalism sat facing six defenders of the working-class position. They were, of course, opposed to the state's taking over the mines. But they were concerned about the low output of labor, and they knew that this output would not improve so long as the worker did not approach his job in a spirit of goodwill and co-operation. How could this spirit of co-operation be created? The expedient of the Whitley Councils came to mind. Let us set up pit committees at the bottom, they said, district committees a little higher up, and a national council at the top. These committees will be invested with no management function. But employers and workers, in equal numbers, will discuss there matters that directly concern the welfare of the worker: wages, the length of the working day, sanitation. And so, thanks to the Whitley Councils, social peace will be assured without recourse to state collectivism or even to complete unionization. One of the six employers' representatives worked out an even bolder plan. To remedy the excessive fragmentation of the mining industry, he asked that it be grouped into a limited num-

191

ber of large regional companies, each of these big companies to be governed by a board on which the state and the trade union would be represented. A joint committee would discuss questions of wages. In each mine, a pit committee would carry out all the functions the Whitley Report had proposed for the new councils. Here again, although more boldly, a system of friendly negotiations between employers and workers was proposed to escape state collectivism.

When on August 19 Mr. Lloyd George rose in the Commons to explain the government's attitude, he began by refusing to consider himself bound by the conclusions of the Sankey Commission. Then, drawing his inspiration from the ideas of Sir Arthur Duckham, he recommended a policy not of nationalization but of unification and, in each of the unified enterprises, a system of joint control. Heading each area group would be a governing body, on which several working-class representatives would sit. At the bottom there would be pit committees, which would have as their sole function overseeing all measures taken to assure the security and health of the workers. In *The Future*, a curious propagandist pamphlet which he published in September,[4] he tried to define the whole of his program of social reconstruction. In vague terms, he urged "the reorganization and the economical direction of the mines": he was asking too that the miners help in shaping conditions of industry. An allusion was made in the pamphlet to the Whitley Councils whose development he urged. In short, the government was offering to intervene between employers and workers, to encourage them to establish peaceful relations in a well-organized industry: he refused to assume responsibility for the operation of the mines.

The mineworkers were indignant and began to think about a strike, appealing to the other unions to join them

4 [I have been unable to trace this pamphlet.]

in a general strike. But the Trades Union Congress temporized and turned over to a special congress the burden of deciding what form of action should be taken to force the minister's hand. The special congress also temporized and referred the question to a second special congress to be held early in 1920 after the meeting of Parliament. Parliament met. Once more, in the debate on the address, Mr. Lloyd George rose to explain his program for the mines, still more modest than his program of August had been; he grew bolder as the apathy of the working masses became more evident. He went no further than proposing an advisory council, on which workers' representatives would sit, to give the government its views on conditions of labor. Unification of the mines and establishing Whitley Councils in each firm were no longer at issue. The mine owners did not want that system. The miners did not want it either. The reason was clear. The August program had done its work: it was a mere smokescreen behind which the government could beat a retreat and repudiate the proposals for nationalization.

The second special congress met in March, and the miners were once more abandoned by the other unions. Would they strike alone? Not daring to do so, they adopted a new tactic: they concentrated all their effort, not on nationalization, which was too abstract really to interest the mass of workers, but on raising wages, a matter that was for them, with the steadily mounting cost of living, a vital necessity. In a strike which was called in October and lasted nearly three weeks, they won concessions. But economic conditions were already changing; with the slump in coal prices, there could be no question of the miners' obtaining a rise in wages. The employers took the offensive.

The system of government control instituted in the collieries during the war would normally have come to an end on August 31, 1921. The government advanced the date and set March 31 as the day when the mine owners would again take charge of their operations. Some days before March 31 the employers notified their workers throughout England of the conditions, varying from region to region, under which they would have to resume work. The workers refused to accept these new conditions, marked by often considerable cuts in wages. The employers said it was a strike. The workers maintained that it was a lockout. Strike or lockout, the crisis lasted three months.

The miners' demands were two. In the first place, they did not want wages to vary according to region; they wanted the same wage for the same work—or at least a fixed minimum wage—for all workers. But there were regions—South Wales in particular—where the employers proved, with facts and figures, that if they paid their workers the same wages that Yorkshire miners drew, they would be ruined. Then the workers proposed that all the profits of all the mining firms be paid into a national pool. From this national pool equal wages could be paid to workers in all regions. In tying the national pool to the national wage, the miners hoped in a roundabout way to raise the question of nationalization of the mines again. But they came up against the categorical resistance of the government and the apathy of the other unions. In the end they got neither the national pool nor the national wage. The mining law passed by Parliament gave the partisans of worker control only the power to set up Whitley Councils in the mines, if they could. Had the system of Whitley Councils been proposed on the heels of the Russian Revolution to bring about the failure of the program of nationalization?

It is the same story so far as the railways are concerned.

The bill introduced by the government in February 1919 to establish a Ministry of Ways and Communications was passed by Parliament, but not without having undergone drastic amendments. The new ministry, called the Ministry of Transport in the final version of the law, lost the

194

power given it in the original bill to nationalize the railways, canals or ports by simple administrative decision. One may doubt that the Prime Minister had many regrets over this modification of the plan he had originally approved. We have seen how the reconstructionist zeal of Mr. Lloyd George had weakened between February 15, the date on which the bill was first introduced, and August 15, the date on which it finally became law. For him and his associates, the problem was no longer how to obtain the necessary powers to nationalize the railways dictatorially. The problem was to get rid of the embarrassing question of nationalization as quickly as possible by returning to the normal prewar system.

Immediately after the Armistice, nationalization of the railways seemed so certain and so near that the Labour Party at first appeared to be uninterested in it. The railwaymen directed their demands and their strikes to questions of wages. Not that it was possible to raise questions of wages without touching the problem of railway organization. At the end of 1919 the government set up a Central Wages Board, half employer, half worker, and a National Wages Board, on which there were equal numbers of managers, workers, and representatives of the consumers, to negotiate concerning wages and conditions of labor. At the same time a Railway Advisory Committee was set up: twelve administrators and four workers, all named by the government. It was going to be necessary soon, however, to face the problem of reorganizing the railways, since the wartime system of government control would expire in August 1921. In June 1920 Sir Eric Geddes, the Minister of Transport, announced the government's plan.

In the last analysis, the government was trying to apply Sir Arthur Duckham's mining plan to the railways: unification and amalgamation, but not nationalization, because, with nationalization, the bureaucratic peril seemed too great. They did not, then, go back to the anarchic prewar system, with many competing companies serving the same localities, their systems linking up by chance. The state obliged the English companies to amalgamate into a small number of large groups. At the head of each group there was a board of management, on which representatives of the employees would sit along with representatives of the stockholders.[5] Could the workers complain about so generous a plan? If it was a far cry from the collectivist system, was it not a first step in the direction of Guild Socialism?

It was on this plan that debate took place. It lasted nearly a year without ever arousing public opinion. In March 1921 the Labour Party offered a counter-proposal: immediate purchase of all the railways by the Ministry of Transport. Once purchased, there would be unitary management of the railways by seven commissioners; the chairman and two other commissioners would be named by the minister, one commissioner by the Treasury, and three others by the government on the recommendation of the three big railway unions. In short, to the government's plan of worker control and no nationalization, the Labour Party opposed a strengthened plan of nationalization with worker control.

But, as we shall soon see, it was only putting up a bold front. On May 3, 1921, in the midst of the miners' strike, an agreement between the railway companies and the three railway unions was made public. Mr. J. H. Thomas, secretary of the National Union of Railwaymen, had carried on the entire negotiation in secret, without even referring to the headquarters of his union. He had agreed with the companies to abandon the nationalization plan. Moreover, he had complied with the companies' wishes and had given up asking that workers be allowed on the boards of management. He was content to retain the two wage boards set up by the government at the end of 1919

[5] [On railways, see the excellent detailed study by E. A. Pratt, *British Railways and the Great War* (1921).]

and, beyond that, to get the establishment of Whitley Councils at three levels—local councils, district councils, and system councils. To those on the labor side who a year earlier protested against Sir Eric Geddes' plan, the minister answered: "What are you complaining about? The collectivism you are asking for is out of date. The future lies with Guild Socialism." To those in Communist circles who protested against the treason of Mr. J. H. Thomas, his socialist defenders answered: "What are you complaining about? We are not Guild Socialists; and it is no part of orthodox collectivism to turn over the management of nationalized industries to the trade unions."[6] Meanwhile, the industries, in whose management the workers had no say, were not even nationalized. The trick had come off, and the system of Whitley Councils had done its work. It had allowed capitalism to play state collectivism and Guild Socialism off against each other and to cancel each other out. In August 1921, in the railways as in the mines, capitalism emerged the victor from a crisis that had lasted for two years.

We have emphasized these two cases of the coal mines and the railways because more than any others they seem to allow us to understand the silent and patient tactics by which the ruling classes in England under Lloyd George were able to defeat the working-class agitation. But many other examples would have to be cited if we were to sketch the complete picture of this liquidation of wartime socialism.

A whole program of legislation was being worked out for legally fixing the conditions of labor; it fell in ruins. Following the recommendations of the Industrial Conference of 1919, the ministry had promised to produce a bill for the legal limitation of the working day to eight hours and the opening of an inquiry into the best means

[6] [I have been unable to find the source of either quotation; again, it is possible that they were constructed as "typical" replies.]

for fixing a national minimum wage. The bill on the eight hour day has not been introduced, and we no longer hear anything about the inquiry. The wartime law that temporarily regulated wages—twice renewed—finally expired without being replaced by permanent legislation. The law that regulated the wages of agricultural workers has been abrogated along with the law that maintained wheat prices for the benefit of the farmers. Finally, the 1918 law on trade boards, which, generalizing the principle of the law of 1909, gave to the Minister of Labour the arbitrary power to create trade boards wherever, in his view, workers were unduly underpaid, had brought protests, and a committee of inquiry was set up to see if it could not be revised. This committee, to which three trade-union secretaries belonged, has just made its report;[7] if it is adopted by Parliament, all the additions that, under socialist inspiration, the law of 1918 made to the law of 1909 seem likely to be abolished outright.

The English taxpayers, overburdened by taxation to a degree that the French taxpayer can scarcely imagine, protested against huge government expenditures and demanded economies. The famous Geddes Commission on public expenditures made its report on March 1 last and proposed reductions of expenditures for the various services which would rise to eighty-seven million pounds—more than two billion prewar francs, more than four billion postwar francs. But how could this policy of all-out economy be implemented without compromising that new policy that gave the state so large an initiative in the social sphere. It seems that the policy whose framework was established by the Electricity Bill of 1919 had not even begun to be put into execution. Under the Housing Bill of the same year, the first programs had been drawn up for the construction of 176,000 houses. Sixty-eight thou-

[7] [*Report of the Committee to enquire into the Working and Effects of the Trade Boards Act* (Cmd. 1645), *Parliamentary Papers*, 1922, x.]

sand were built, sixty-nine thousand are under construction, and thirty-nine thousand remain to be built and perhaps will be built, if the money can be found. But the Ministry has just declared that no new building plans will be made and envisages the possibility of selling the houses already built at half price to lower the costs which are still accruing—more than ten million pounds a year for sixty years. Finally, the Education Act of 1918 seems to have fallen into desuetude. Only the London County Council has begun to apply it and to set on foot the organization of adult education courses that was to raise the age-limit for compulsory education of all children in the capital to eighteen. But in the past year, it has already limited compulsory education to the age of fifteen; and it is possible that in the wake of recent municipal elections, clearly unfavorable to the Labour Party, the adult education courses will soon be completely eliminated as an economy measure.[8]

Mr. and Mrs. Sidney Webb, Mr. Bernard Shaw, and Mr. H. G. Wells remain today, as they were ten or twenty years ago, convinced collectivists. They are continually publishing works of science, plays and novels to propagate their doctrines. But they are in their sixties, and it is always wise to ask if their ideas are those of 1940 or those of 1900. Let us look at them more closely. In two fine works, too little known in France, which they have just published—A *Constitution for the Socialist Commonwealth of Great Britain* (1920) and *The Consumers' Co-operative Movement* (1921)—Mr. and Mrs. Sidney Webb have made many concessions to syndicalism; must we not see in that the sign of some restlessness of mind? The most striking work Mr. H. G. Wells has published since the war,

[8] For all the repercussions of the new policy of economy on the social program of 1919, see *Labour and National "Economy,"* published by the National Joint Council of the Trade Union Congress, the Executive Committee of the Labour Party, and the Parliamentary Labour Party, 1922.

the most striking perhaps that has appeared in England, is his audacious *Outline of History* (1921), which begins with the nebula and ends with the Treaty of Versailles. Are its last chapters conceived in a socialist spirit? Mr. H. G. Wells would no doubt insist that they are and would not fail to produce many extracts to support that contention. Yet why does this perpetual denunciation of Roman imperialism, this glorification of Anglo-Saxon liberalism inevitably make me think, when I read his *History*, that I am dealing with a disciple, not of Karl Marx or even of the Webbs, but of Buckle and Herbert Spencer?

There is another generation, younger than the Webbs, Bernard Shaw, and H. G. Wells, whose socialist faith remains intense. The founder of Guild Socialism, Mr. G. D. H. Cole, is one of them; to point out the use that capitalism has been able to make of his criticisms of bureaucratic collectivism is not to question the strength of his belief. Can one imagine a socialism more radical than that whose principles Mr. R. H. Tawney has just set out in his vigorous little book *The Acquisitive Society?* But both men are over thirty. Theirs is a prewar socialism. It has been strengthened by the war, or, to speak more precisely, by the lessons of wartime administration. What progress state socialism was making then! Would it be possible, once peace was re-established, for the ruling classes to go back on so much progress? But now peace is re-established, and we have seen what a reaction has taken place. In this time of disenchantment, what are the young people thinking about—not those of thirty, but those who are only twenty? All the information I have received agrees in portraying them as perplexed and awaiting some new prophet, or as skeptical and professing a kind of cynical positivism. They are reading Freud, not Karl Marx. If there is an older man to whom they turn, it is the eccentric Bertrand Russell. At times, he has certainly been willing to wear a socialist label, out of hatred for the tyranny of the power of wealth. I doubt, however, that he still wears it today, and I am sure that if in fifty or a hundred years someone writes the history of modern English thought, he will class Bertrand Russell among the individualists and libertarians, not among the socialists.

The Labour Party is more solid than ever: nothing has happened to shake the vast organization, based on parliamentary constituencies, which it set up in 1918 and improved in 1919 and 1920; if it lost seats in the last municipal elections (the wretched financial management of some Labour corporations explains this failure), it has won a good many victories in by-elections over the past twelve months which have given it the chance to reinforce its parliamentary representation. In the next general election, it hopes to double, perhaps to triple, the number of members who will speak for working-class interests in the House of Commons. The Trades Union Congress, representing more than six million workers, has also strengthened its constitution; it has formed a General Council— similar in many respects to the Comité Confédéral of our Confédération Générale du Travail—capable of taking decisions in the name of all the organized workers without being obliged always to refer them to a Congress. There is, moreover, none of the opposition between the political organization of the workers and a rival, purely syndicalist organization, such as one finds in France. Never has there been a closer union between politicians and trade unionists. In agreement with the Executive Committee of the Labour Party, this new General Council has formed a National Joint Council to decide on common policy; and the walls have been pulled down (I speak literally, not figuratively) between the house in Eccleston Square, in which the offices of the Trades Union Congress are located, and the house in which the offices of the Labour Party are to be found. But that is precisely what is interesting and what we must try to explain—how the collapse of wartime collectivism can coincide with the methodical strengthening of working-class organization.

Of all the working-class parties in the world, the English Labour Party is the least doctrinal. It is a class party which defends the interests of the working class from day to day, and if the demands of this class happen as a rule to agree with socialist principles, it can happen too that at times such harmony does not exist. Then the English Labour Party, precisely because it is so undogmatic, is less embarrassed than any other labor party would be by throwing its specifically collectivist program into the background. It cannot be said that the recent liquidation of the laws that brought all the industry and commerce of the kingdom under national control was accomplished over the resistance of the trade-unionist and Labourite leadership. It was done with the connivance—let us go further and say with the collaboration—of that leadership.

We have seen the part played by Mr. J. H. Thomas in the final settlement of the railway question. Again, it was he who, between the autumn of 1919 and the spring of 1921, used all his authority to prevent the railwaymen, the transport workers, and the rest of the trade unions from joining forces with the miners and thus extorting nationalization of the mines from an intimidated government. The Cabinet repaid his many services by making him a Privy Councillor. The Communists denounced his treason and accused him of having sold out. But the Communists do not count for much in England. He got a judgment for libel, and, in spite of government favors, in spite of these revolutionary attacks, he is still secretary of the National Union of Railwaymen. With Mr. Henderson and Mr. Clynes, as conciliatory and moderate as he is, he remains one of the important figures in the Labour Party. What, then, is the present policy of the party, as these three opportunists have defined it? It is governed by the economic conditions of the time; and because these conditions changed abruptly two years ago, the economic policy of the party had to change too.

For the past twenty years the whole economic history

of western Europe has been dominated by one important fact, the rapid rise in the cost of living. That fact does not date from the war, although since the war it has taken on a character of unprecedented seriousness. Since the war, it is to be explained by the unlimited issuing of paper money at the same time that production has declined. Before the war, it was to be explained by the increasing output of gold mines. It is a fact that necessarily has revolutionary consequences on the distribution of wealth. Anyone at all who must live on a fixed salary or on the fixed income of a fortune acquired previously is in financial difficulties and has the sense of belonging to a declining class. Over against the distress of such people stands the opulence of all those people—industrialists or merchants—with something to sell: hence the rapid rise of a class of *nouveaux riches,* who turn those with older wealth out of their houses and estates. But where shall we put the wage-earners? Are they victims or beneficiaries of the new state of things? Being very unstable, their situation is hard to define. If they can raise their wages by striking or threatening to strike, that rise follows the rise in the cost of living which brought it on, when it should precede it, if the workers are to be really satisfied. In short, repeated rises in wages give the worker an impression of strength. But in pursuing a prosperity that always eludes him, he remains a malcontent dreaming of new victories. He is a revolutionary.

Then a crisis occurs. Manufacturers and merchants can no longer get rid of their stocks. They lower—as little as possible—the selling price of their products. They lower—as much as possible—the wages of their workers; they cut down—again as much as possible—the number of workers. If the workers strike to protect their wages, the strike hardly hurts the employer. For one thing, it is certain to fail; for another, it reduces the number of workers just when the employers want to restrict production. It only adds voluntary unemployed to the already immense number of involuntary unemployed. The number of the latter, although it tended to rise slowly in England in the course of 1920, had not yet gone beyond two hundred thousand at the beginning of autumn. Then it rose rapidly, passing half a million at the end of November, a million at the end of January 1921, a second million at the end of May. Since then it has kept close to that figure, accidentally falling for only a week below a million and a half. The problem of unemployment has drawn all the attention of working-class leaders.

The collectivist arsenal certainly contains some remedies that can be tried to solve the problem. In socialist circles there is sometimes vague talk of a system by which the government, the great entrepreneur, would undertake public works on the basis of the state of the labor market. It would slow them down in times of industrial activity; it would speed them up in time of crisis to make work for excess manpower. But, even admitting that the states of western Europe could ever be capable of following so rational a plan, the long-term projects involved cannot be undertaken as emergency measures in the present crisis. The state did not have the necessary funds in reserve before the crisis for employing two million unemployed today. Were the funds to be got from taxation? The middle classes were already in revolt against excessive taxes. Some other remedy is called for.

Before the war, going beyond the German model, England had set up a system of insurance against not only accidents and illness but also unemployment. As a first experiment, the law of 1911 had organized this system, resting on a three-way contribution by employers, workers, and the state, for the benefit of three large categories of workers in building, engineering, and shipbuilding, totaling 2,250,000 workers. Then, in 1916 the government extended the benefits of the law to a million and a half workers employed in certain war industries. Finally in 1920, at the moment when the crisis was about to break, a comprehensive law was passed, applicable to everyone already covered by the health insurance law, a total of twelve million workers. What has been done since the beginning of the crisis is to extend the benefits of this legislation to the wives and children of unemployed workers. To this end, in November, a fund was created for a period of six months, and the provisions of this special law have just been incorporated into a general law to remain in force until June 1923. Thus the transition has been openly made from the system of social insurance to a system of pure and simple relief.

But a weekly dole of fifteen shillings, even augmented by a further five shillings for the wife and a shilling for each child over fourteen, will not rescue the worker from poverty. Even if the allocation were raised to a pound by increasing the state's contribution, as the Labour Party demands, it would not be enough. Instead of being satisfied with expedients designed to make the evil barely supportable, would it not be possible to find a radical solution that would eliminate the evil? There is one, and one that involves no state intervention. It is to regain for British industry the markets it supplied before the war or to find new markets in place of the old. Why are these markets so difficult to find? The pacifists say that it is the fault of the war, or, to speak more exactly, of the disorder in Europe that followed the war. Variation in the exchanges: the countries whose exchanges have collapsed have lost all their purchasing power. Instability of exchanges: so long as that instability lasts, long-term commercial transactions with foreign countries are impossible. For England, the real problem is not balancing the budget, to be solved by huge German contributions; it is unemployment, to be solved by restoring the countries of central and eastern Europe and reopening their markets. So ideas already a century and a half old have returned to favor, ideas dear to those who have arrogated to themselves the name of "economists." An individual does not grow rich by piling up money, but by work and by exchange with other workers, whose prosperity is the condition of his own prosperity. Adam Smith and Ricardo taught this doctrine. Their teachings were popularized by Richard Cobden three-quarters of a century ago, and by Norman Angell, the author of *The Great Illusion,* on the eve of the war; today John Maynard Keynes is their successor. The Labour Party has adopted these ideas. But are they the Labour Party's? Far from being socialists, Adam Smith and Ricardo, Richard Cobden, Norman Angell, and Maynard Keynes are doctrinaire liberals, conscious opponents of socialism.

We dare not say that this decline of the socialist idea in England, to which our study of the facts repeatedly leads us, must be permanent. The socialists can argue that the rapid development of state collectivism after 1914 was an abnormal phenomenon that had nothing to do with the regular progress of socialism; that the apparent reaction is only a return to normal peacetime conditions; and that, once this return is effected and the economic crisis solved, European collectivism will again move ahead. Perhaps. It is no less true that the Labour Party has just missed a singularly favorable chance quietly to bring about the nationalization of railways and mines. And, the occasion having been lost—lost, as we have tried to show, with its connivance—the party finds itself in a paradox. Firmly set for electoral battle, it has become the Parliamentary opposition to the coalition of bourgeois parties. But when it tries to define a program capable of rallying the masses at the next general election, it falls back, not on a specifically socialist program, but on the old program that half a century ago had been that of bourgeois liberalism in England. Peace and Plenty. Plenty through Peace. Peace with the enemy in Germany and Russia, with the rebels in Ireland, in Egypt and India. Peace everywhere, forever, and at any price.

Since this article was written, the Labour Party has just held its annual conference at Edinburgh, June 27–30. Motions in favor of nationalization of the land, of the mines, of the railways, and of all means of production, distribution, and exchange have been submitted for its approval. It is probable that they passed: why should the conference refuse to perform the ancient ritual? But the summary minutes which I have before me do not even take the trouble to tell me if they did: so little interest does the question arouse at present, in the public at large or in the Labour Party itself. Can we forget that in April the Independent Labour Party eliminated from its program any mention of the nationalization of means of production? Of course, we must not confuse this tiny sect with the great Labour Party which engulfs it, but it was under pressure from this sect thirty years ago that the Trades Union Congress first came out for complete nationalization.

At the very time when the Labour Party Conference was sitting, six leaders of the party published their program under the title, What We Want and Why. We still know the publication only through a first review. The book seems, however, to be clearly collectivist and in particular to demand nationalization of the railways, with worker participation in management; it regrets that the most favorable circumstances were not seized two years ago to bring about this reform. But imagine our surprise when we learned that the article dealing with nationalization of the railways is by Mr. J. H. Thomas himself! Really, the mysteries of British parliamentarianism are unfathomable! Did Mr. J. H. Thomas send autographed copies of What We Want and Why to the directors of the companies with whom he signed the agreement of May 1921?

E. H.

July 2, 1922

THE WORLD CRISIS OF 1914–1918:
AN INTERPRETATION[1]

I. *Towards Revolution*

Allow me, before I begin, to express to you my feelings of gratitude. That the University of Oxford should have made me, three years ago, an honorary Doctor of Letters, that the Rhodes Trustees should have made me their Memorial Lecturer for the year—such honours heaped upon me make me feel, I assure you, more modest than proud; they do not induce me to think myself a greater man than I am. My work has been a work of patience: my patience you have meant to reward. You will readily understand how high a value an historian of the English people must set upon this reward, coming as it does from the very center of English learning. He accepts it as something more than a reward for his past work; he accepts it as an encouragement for the future. For his work is far from having come to its end. Whether he will ever be able to finish it depends upon his being favoured with the requisite strength and health and freedom from anxieties, blessings that it is not in your power to bestow on him. But it requires also self-confidence and continued patience. These you can and do provide him with, for which he thanks you heartily.

But it is not only on my own behalf that I wish to ex-

[1] [The Rhodes Memorial Lectures, Oxford University, 1929. The lectures were published in 1930 by The Clarendon Press, which has generously permitted this republication. The lectures, originally given in English, appeared in a French translation in the original edition of *L'ère des tyrannies*.]

press my gratitude to you; it is also on behalf of my native country, France. The first Rhodes Memorial Lecturer was a Canadian statesman, one of the leading figures of the British Commonwealth of Nations. The second was an eminent American scientist, who belonged, if not to that Commonwealth, at all events to what might be called the Commonwealth of the English-speaking nations. But you have now remembered that this is the century of the League of Nations. You have thought that it might be well if you looked for a third lecturer outside the circle of the English-speaking world. Cecil Rhodes, who, if he was anything, was a man of imagination, would have certainly approved of the idea. And finally, having taken this decision, you have invited a Frenchman to come; for which, again, I thank you. Your purpose has been to give the Entente its true interpretation, not as a passing diplomatic contrivance, but as something more lasting, because more spiritual, not founded, let us hope, upon fear of a common enemy, but upon the more positive qualities of charity, hope, and faith. Charity towards mankind as a whole, hope in the future welfare of the human race, faith in the possibility of furthering, through co-operation between nations, the cause of knowledge and culture, of everything that the eighteenth century, the most Anglo-French century in history, called by a fine name, "enlightenment"—*les lumières*.

It is in this philosophical spirit that I mean to approach my difficult subject. I shall not deal with individuals. I shall not dwell upon the story of the last week before the war, dramatic as it is. I shall disregard the suggestions made retrospectively by a host of well-meaning critics, as to what such and such a sovereign, or prime minister, or foreign secretary, should, on this particular day, at this or that particular hour, have done or not done, said or not said, in order to prevent the war. Pills to cure an earthquake! The object of my study is the earthquake itself. I shall attempt to define the collective forces, the collective feelings and movements of public opinion, which, in the early years of the twentieth century, made for strife. I say purposely "strife," not "war," because the world-crisis of 1914–18 was not only a war—the war of 1914—but a revolution—the revolution of 1917. It may therefore be well for me, at the outset, to draw your attention to some aspects of those two important notions—"war" and "revolution."

My first point will be that there is a striking resemblance between the two notions. Suppose there is, at a given period, a fairly complete equilibrium between the political and the economic condition of a nation; that the distribution of political power among the several classes within the nation corresponds substantially to the distribution of economic power. Suppose, then, that, while the distribution of political power remains the same, and cannot by any normal means be readjusted to meet altered circumstances, the distribution of economic power is greatly altered. Suppose, for example, that the bourgeoisie, as in eighteenth-century France, acquires an immense increase of economic and cultural power without any corresponding increase of political power. There will come a strong temptation, almost as irresistible as a law of nature, for the class that is at a political disadvantage to resort to violence and revolution, until a new equilibrium is reached. Suppose, again, that, at a given time, the territorial distribution of the soil of Europe among the nations corresponds approximately to their respective military, economic, and cultural strength, and is in substantial harmony with the sentiments of the large majority of the subjects of each state. But suppose that, presently, one nation is found to have gained immensely in military or economic strength at the expense of one or many of the others; or that, within the limits of one or more nations, new nationalities have become self-conscious and wish to express themselves as independent states. For such a disturbance of equilibrium man has not as yet discovered any method of peaceful adjustment. It can be rectified only by an outburst of violence—called, in this instance, not a revolution, but a war—to be followed by the establishment of a new equilibrium of a more or less lasting character.

In the second place, just because the notions of war and revolution are closely allied, it is often difficult to distinguish between a revolution and a war. A nation, Ireland or Poland, which has been absorbed into an empire, wishes to assert itself as an independent state, and rises in arms against those who are, according to the written constitution, its legitimate masters. Should this rising of a nascent nation be called a revolution, or a national war? Or again, a revolution may extend beyond the narrow limits of the country where it began. French armies, for example, in 1792 and the following years appeared in Belgium and the Rhineland, and were everywhere acclaimed by the democratic party, while their opponents fled for their lives. Was this a war, in the purely military meaning of the word, or the propagation of a revolution?

It is thus apparent why all great convulsions in the history of the world, and more particularly in modern Europe, have been at the same time wars and revolutions. The Thirty Years' War was at once a revolutionary crisis, a conflict, within Germany, between the rival parties of Protestants and Catholics, and an international war between the Holy Roman Empire, Sweden, and France. The Great War (as, until quite lately, it used to be described in England) which lasted from 1792 to 1815, having begun as a social revolution in France, became a war which spread throughout Europe, until national revolutions, or wars, recoiling against France, drove her back, after one of the most amazing successions of triumphs and disasters in history, within her former limits. The last great and greater war, which is my present subject, has similar characteristics. I shall therefore, in my first lecture, define what the forces were which, at the beginning of the century, made for revolution. I shall define, in my second lecture, what the forces were which made for war. I shall then endeavour, in my third and concluding lecture, to show how a knowledge of the two sets of forces may help us to unravel the tangled plot of the four years' world crisis.

What were the collective forces that made for revolution? One word sums them up, a word in world-wide use, "socialism," which is the easier to define since its meaning has, so to speak, crystallized into a single doctrine. A man, who, whatever we think of his teaching, was certainly a man of genius, the most internationally minded of all internationalists, had founded his system upon his thorough knowledge of the dialectical method of Hegel and his German followers of the left, of French socialism, and of English economics. It may be well to recall, however briefly, the essence of Karl Marx's doctrine. The main feature of modern civilization, as he sees it, is the class war, the war between capitalists and wage-earners. The capitalists own all the means of production; they are in a minority, and an ever-dwindling minority, it being the law of industrial competition that the smaller concerns are always defeated by, and absorbed into, the larger. Their function is a beneficent one, inasmuch as, through their power of organization, they have increased, to an almost incredible degree, the wealth-producing power of mankind. But they have not fulfilled this beneficent function for the immediate benefit of mankind, taken as a whole. They have fulfilled it through the methodical exploitation, oppression, and pauperization of the wage-earners. Mankind will only take its revenge on the day, which is bound to come, and the coming of which capitalism is unconsciously preparing, when the exploited masses will have become such a crushing majority, as compared with the constantly diminishing, and finally insignificant, number of their exploiters, that they will find it easy, at the cost of a supreme upheaval, to come at last into their inheritance,

213

to get control of the concentrated industries, and work them henceforward, not for the profit of the few, but for the benefit of all.

The doctrine of Karl Marx has always struck me as unfair, because it directs the hatred of the multitude against that particular class of capitalists, the captains of industry, whose activity has been the most positively beneficent, to the exclusion of many more parasitic forms of capitalism. But it is easy to understand why it made a powerful appeal to the emotions of the working masses. It fitted in exactly with the conditions that prevailed in the newly industrialized districts of Western Europe. There, huge masses of suddenly congregated wage-earners faced minorities of arrogant task-masters, monopolizers of wealth, upstarts of industry. The doctrine provided them with reasons for hating those whom they hated instinctively. Little by little, it was forgotten that there had been socialists in France and England before Karl Marx had begun to write. "Marxism" and "socialism" became synonymous words.

This development was especially pronounced in the leading European country, Germany. There a powerful party had been expressly based upon orthodox Marxism; and socialists in the neighbouring countries had been working, more or less successfully, to imitate the German Social Democratic Party, just as soldiers, industrialists, and social reformers had done their best to imitate the methods of German militarism, German industrial organization, and German social legislation. The Social Democratic Party had first been founded in 1875 under another name, with a still indefinite programme and imperfect organization. Then it had undergone a long ordeal, lasting over ten years, of Bismarckian persecution. But from this ordeal it had emerged triumphant, at the moment when Bismarck was dismissed by the young William II, and a new regime of toleration began for the Social Democrats. Already a million and a half electors voted for the Social Democratic candidates; a figure of three millions was reached at the general election of 1905; the fourth million in 1912. Here was a great country, the greatest country in Europe, with more than four million voters eager to send to the Reichstag members of a party whose programme was strictly revolutionary.

Now, the constant and impressive growth of the German Marxist party raises an important problem. There have never been, in any great country, four million revolutionists; there certainly were not in Germany, when the twentieth century began, four million enemies of religion, conscious antipatriots, eager for the rapid abolition of private property. What the Social Democratic Party did, was to provide an outlet for discontents of all kinds and of all degrees of intensity; and it only succeeded in doing so, and in keeping together such a huge and mixed body of extremists and moderates of many sorts, through a clever use of the Marxian doctrine itself. For, if Marxism is in its very essence revolutionary, the leaders of German Social Democracy always reminded their followers that it was also a fatalistic doctrine. Socialism was bound to come, but only at the time when the natural process of capitalistic concentration had reached its ultimate development. Then the catastrophe would happen; but it would be dangerous and absurd to anticipate the date and mislead the masses into premature insurrection, which could result in nothing but failure. Thus did the German Social Democrats play a clever and successful game, constantly making new recruits, constantly teaching them patience at the same time as hope, pursuing a policy not so much of revolutionary action as of revolutionary expectation, a policy of waiting.

But the game was a difficult one, and after the general election of 1912 the question had arisen how long the party, numerically formidable as it had become, could continue to play it. It is legitimate for historians to ask, whether one of the reasons—we are far from saying the main reason—why the German military aristocracy decided, in July 1914, to run the risks of a great European war was not a growing sense of discomfort under the increasing pressure of Social Democracy, and a surmise that a bold attempt to give a set-back to socialism, by asserting themselves once more as the party of war and victory, might prove the wisest course. There was indeed something paradoxical in the structure of the German Empire. Here was a highly industrialized country, the most highly industrialized of all the nations on the continent, subjected to a political régime of feudalism and absolutism. Here was an empire founded, in 1866 and 1871, upon the basis of manhood suffrage, but in which Prussia, the leading state within its boundaries, was condemned to an electoral system that was a mere travesty of democratic institutions; in which ministers were responsible not to the elective assembly but to the hereditary sovereign; in which a minister was not regarded as having even a right to resign, but must wait until it pleased the King and Emperor to dismiss him. Here was one of those cases of apparently precarious equilibrium which demand a revolution; and, since the only party in the state that stood for democracy pure and simple was at the same time a socialistic party, it is difficult to see how the political crisis could fail to be attended by some social upheaval.

We shall see by and by how both these things happened. Nobody, however, would have been prepared to say during the years immediately preceding 1914 that Germany was the center of the European revolutionary spirit. The revolutionary centers of Europe had to be sought elsewhere, westward and eastward, in France and in Russia.

Let us begin with France. The political and social conditions that prevailed here were very different from those which prevailed in Germany. When the twentieth century opened, manhood suffrage had been established in France for more than half a century. France had been, nominally, even under the Second Empire—since that Empire was a monarchy founded on a plebiscite—and after 1871, in reality, a country where all administrative and legislative functions depended directly or indirectly upon popular election. With what results? When they considered the results, revolutionists could not help feeling bitterly disappointed. They saw revolutionary socialists, once admitted into a democratically elected Chamber of Deputies, become parliamentarians instead of revolutionists, political radicals instead of socialists, and, too frequently, moderates instead of radicals. They noticed that Bismarck's social monarchy had provided the working classes with more effective laws of protection against the risks of industrial life than had French radicalism. They wondered whether these failures of French democracy were not inherent in the very nature of democracy. Electioneering involves catering for votes of all kinds—even bourgeois votes. Membership of Parliament entails concern in a mass of questions—national, diplomatic, military, religious—that have nothing to do with the purely economic problem of the welfare of the working classes. Hence the rise of a new doctrine, called syndicalism, which really opened a new era in the history of socialism, and which has only lacked, in order to be appreciated at its full value, a prophet of the calibre of Karl Marx. The syndicalists condemned as barren what they called the indirect action of the state; they forbade trade-union leaders to seek admission to democratically elected assemblies in the fond hope of acting indirectly, through state interference, upon the employers of labour. If these leaders really meant to remain in contact with labour and faithful to the militant spirit of the class war, their duty was consistently to ignore politics and stick to the method of "direct action" against the employers. Let the workmen, by persistent pressure on the capitalists, exerted in workshop and factory, through collective bargaining, boycotts, and strikes, conquer higher wages, shorter hours, more control over the conditions of labour and the management of industry itself; let them group their trade unions, or *syndicats,* into federations coextensive with the nation, and these federations into one single federation of all trade unions, the Confédération Générale du Travail, endowed with executive powers. The day would come when, after a final revolutionary general strike, the General Confederation of Labour would achieve the annihilation of capitalism and become a pure industrial democracy, a society of producers, divested of all the political functions which appertained to the military state of the past.

Our picture of French revolutionary syndicalism is, however, not yet complete. A schoolmaster in Burgundy, by name Gustave Hervé, started another school of revolutionary tactics, which came to be more or less completely adopted by the syndicalist extremists. His formula was the military strike, the strike of soldiers against their officers; and, so long as he confined himself to persuading soldiers that they should decline to act as strike-breakers, there was undoubtedly a close resemblance between his ideas and those of revolutionary syndicalism. But he went further, and advised the soldiers if ever war came to be declared not to act the part of conscientious objectors and, in a Tolstoian spirit, merely decline to fight: he wanted them to retain the weapons that circumstances placed in their hands, and, instead of making war, turn them against the government of their own country, against militarism, patriotism, and capitalism. This was a notion that had very little resemblance to the syndicalist notion of a strike; it reminds us rather of the old formula of the Jacobin or Blanquist *coup de main* upon the central organs of government, in order to force a revolution upon a nation through the political action of the state. But the fact was that both notions appealed to extremists, and also that the word "strike" was used in both connections, so that it often became difficult to distinguish Hervéism from syndicalism. The double programme of a general strike of workmen and soldiers was indeed to be applied, and succeed, as we shall see, in another country than France. But it was in France, during the last ten years of the nineteenth century and the first ten years of the twentieth century, that the scheme was conceived.

It was no sooner conceived than it spread like wildfire to many countries outside France. It spread to Spain and Italy, where orthodox Marxism had always found it difficult to hold its own against more revolutionary forms of socialism, and had often been compelled to come to terms with them. It became particularly vehement in Italy at the time of the Tripoli War, towards the end of 1911. A brilliant agitator successfully organized a general strike of the whole body of workmen in the town of Forlì, which lasted several days, as a protest against the war. He thus came to the front, and was soon afterwards promoted to the post of editor of the important Roman socialist paper, the *Avanti;* he gave it a distinctly revolutionary tone, and largely increased its sale. His name was Benito Mussolini.

Syndicalism spread also to the Anglo-Saxon world. It spread to the United States, where the so-called Industrial Workers of the World propagated, among the masses of the unskilled proletarians, the idea of the revolutionary strike, as against the ultra-moderate methods of the American Federation of Labor. The Industrial Workers of the World in their turn found imitators in Australia, where Labour governments were getting into trouble with their workmen, and where the discontented workmen were glad to find in syndicalism a useful weapon with which to fight their Governments. Here two Englishmen, Ben Tillett and Tom Mann, came into contact with the syndicalist agitators. They had been, twenty years before, active revolutionists in London, had failed to accomplish their designs, and had left their country in disgust. They now became converts to the new doctrine, and brought it back to England, which it had already begun to permeate more directly from across the Channel. In the critical summer of

1911, when the "die hards" were fighting in the last ditch against the Parliament Bill, when the *Panther* was at anchor before the Moroccan harbour of Agadir, and the British government really believed in the possibility of an immediate war with Germany, Ben Tillett and Tom Mann became the leaders of a series of big strikes among transport workers and railwaymen, strikes that contained an element of violence quite new in England and bore the mark of a foreign influence. Then came, in the following winter, the general strike of the miners, and in 1913 the general strikes in South Africa and Dublin, which so strangely and unexpectedly cut across the feud between English and Dutch overseas, between Protestant and Catholic in Ireland. Then followed, during the first months of 1914, the new move among transport workers, railwaymen, and miners towards the formation of what was called the Triple Industrial Alliance, designed to exert a joint pressure upon the associations of their respective employers and eventually to organize the general strike. Of course, their aspirations were not the same as those of the continental extremists and utopians. Their very definite objects were their immediate interests—higher wages, shorter hours, and recognition of the trade unions. The situation was nevertheless alarming: the nation was facing a situation approaching in gravity the crisis that was not reached until 1926, after years of trouble and suspense.

Still more serious was the position in the east of Europe, if Russia may be really considered as part of Europe. But you must not expect me to dwell, in this connection, on the history of the beginnings of Bolshevism before the war. Suffice it to say that there was, from 1903 onwards, a Bolshevist Party; but it was a small party—one-half of the Social-Democratic Party; and the Russian Social-Democratic Party was very far from forming the whole of the Russian socialist movement. I compare the influence of the Social Democrats (Bolsheviks and Mensheviks combined) in the revolutionary movement to that of the Baltic

Barons in the reactionary circles. The Baltic Barons were a German, an exotic element: their aim and function was to introduce the orderly, if brutal, methods of German bureaucracy into a semi-Asiatic, inefficient, anarchical, and corrupt society. The Russian Social Democrats were likewise an exotic element: they were adepts of Marxist Socialism and admirers of German science, conscious enemies, as the Baltic Barons were, of eastern nonchalance and inefficiency. They understood, and explained, that the time had not yet come for a socialist revolution in Russia. The country, according to Marx's philosophy of progress, had first to go through a long and painful process of westernization and industrialization. Not so the really powerful, and authentically Russian, Social-Revolutionary Party. They despised the west and thought it the legitimate pride of Russia that the evils of industrialism and competitive civilization were unknown to her. Their socialism was agrarian. They believed that whereas western socialists were inventing complicated and pedantic systems in order to escape the horrors of factory life without abolishing the factory, the Russian *moujik*, in the simplicity of his primitive mind, had hit upon the true formula of unadulterated communism. The *mir*, the village community, had only to be maintained, or restored where it was in risk of being destroyed by the impact of western individualism, for the social question to be solved. As to the methods to be used, the Social Revolutionaries condoned, if they did not actually encourage, the anarchist method of terrorism and wholesale assassination. Not the murder of this or that particular statesman, in order to put another more popular man in his place, but the murder of official after official, indiscriminately, so as to throw the whole of society into a state of constant panic, dislocate the machinery of government, and prepare the advent of universal liberty through universal anarchy.

In fact a revolution had already occurred in Russia, a most formidable revolution, in 1905–6, at the end of the disastrous war with Japan. It had looked for a time as if Tsarism would be unable to weather the storm. But the storm had been weathered after all. And it is a legitimate question whether the revolutionary movement in Russia did not reach its climax about 1905 and subside afterwards. Perhaps also the syndicalist agitation, which raged in France between 1906 and 1910, was only the aftermath of the Russian Revolution, just as the English agitation of 1911 was only the aftermath of the French upheaval. No definite statement on such points is possible; but certainly no responsible statesman would have said, at the beginning of 1914, that he felt safe against the perils of some kind of revolutionary outburst. In Russia the recent assassination of Stolypin was a dangerous symptom; so was the big strike that broke out in the streets of St. Petersburg, just as President Poincaré was paying a state visit to the Tsar, in July 1914. Hervéism was still rampant in the rank and file of the French army: in England, the Industrial Triple Alliance was openly preparing to blackmail the community into submitting to its claims. "Beware," Sir Edward Grey warns Count Mensdorf on the 23rd July 1914; "a war would be accompanied or followed by a complete collapse of European credit and industry. In these days, in great industrial states, this would mean a state of things worse than that of 1848."[2] "Beware," Lord Morley a few days later warns his colleagues, "in the present temper of Labour, this tremendous dislocation of industrial life must be fraught with public danger. The atmosphere of war cannot be friendly to order, in a democratic system that is verging on the humour of '48."[3] In 1848 a revolution had begun in Paris that spread through the whole west of the continent and was altogether republican and socialistic in character. But what

[2] *British Documents on the Origins of the War,* vol. xi, p. 70.
[3] Viscount Morley, *Memorandum on Resignation,* August 1914, p. 5.

now happened was not a revolution but a war; not even, as in 1789, a revolution followed by wars, but a war that, for a time at least, threw the revolutionary peril into the background. Hence we are entitled to conclude that, powerful as were the forces which, in prewar Europe, made for revolution, the forces that made for war were still more powerful.

II. *Towards War*

Having made an attempt, in our first lecture, to define the collective forces which, before the beginning of the world crisis of 1914, made for revolution, let us try to define those which made for war.

The so-called economic, or materialist philosophy of history suggests a first interpretation. We should, if we adhered to this philosophy, regard the collective forces that made for war in the light of an economic phenomenon. The structure of a capitalistic society is such, we should say, that, in a given nation, the home market is unable to absorb the whole produce of the nation's industry; if it could do so, this would mean that wages were sufficient to purchase the entire produce of labour, since wage-earners of all grades form the vast majority of the nation. But if that were so, where would the capitalist find his profit? The profit-seeking instinct will therefore compel him to look for foreign markets, among nations less industrially developed than his own. As these other nations become, one after another, more industrialized, he will find new outlets for his goods in the non-civilized parts of the world, fit for colonization, but not for immigration. But the time will presently come when many nations will be competing for these colonial markets, and the world will have become too small for the scramble. Hence war, the natural result of industrial over-production and international competition.

I am no believer in the materialist conception of history. This is, of course, not the place for a philosophical discussion of the subject, which, in order to be thorough, would require not one lecture but a whole course of lectures. I shall only draw your attention to a few facts, belonging to the period immediately before the war, which I believe will convince you how little this theory accounts for the real course of history.

The danger-spot in Europe, from 1904 to 1911, was assuredly Morocco, the field of a keen competition between France, whose rights were upheld by England, and Germany. Was it a case of French capitalism versus German capitalism? In 1909 the two governments came to an agreement: some kind of political preponderance in Morocco was allowed to France, and the French and the Germans agreed to exploit in common the natural resources of north-west Africa. This agreement met with no opposition from the magnates of industry in the two countries. Behind the diplomatic document there was a pact of alliance between the great Krupp firm and the Schneider firm, the great industrial houses that provided their respective countries, in the Ruhr and at the Creusot, with their military armaments. The agreement of 1909 broke down, in France at any rate, because of the fierce resistance of the French nationalists, who thought it too international, and of the French socialists, who thought it too capitalistic. Here therefore we find industrialism making for peace between France and Germany, defeated only by other forces, non-economic in their nature and stronger than industrialism.

The agreement broke down. A French army marched upon Fez. Germany sent a warship to Agadir. It looked as if Germany wanted war, and was armed and ready for immediate war. Suddenly, the German government dropped the greater part of its African claims, and accepted a very moderate compromise. It is generally admitted that this unexpected change of attitude was due to the fact that, just when war was in sight, there was a panic on the Berlin stock exchange, and the German government was assailed by terror-stricken stockbrokers, merchants, and industrialists, who explained that war spelt ruin for them and disaster for the country as a whole. Once more capitalism meant peace; this time capitalism was the more powerful force and averted war.

But those who uphold the economic theory of the origins of the war are also those who think of it as having been mainly a war between England and Germany. What, then, of the relations between England and Germany? Is it true that, as many Socialists on the continent used to say, the English capitalists, the merchants in the city, wanted war? What strikes the impartial observer is, on the contrary, a constant and eager yearning after peace on the part of the mercantile and industrial community. "Trade follows the flag" may have been a popular motto a few years before, at a time when, oddly enough, the English imperialists favoured an alliance with England's chief competitor in the markets of the world, Germany. But now the popular motto was that "war did not pay." A clever and clear-headed writer, in a book whose sale in England and out of England was enormous, set himself to dispel "the optical illusion," "the Great Illusion," according to which it was possible to make money out of a victorious war. It had perhaps been possible in primitive stages of society, when the conqueror could enslave the individual members of a defeated tribe. But, in a modern world, based upon exchange, the victor could not even extract tribute from the vanquished without running a great risk of ruining, not the latter, but himself. This theory made headway among the merchants and financiers. On the very eve of the war, we see bankers, stockbrokers, leaders of the cotton, steel, and coal industries, crowding into the room of the Chancellor of the Exchequer, and expressing terror at the prospect of England's drifting into the conflict.

However, the conflict came, and England plunged into it; and these facts raise a problem as to the value of Norman Angell's type of pacifism. For, whereas the upholders of the economic theory of the causes of war believed that, just on account of its highly industrialized structure, the western world was heading towards an inevitable and imminent war, Norman Angell, on the contrary, because he thought that the commercial structure of Western Europe made for peace, believed in the permanent stability of a peace that had already lasted forty years. Are we not therefore entitled to declare that the facts have very rapidly belied his theory? Did not the three great capitalistic nations of Western Europe, only four years after Norman Angell's optimistic prophecies, actually go to war? To this question my answer will be the further question: "Did they? Did Germany, France, and England go to war?" Or perhaps I may put my question in a less paradoxical form, and ask: "Supposing Germany, France, and England had, by themselves, made up the whole world; supposing there had been, on the surface of the globe, only these three nations, and the deep sea all round them, would they have gone to war?"

There is perhaps something to be said in favour of a theory current before the war, according to which the system of "armed peace," resting as it did upon compulsory military service and manhood suffrage, contributed, ruinous though it was, to the maintenance of peace, since those ultimately responsible for the declaration of war were also those who would have to face all the risks of the war, when once it was declared. On many occasions, indeed, during the forty-odd years that followed the Franco-German War of 1870, it had seemed that Germany and France, or France and England, or France, England, and Germany, had reached the very brink of war. Sometimes one nation had suffered a severe diplomatic reverse;

226

sometimes a compromise had been patched up; always the rival nations had stopped short of coming to blows and slaughter. By about 1914 the strain of the situation was certainly becoming intolerable, and doubt whether peace could long be maintained was widespread. But why did the German government in 1913 decide in favour of that formidable increase of their military strength, which seemed, at last, to make war inevitable? The decision had nothing to do either with the naval competition between Germany and England, or with the quarrels between Germany and France about Morocco or about Alsace. What decided the German government to prepare for an eventual European War was a crisis that was brewing, not in the highly industrialized and capitalistic West, but among the primitive communities of the southeast of Europe. War came to the West from the East; it was forced upon the West by the East.

Peace hinged, all through the interval between the Prussian wars of the sixties and the Great War of 1914, upon the relations of Germany and Russia. There was an old tradition of intimacy between the courts of St. Petersburg and Berlin, which was completed in the days of the Holy Alliance by an intimacy with Austria. This conspiracy between three autocratic monarchies was hated and deemed "unholy" by all liberals in the West. But it undoubtedly made for peace. The three monarchs had never forgotten the Jacobin wars of conquest of the last years of the eighteenth century; they felt—not mistakenly —that revolution and war are two very closely allied notions; they considered their alliance as a system of mutual insurance against the peril of revolution and war. The system endured down to the very eve of the war of 1914 in attenuated and modified forms. Bismarck added to his alliance with Austria an alliance with Russia. When he fell, the treaty of alliance with Russia was not renewed; but, after a very short interval, the friendship between Germany and Russia became once more so close that it practically amounted to an alliance. The conclusion of the "Entente" between England and France, directed against Germany, did not, in spite of France being Russia's ally, make Russia's relations with Germany cooler. The Russo-German friendship even survived the Anglo-Russian Convention of 1907, a very artificial and superficial *rapprochement*, which did not prevent Russia from concluding with Germany, in 1910–11, at the very time of the Agadir crisis, an arrangement concerning the Baghdad railway, amounting to a Russo-German entente in the Middle East. The breach only occurred in 1912. And what was its cause? Was the breach an effect of rival dynastic purposes? Nobody in St. Petersburg dreamt of conquering German territory; neither did anybody in Berlin dream of aggrandizing Germany at the expense of Russia. The two governments had, in this respect, only one common purpose, which was to keep Poland in a state of disruption and subjection. What happened, from the end of 1912 onwards, was that both governments were carried away by great waves of collective feeling. To understand the nature of these collective forces, which were the real cause of the Great War, you must allow me to carry you farther into the East, into the Far East of Asia.

An epoch-making event happened in 1905, when Japan destroyed the Russian fleet, defeated on land the Russian army, and expelled Russia from the coast of the gulf of Petchili. The Russo-Japanese War sent a thrill through the whole Asiatic continent. It now appeared that the Europeans were not the demigods they believed themselves to be, and had so long, by armed pressure, compelled the whole non-European world to believe them. At last the East was asserting itself against the West, and shaking the yoke of the white European. Let us not attempt to translate the fact into the phraseology of historical materialism. This was not a case of Japanese capitalism fighting Russian capitalism. The quarrel was between nation and nation, culture and culture. The basis of history is idealistic, not materialistic; and idealism makes revolutions and wars.

There was, however, one difference between Japan and the rest of Asia. A feudal aristocracy, a military monarchy, had always known how to keep Japan free from invasion. Everywhere else effete aristocracies and corrupt monarchies had allowed themselves to be conquered by European armies or bought by European gold. It was therefore impossible that the peoples in Asia should turn to their aristocracies and monarchies for help against Western oppression. They had to rely upon themselves, and do what, at that very moment, as an after-effect of the defeat of their armies in Manchuria, the Russians, themselves a semi-Asiatic people, were doing, revolt against their rulers, and save the nation by the introduction of free institutions. We thus observe in Asia, during the last ten years before the war, a renascence of those ideas of militant liberalism and democratic nationalism which, during the first half of the nineteenth century, had played so important a part in the history of Europe. In Europe, at the beginning of the twentieth century, one might have been tempted to call those ideas old-fashioned, for international socialism paid only lip-service to the principle of nationality. But in Asia, just at this time, they began again to shake the world.

The revolutionary movement compelled the imperial government in China, as early as 1906, to promise political and administrative reforms, and to prepare the draft of a constitution. It became more intense after the death, natural or otherwise, in 1908, of the Empress-dowager. In March 1911 the monarchy accepted the principle of a responsible cabinet. In 1912, a year after the Emperor had abdicated, the republic was proclaimed. Thus it was that in the Far East the most ancient of the great military monarchies in the world fell to the ground.

In India there had already existed, during the previous

twenty years, a National Congress which had as its program home rule for India, to be obtained by peaceful propaganda and legal means. But the Indian nationalist movement took a more revolutionary form after the victory of Japan and the Russian Revolution. Gandhi, undoubtedly inspired by the teachings of Tolstoy, preached passive resistance to the orders of an alien government; and then, in conjunction with Tilak, a boycott of European merchants and European goods. The boycott rapidly degenerated into more violent forms of aggression, including bomb-throwing after the Russian model. In 1907 the revolutionists swamped the National Congress; and the British Government, realizing at last the seriousness of the movement, adopted a policy of concession. Two natives were admitted into the Executive Council of the Viceroy, and elected members were admitted into the Legislative Council of the Viceroy and the provincial legislative councils.

In Persia, as early as 1906, the Shah, accused of selling his country to Russia, was murdered; and his successor was subjected to the control of a popularly elected assembly, or *Medjlis*. He tried to shake off the yoke, dissolved the *Medjlis*, and, with the help of a Russian army, besieged the leaders of the nationalist army in Tabriz. He was in his turn deposed; and a new Shah, only twelve years old, was placed once more under the control of the *Medjlis*. Later on, the reactionaries, under the deposed Shah, and with Russian assistance, were to take their revenge, and finally suppress the *Medjlis*. Nevertheless we see in Persia the triumph, however precarious, of a party that stood at the same time for political and for national liberty.

In 1908 the agitation reached the Bosphorus and the very borders of Europe. The Young Turk party provoked a military insurrection, and compelled the Sultan to reestablish the Constitution of 1876, based upon a popularly elected Parliament. The object of the so-called "Union and Progress" Committee, which carried out the revolution, was to strengthen Turkey by reconstructing it on the western model, and to transform it into a unified nation, whose inhabitants would be equal citizens, irrespective of race, creed, or language. They did not succeed in strengthening Turkey. Austria annexed Bosnia. Italy annexed Tripoli and the Dodecanese. Then the revolutionary principle of nationality recoiled, so to speak, upon Turkey. An insurrection broke out in Crete, another in Albania. Finally, Serbia, Montenegro, Greece, and Bulgaria entered a league for the partition of those provinces of the Turkish Empire which they claimed in virtue of the principle of nationality. Thus began, towards the end of 1912, what may be called a war, in so far as it was a struggle between Turkey and four foreign nations, or a revolution, in so far as the inhabitants of Turkey rose in arms, not against the invader, but against the Turkish army. We will pass over the gruesome tale of the two Balkan Wars. Suffice it to say that, by August 1913, the Turkish Empire, so far as its European possessions were concerned, was shattered.

A great historian, Albert Sorel, wrote as early as 1878, the year of the Congress of Berlin: *"Le jour où l'on croira résolue la question d'Orient, l'Europe verra se poser inévitablement la question d'Autriche"* ("Once the Eastern Question appears to be solved, Europe will inevitably be confronted with the Austrian Question"). The collapse of the Ottoman Empire had now begun, and the time had come for the collapse of the Austro-Hungarian monarchy in its turn. The dual monarchy included a majority of alien races subjected to the control of two dominant races, German and Hungarian. The subject races had already long been restive; and from the moment when the Austrian Government in 1909, and the Hungarian Government in 1911, had granted manhood suffrage to their subjects, both parliaments, in Vienna and Budapest, had become pandemoniums of rival nationalities. Now that the victory of three million emancipated Serbians had doubled the territory and population of their country, how could five million Czechs, six million southern Slavs, subjects of Austria and Hungary, refrain from the dream of following their example? Sedition was rife all through the Slavonic parts of the Austro-Hungarian Empire.

The Hapsburg monarchy was thus confronted with an anxious problem. Should it submit to the coming catastrophe, and passively allow its possessions to be dismembered? or boldly take the initiative, declare war upon Serbia, and absorb it into the Slavonic part of the Monarchy, which would thus be transformed from a dual into a triple state, no longer Austrian and Hungarian, but Austrian, Hungarian, and Slavonic? Such a plan was favoured by the military party, which gathered round the heir to the throne, the Archduke Franz Ferdinand. But every one knew, who chose to know, that, whenever Austria declared war upon Serbia, Pan-Slavist sentiment would become too strong for any Russian government to resist its pressure. Every one knew, who chose to know, that whenever Russia gave so much as a sign of declaring war upon Austria, Pan-German feelings would compel the German government to enter the lists in its turn; and that the Austro-Serbian war would become a great struggle for the supremacy of Teuton or Slav throughout Central Europe. It was likewise common knowledge that Germany, whenever she declared war upon Russia, was resolved not to tolerate the existence in the west of an army that was after all the second best army in Europe; that she would first march upon Paris and annihilate France as a military power, before rushing back to the east, and settling matters with Russia. Again, every one knew, who chose to know, that the German general staff very wisely judged the Franco-German frontier between Luxembourg and Switzerland too narrow for the deployment of the German army, which would have to cross the territory of Belgium if it was to strike the necessary lightning blow at

France. And everybody understood that if ever the Belgian coast and the northern coast of France were to fall under the domination of Germany, Great Britain, feeling her prestige and her security in danger, would enter the war on the side of Belgium and France. Every one knew, who wished to know, not only that a European war was imminent, but what the general shape of the war would be.

How, then, should we account for the fact that neither the first nor the second Balkan War degenerated into a general war? England was eager for the maintenance of peace. The German government was afraid of an Austro-Serbian war, which might bring about a breach between Austria and Italy, and dislocate the Triple Alliance. But the main reason was perhaps that there remained, at the three courts of Berlin, Vienna, and St. Petersburg, enough of the spirit of the Holy Alliance to make the three military governments feel that a war between them would have the character of fratricidal strife, that it might spell disaster to all three, and that peace was the safest course for the preservation of monarchical order in Europe.

Then, after ten months of peace, came the murder of the Archduke Franz Ferdinand and his consort. It was committed in the streets of Serajevo, where the Archduke was paying a visit that was in itself an act of defiance to Serbia. Two Bosnian revolutionists were the murderers. Was the murder planned in Bosnia? If so, we may call it indifferently a revolutionary deed, the murder of a tyrant, or the germ of a war of independence. Was it, as is probable, planned in Serbia? If so, we may call it either the revolutionary assassination of a would-be tyrant, or the signal for a national war of Serbia against the oppressors of Bosnia. One thing, at all events, is certain. The Great War was a war for the liberty of the peoples from its inception: not from the day when German armies violated the neutrality of Belgium—this was only an incident in the course of a war that had already begun—but from the day

233

when, with the murder of the Archduke Franz Ferdinand, the insurrection of the southern Slavs began. It was then that the central empires took the responsibility of declaring war upon Serbia, Russia, and France. But why did they take this awful responsibility? The question can be answered only if put in another form. We should ask, not *who*, but *what* was responsible for the three declarations of war; and the answer should be: "The rotten condition of the Austro-Hungarian Empire, the fact that the revolutionary principle of nationality was at work within its limits, and that it was about to break up into a number of independent States." If so formidable an event as the dismemberment of Austria occurred, nothing short of a miracle could prevent its developing into a general war. European diplomacy did not work the miracle. And there was war.

III. *War and Revolution*

Our purpose being to understand the causes of the world crisis of 1914–18, we have focused our attention, not upon the acts of individual statesmen, not upon the incidents of diplomatic history, but upon the general movements of public opinion, upon the collective forces which, before the crisis began, made for strife. We have thus been brought to distinguish between two different species of forces. Some of them set class against class within each nation, or, to speak more accurately, cut across nations, and set class against class all over Europe, irrespective of nationalities. Others were exclusively national, they united all the classes within each nation against all the classes, equally united, within every other nation. Which were the more powerful? From what happened in 1914, it appeared that national warlike emotions influenced the human mind more deeply than international revolutionary emotions. But these latter feelings were only submerged for a time, not annihilated; they were soon to come to the surface again, with an intensity increased by the sufferings of the war. The two played an equally important part in the evolution of the crisis. My aim, in this third and last lecture, is, if not to tell the history of the war, at least to give you some hints towards a new way of approaching its history, through the knowledge of the action and interaction of these forces.

The history of the war I shall divide into two parts, before and after the Russian Revolution of 1917. The tale of the first part I cannot begin otherwise than by inquiring what happened to the great Napoleonic scheme planned by the German general staff, with a view to achieving a rapid and crushing victory. The plan failed. It failed in the west at the battle of the Marne. And of course many causes contributed to the French victory of September 1914. The French believed (quite mistakenly, but the belief, although mistaken, was very effective) that a huge Russian army was marching upon Berlin. They knew that one hundred thousand British soldiers were fighting at their sides, the promise of more to come. They might have realized (in fact, they thought of it very little, since the idea of a prolonged struggle had not yet entered their minds) what a tremendous asset on the Allies' side was England's sea power, which enabled her to besiege Germany and reduce her to starvation. But, take it all in all, the French victory of the Marne was emphatically a victory of nationality, a victory won by the French nation over German imperialism. The Germans failed also in the east. There was no victorious march upon St. Petersburg, following a march upon Paris. A Russian army that had invaded East Prussia was thrown back into Russian territory. A confused warfare followed, neither upon German nor upon properly Russian territory, but upon the plains of Poland, an uninteresting and aimless struggle between German and Russian imperialism.

There were other parts of what may be called the European battlefield, where it looked as if the triumph of the central empires was, at least temporarily, more decisive; but these triumphs were also the most precarious, just because they were victories won against nationality.

Germany had not declared war in order to conquer Belgium; but man is so made that, when he has got hold of something, he is not prepared to let it go; and, now that practically the whole of Belgium had been occupied by the German army, no responsible statesman in Berlin would, while the war lasted, have admitted the possibility of peace being signed without Belgium being, more or less radically, annexed to Germany. But was the thing feasible? Was it conceivable that Germany could absorb six million foreigners, one part of them French-speaking, none of them German-speaking, with an already long tradition behind them of national independence and democratic government? Germany, if victorious, was bound to make the attempt, and to fail. Such was the nemesis of victory.

In the south, an Austrian army swept Serbia out of existence. The entry of Italy into the war had but insignificant military results. Later on, Rumania in turn joined the Allies, only to be invaded in her entirety. The army which, in 1916, invaded Rumania was in fact a German, not an Austrian, army; and the plains of Hungary would twice have been overrun by the Russians if German assistance had not saved Hungary and Austria from destruction. It was therefore Germany's military power that was the salvation of Austria. So long as the German armies were there she would be safe from dismemberment. But the German armies could not remain there for ever. As soon as peace was signed, and Germany demobilized, it was highly probable that Austria-Hungary would break into pieces; the peril had only been deferred.

Such was, indeed, the strength of the national idea that Germany found advantage in appealing to it, in order to

236

weaken her enemies materially and morally. The Germans not only denounced French imperialism in North Africa and British imperialism in Egypt and India; nearer home, in Europe itself, they found the way to exploit nationalism against Belgium, England, and Russia.

Belgium is, to a certain extent, an artificial nationality. One part of it, the larger part, is Flemish, Teutonic in blood and language; the smaller part is Walloon, and speaks a Romance dialect, the most northern of all the Romance dialects. Germany knew how to play off the Flemings against the Walloons; she created, in the Flemish part of Belgium (with more success than we cared to realize in France and in England), an activist party, which claimed and obtained an administrative division of Belgium into two heterogeneous regions.

Ireland had been, all through the nineteenth century, in a state of chronic rebellion against her Saxon conquerors from England and Scotland. The country in July 1914, just before hostilities began with Germany, was on the very verge of actual civil war. As soon as war was declared by England upon Germany, mixed feelings of chivalry and political interest made Ireland loyal for a time. But it was for a short time only. Germany began to play the game that France had played in other wars; she made use of the Irish against England. In April 1916 there appeared on the western coasts of Ireland a German auxiliary ship, in conjunction with a German submarine, under the guidance of an English visionary, Sir Roger Casement. The ship was sunk and Casement was arrested, but four days later formidable disturbances broke out in Dublin, where the battle lasted four entire days, with serious loss of property and human life. From this moment the absolute, or practically absolute, independence of Ireland was an issue that could no longer be evaded.

The case of Poland presented the German war propagandists with a triumphant argument, when they wished to confute the legend that Russia was fighting for the liberty of the Slavs, of all the Slavs. In no part of Poland were the Poles so badly treated as in that which had become Russian, neither in Prussian Poland, where they were at all events free from religious persecution and from subjection to a universal state of barbarous illiteracy, nor in Austria, where they enjoyed complete liberty, both of language and religion. We need not be surprised, therefore, to see Pilsudski, the future Polish marshal, enlisting in the Austrian army in order to fight for the liberty of Poland; the central empires re-establishing full linguistic liberty throughout the whole of that part of Poland that had formerly been Russian; and in November 1916, when practically the whole of Russian Poland had fallen into the hands of the combined armies of Germany and Austria, both the victorious governments announcing their intention of immediately transforming these Russian possessions into an independent state with a hereditary monarchy and a constitution.

Such was the situation towards the end of 1916. Germany had not gained the lightning victory for which she had gambled in July 1914, and she knew it to be more and more impossible, as the months went by, that she should ever make good her initial failure on the Marne. She was therefore eager for a peace, which in her view would have been a peace of compromise, but which it was impossible for the Allies to see in that light, since Germany was everywhere, to the south as well as to the east and west, in armed occupation of territories belonging to the enemy, and therefore felt herself in a position to dictate the terms of the compromise. At this time begins the second phase of the war, marked by two important events: the United States entered the war; Russia, after a revolution, withdrew from it.

It is useless for me to insist on the importance, in the history of the war, of the first of these two facts. It was the entry of America into the war which, at last, made

238

the victory of the Allies a decisive victory. Until the first weeks of 1917, America, in spite of the British blockade, had persisted in doing her best to revictual Germany through Scandinavian harbours: in fact, her real quarrel had been, not with Germany, but with England for violating the "freedom of the seas." Now, as a result of German recklessness, and of the resolve of the German general staff to intensify the submarine war against all neutrals (the Americans included), as well as against the Allies, the United States accepted the English conception of the blockade, and rigorously applied all the rules against which they had persistently protested while suffering under them as a neutral power. The isolation of Germany from foreign sources of supply consequently became absolute. Moreover, the appearance in Europe, during the spring of 1918, of millions of young Americans, raw and untrained recruits, no doubt, but young and fresh, made the situation of Germany on the battlefields hopeless, even before the Allies had had time to carry the war into German territory.

But the Russian Revolution is the historical event of which I should like more particularly to emphasize the importance, for reasons that will appear presently.

In order to understand its antecedents, it is necessary that we should go back to the beginning of the war, when the revolutionary feelings of the working classes seemed powerless in presence of the instinctive appeal of national solidarity. In vain did some individual leaders, or groups of leaders, try to remain doctrinally faithful to the principle of unconditional peace. Those who did so were swept aside by the patriotic enthusiasm of the masses. The majority even of these men were themselves carried away by the warlike feelings of those around them. And there is this to be said in favour of the socialists who helped to fight the battles of their respective countries, that some measure of socialism permeated the policy of all the belligerent countries. Their governments everywhere found it necessary to bring under control all means of communication and transport, all imports and exports, the mines, and whatever branches of production were necessary for the feeding, clothing, and arming of their armies. Moreover, in order to conciliate the working classes, they took the trade-union secretaries into their confidence, and ran the whole of the controlled industries in full and explicit agreement with the workmen's organizations. Some socialists fondly hoped that the war had worked a miracle and that, when peace returned, Europe would perhaps discover that a permanent régime of state socialism combined with syndicalism had come into being without the horrors of revolution, if not without the horrors of war.

The proletariat, however, very rapidly became restless again. The workmen were well paid, but were subject to a system of stern military discipline, and were given to understand, when they complained, that their leaders had signed agreements with the representatives of the different states by which the members of the trade unions renounced the right to strike. Intransigent pacifists came into touch with discontented workmen; and there grew up a body of revolutionary feeling, directed both against capitalism and against war. On the continent, some of the revolutionists managed to pass into Switzerland, and there meet and discuss in common the possibilities of a rapid return to peace. Not that they agreed even among themselves. At Zimmerwald in Switzerland, just one year after the Marne, while some internationalists were examining what kind of pressure might be brought to bear upon their respective Governments in favour of peace, they were interrupted by one of them, a man of Mongolian type, indolently stretched upon a sofa. "Peace! why do you talk of peace? You cannot have peace before you have social revolution! Go home, every one of you, and start the revolution." "It is easy enough for you to talk," answered one of the German delegates, "you are in exile, and very far indeed from your native country. The only logical thing for you to do would be to go to Russia yourself and start the revolution. But I won't give you that advice, knowing what would happen to me, if I went to Germany and preached revolution. There would be no revolution. But I should be shot next morning." The other man, not many months later, went to Russia, and did the thing. He was Lenin.

The Russian Revolution began in March 1917, with a general strike of workmen in Petrograd, followed by a general strike of soldiers at the front. It was a revolution which conformed to the syndicalist and Hervéist plan, a revolution against war and capitalism, conducted by councils of workmen and soldiers, now known throughout the world as soviets. After a futile attempt to dissolve the *Duma*, the Tsar abdicated; and there followed, under the nominal direction of a provisional government, six months of universal love, universal anarchy, and murder at every street-corner. A time came when the régime had to end, as all such régimes do, in some kind of dictatorship. There was a first attempt at a *coup d'état* by the military, under Korniloff, which failed, another by the Social-Democratic Bolsheviks, under Lenin, which succeeded. Twelve years have passed, and the proletarian dictators are still in power in Moscow. What were the effects of the Russian Revolution upon the destinies of the war?

In so far as the effects were unfavourable to the cause of the western Allies, they are obvious. Long and dreary months followed the Revolution in Petrograd, during which it looked as if the results of the Russian defection more than counterbalanced those of America's intervention. On the one hand, more and more German troops were liberated for use on the western front, until, after the peace of Brest-Litovsk, in February 1918, there were practically no German troops left in the east. The French, the Italians, the English, and the French again underwent, from April 1917 to May 1918, a succession of severe defeats. In another and more subtle way, Russian revolutionarism exercised a pernicious influence upon the morale of the allied nations in the west. The French and British governments sent socialist envoys to Russia with the object of keeping the Russian socialists faithful, in the name of democratic solidarity, to the cause of the anti-German coalition. What happened was that the will to win the war was weakened in the minds of the French and British envoys. They came back converted to the cause of peace, some of them even (the French, if not the English) to the cause of Communism. There were mutinies in the French army in 1917. There were more and more strikes in England, inspired as much by war-weariness as by conscious anti-war propaganda.

But there were other aspects of the Russian Revolution, which should also be taken into account, and which were favourable to the cause of the Allies and to their final victory.

In the first place, the Revolution helped to bring about America's entry into the war. It was on the 3rd February 1917, four days after Germany's announcement of an intensified submarine war, that diplomatic relations were broken off between America and Germany. But war was not declared; and many weeks followed during which the States hesitated to plunge into the conflict. It was only on the 21st March, that is, one week exactly after the abdication of the Tsar, that President Wilson invited Congress to hold an extraordinary session, to begin on the 2nd April; and in his message to Congress, President Wilson sang the praises of the Russian Revolution. The United States were the only great power that had joined in the fray without aims of conquest, either in Europe or elsewhere; they wanted a disinterested and idealistic cause to fight for. It was difficult to represent the war as a war against imperialism, so long as one of the Allies—and in some ways the most formidable—presented all the features of oppressive imperialism at its worst. Thanks to the fall of Tsarism, the war could be fought on the democratic lines of President Wilson's Fourteen Points. It is even a question whether President Wilson's programme was not, to a certain extent, directly or indirectly, consciously or not, influenced by the new Russian formula of "a peace without annexation or indemnity."

In the second place, Bolshevik influences permeated Germany, just as they permeated France and England; only the permeation was deeper and more direct. In August 1914 the nation (including the Social Democrats) had been practically unanimous in favour of the war. A single eccentric Social Democrat had abstained from giving his approval to the government, and round him had thereafter clustered a small body of revolutionary extremists, the Spartacists. They became, after March 1917, the nucleus of the German Communist Party, which copied the Moscow model. As time went on, an ever-increasing minority of Social Democrats had refused to grant to the government the war credits that it demanded. It was, however, only after the Russian Revolution of March 1917 that they broke away from the majority, and formed a separate party of "Independent Social Democrats" based on a programme of immediate peace. There was a serious mutiny in the navy in July 1917, the leaders of which were court-martialled and shot. And the government, for their part, came to realize that they must bow before the storm. It now became apparent how precarious was the Bismarckian political constitution of Germany, since it proved unable to resist the strain of a prolonged war or of an incipient defeat. In July 1917 Bethmann-Hollweg resigned, and three phantom ministries in succession leant, each a little more than its predecessor, upon the parties of the left. Bills were introduced by the government for the thorough democratization of the Constitution of Prussia, and for the introduction of the principle of ministerial responsibility into the Constitution of the Reich. Finally, when, in the autumn of 1918, the German army in the west had been repeatedly beaten and disaster was in sight, a revolt broke out among the sailors at Kiel. Councils of soldiers and workmen were formed throughout northern Germany. The Kaiser fled to Holland, and the Armistice was signed in November, with a Republican and Socialist German Government. In Austria, where the final catastrophe of the central empires really began, there were social and national revolutions combined. What is called the battle of Vittorio Veneto was merely the breaking up of the Austro-Hungarian army into its component elements; each of them rushed back to its separate national home, there to promote the social revolution in Vienna and Budapest, or the national revolution in Prague and Agram.

After protracted negotiations among the Allied and Associated Powers themselves, the Treaty of Versailles was published to the world, and signed by Germany. Some of the critics of this very much abused document have protested against its revolutionary character, carving brand-new nations out of the old states to whose existence Europe had grown accustomed. The question is how a revolutionary war could end otherwise than in a revolutionary treaty. The treaties that created a free Poland, a free Czechoslovakia, a free Yugoslavia, that liberated Alsace from Germany and the Trentino from Austria, were based upon the principle of nationality; they represented the triumph of everything that the liberals of the nineteenth century had fought for. Not that war came to an end with the signature of the treaties. It dragged on in Russia, where you may choose to call it either a civil war between Communism and the Russian enemies of Communism, or a national war, by which Russia asserted her independence, as against what was really the foreign intrusion of England and France. Then Russia, freed from internal peril, endeavoured to transform her defensive wars into an offensive war of Communist propaganda, directed against Poland and Germany. This new war failed under the walls of Warsaw. Perhaps, it may be said that the world crisis did not really begin in 1914 and come to an end in 1918. It began in October 1912, with the first Balkan War; it came to an end only in August 1920, when the last of the postwar treaties was signed at Sèvres, when the Bolshevik army was defeated in Poland, when an attempt at a Communist revolution in Italy proved abortive, and the rise of Fascism began. Throughout, it had been a war of nationalities; and the Russian Revolution had acted as a solvent of imperialism for the benefit, not so much of Communism, or even of socialism, as of nationality.

My tale having come to an end, I should like, in conclusion, to add a few words of warning against a possible misinterpretation. What does my method amount to? I have looked for the "causes" or "responsibilities" of the war, not in the acts of individual statesmen, but in collective anonymous forces, against which individual statesmen were powerless. Now, happy as may have been, happy as I think have been on the whole, the European results of the war, it would be absurd not to realize, as the Soviet government is constantly reminding us—usefully if unpleasantly—that there is still a labour unrest to be appeased, and that there are still oppressed nationalities to be liberated. Should statesmen, then, be content to wait passively until collective anonymous forces once more assert themselves, and a new war, a new revolution—something like a flood or an earthquake—submerges and shakes the world once more? Does my interpretation of history imply the bankruptcy of statesmanship?

It means rather, if you understand me well, a shifting of responsibility for the evils under which mankind labours, from the statesmen to us, the common people, ourselves. The wisdom or folly of our statesmen is merely the reflection of our own wisdom or folly; and, if you agree with me—as I believe you do—that justice in political affairs should be bought with a smaller waste of property and human lives than is involved in a revolution, a war, or a revolutionary war, you must realize that that result will only be secured after there has been a change in our minds.

Let us substitute a spirit of compromise for a spirit of fanaticism. England, in these matters, does indeed show us the road to peace. For more than two centuries England has had no revolution; it looks as if she were, so far as it is possible to pass such sweeping judgements upon human affairs, safe for ever from the peril of revolution. Modern English history thus proves that it is possible to extirpate class and party fanaticism. Why not make an attempt to use British methods to solve the problem of war as well as of revolution? The institution of the League of Nations is such an attempt. In Geneva, representatives of all nations are invited to meet, and try to solve in a spirit of compromise problems that until now have been solved only by war; and, if they fail, to submit to the arbitration, counsel, or command of the Parliament of Man.

But compromise is not enough. National fanaticism is something far more formidable than class fanaticism. England has eliminated the one, but not the other. She may have been, during two centuries, a nation without a revolution; it can hardly be said that she has not been a war-like nation. Even during the last quarter of a century, when mankind has seemed more anxious than ever before to find some way out of war through arbitration and compromise, has any government, that of England included, subscribed to any peace pact, even to the Covenant of the League of Nations, without making, explicitly or implicitly, some reservation? I stumbled, only the other day, upon a debate which took place in the House of Commons a few months before the war, the protagonists being the well-known Irish free lance, Tim Healy, and Lord Hugh Cecil. "What is nationality?" interrupted Lord Hugh Cecil. "I will tell the noble lord," answered Tim Healy, "what nationality is. Nationality is a thing which man is ready to die for." Aye, and to kill for also, and there's the rub. But the fact remains, that man is not wholly made up of common sense and self-interest: such is his nature that he does not think life worth living if there is not something for which he is ready to lose his life. Now I see that millions have been ready, during the great world crisis, to give their lives for their respective countries. How many millions, hundreds of thousands, thousands, hundreds—would even a hundred be ready to die for the League of Nations? Well, this is a serious matter. So long as we have not evolved a fanaticism of humanity, strong enough to counterbalance, or absorb, the fanaticisms of nationality, let us not visit our sins upon our statesmen. Let us rather find reasons for excusing them, if they occasionally feel compelled to submit to the pressure of our disinterested and fanatical emotions.

SOCIALISM AND THE PROBLEM OF DEMOCRATIC PARLIAMENTARIANISM[1]

Will you allow me to preface this address with a few words of explanation? It is about a couple of months since I was asked to give you an address, and the title suggested was "British Policy Since the War." I said yes as concerned giving the address, but I protested against the hugeness of the subject. To deal with the whole of British policy since the war in one hour was beyond my capabilities. So I suggested in my turn that I might limit myself either to foreign policy or to home policy. I thought first of making foreign policy my subject, but it so happened that round about Easter in Paris there was an Anglo-French conference of historians; the programme was put into my hand and I saw that all the lectures—four by Englishmen and two by Frenchmen—were devoted to foreign affairs. I felt this was a bad symptom. Foreign affairs, whatever you may say, generally means war. So I dropped my original idea and set to work on British internal policy. After all, the internal structure of society is well worth study—indeed more so than the external relations of nations.

My troubles did not end there. I, being a Frenchman,

1 [An address given at Chatham House, London, April 24, 1934. It was published in *International Affairs*, July 1934, pp. 490–502. Permission to reprint the address here was generously given by the Royal Institute of International Affairs. The brief transcript of the discussion following the lecture, printed in *International Affairs*, pp. 502–507, has been omitted here. The lecture, given in English, appeared in a French translation in the original edition of *L'ère des tyrannies*.]

249

was asked to give an address here on British policy. The custom at Chatham House, I thought, was to ask a Hungarian to speak on Hungarian affairs, a Japanese on Japanese affairs, a Frenchman on French affairs, and so on, but I am expected to expound to you English affairs. This is placing me in a rather difficult situation. I do not feel to-night like an expert addressing a body of laymen, but like a layman addressing a body of experts. My way out of the difficulty has been to choose a universal subject— a European problem—and to see, from a viewpoint that is not English, what shape this problem takes in England. What that universal problem is I shall explain, being an historian, not in logical or philosophical terms but through a series of historical facts.

In France, in the middle of the nineteenth century, we had what you would call a socialist revolution. After a few months we had Louis Napoleon. Italy went, after the World War came to an end, through something which again you might call a socialist revolution; the result was Mussolini. In Germany, the Socialists practically ruled the country for ten years; and the result was Hitler.

Let us take things another way. Let us suppose that at the end of the nineteenth century there had been a large Social Democratic party ruling Germany; do you think you would have had Bismarck's big Insurance Acts? Or suppose that in 1905, instead of a small Labour party exerting only some sort of moral pressure upon the old parties, you had had a large Labour party with something like a majority in the House of Commons, are you sure that you would have had the Budget of 1909 and the National Insurance Act of 1911? Suppose that in the United States there was a Labour party worth speaking of, do you think you would have had, for good or evil, the Roosevelt experiment? I doubt it.

What is the reason for the paralysis and inefficiency of socialist parties in the west? That is the problem which I put to myself and am going to try to clear up for you this

250

evening. If sometimes there is bitterness in my observations, it will not be the bitterness of hate but the bitterness of disappointed expectations.

Let us begin by taking the fortunes of the Labour Party in England since the war. I might tell the story in an optimistic tone; nothing easier. I would show how the war providentially worked in favour of the British Labour Party in two different ways. On one side all the anti-war groups and all those who after the war were discontented with its results flocked into the Labour Party. On the other side, the war itself had given a strange lesson in state socialism to all classes; the most conservative classes had put into the hands of the state, in order to keep things going and make them hum, an amazing number of functions which they would never have thought of before the war. Thus, as an effect of the war, two powerful streams flowed into the main Labour stream. Statistically I would point out to you that before the war there were less than forty members of the Labour Party in the House of Commons, and probably not over half a million Labour voters in the country. After the war, at the first election, there were two and a half million voters. Three years later there were more than four million voters. At the end of 1924 there were five and a half million and in 1929 Labour had more than eight million voters. Then comes the fall, but at the last general election more than six million Labour voters were still left. Is it not legitimate to infer that the future is with the cause of Labour and with British socialism?

But when I tell my students in Paris the story of the British Labour movement since the war, I tell them quite another story—a rather blank and depressing story from the point of view of Labour. In my eyes the story is one of a succession of violent attacks repelled by very successful counter-attacks—a succession of big defeats. Let me give you a summary of the story of the four big defeats of Labour since 1918.

The first great offensive of Labour after the war was a matter for the trade unions rather than for the political party. The Labour members of Parliament stared at the thing from outside and were not the leaders of it. The Triple Alliance of transport workers, coal-miners and railwaymen leagued themselves together to paralyse the whole economic life of the nation and to force the owning classes into submission. I remember those days vividly, having made a long stay in England at the time. Everybody expected before long to see a universal eight-hour day bill passed by Parliament and a minimum wage established for the whole nation. Everybody expected to see the nationalisation of the railways and mines, and not only nationalisation but also workers' control through the Whitley Councils both in nationalised industries and all through the industrial régime of England. What happened? The whole thing blew out, and after two years of abortive strife what was the result? A seven-hour's bill for the coal-miners, a large measure of amalgamation—not nationalisation—in the railways. That was all—practically nothing. The very able statesman who had out-manoeuvred the Labour Party and the trade union movement in England was Mr. Lloyd George, and the Labour Party have never forgiven him for it. The Conservatives might have been very grateful to him for that, but on other grounds they disliked him; in 1922 he disappeared from the scene, after having defeated the Labour Party.

Then comes what I call the second attack of Labour, this time on the political ground. You remember how at the elections at the end of 1923, the Conservative Party did not have a majority of votes in the House of Commons and the main opposition party was no longer the Liberals but Labour. Liberals and Conservatives and Unionists combined to put power into the hands of the Labour Party. Mr. Ramsay MacDonald accepted office and succeeded in a very short time in producing what was politically, intellectually, morally and socially a highly respectable cabinet. Then what happened? Well, the aim of both Liberals and Conservatives in putting Mr. Ramsay MacDonald into power was the very definite one of getting the French out of the Ruhr. As soon as that had been accomplished Conservatives and Liberals began to find that Mr. MacDonald was committing Great Britain to the League of Nations a little more than was necessary, and that he was working for a *rapprochement* with Soviet Russia, which was not exactly desirable. So they combined to overthrow him and he disappeared. This was the second defeat of the Labour Party. There have been worse defeats in the history of the Labour Party: it had, at all events, achieved one result, in proving that it had been, and might eventually become again, a party able to govern the nation. But it was a defeat all the same.

Then comes offensive No. 3, and this time a disastrous defeat, on trade union ground again, not political ground. The mining problem once more came to the front. You must realise that during 1922 and 1923 your collieries were enjoying happy times. There was, first, a big strike of anthracite miners in Pennsylvania; then there was the occupation of the Ruhr and the passive resistance of the German miners. Both events were favourable to the keeping up of the prices of British coal. But when the question of the Ruhr had been settled and the German miners began work again, competition increased; the price of coal fell, and the condition of the British collieries became critical. The coal-owners wanted longer hours of work in the mines and lower wages. The socialists demanded the resumption of royalties by the state, nationalisation of the mines, or at all events the reorganisation of the collieries of the country on a unitary plan. It looked as if the clash was coming in 1925. It was avoided for a time by the happy intervention of Mr. Stanley Baldwin, but after eight or nine months the General Strike began. The General Strike lasted little more than a week; the desperate stand of the miners, left to themselves, lasted a little under seven months. What the result was you all know. Not only did the miners obtain nothing of what they asked for, but they had to submit to reduced wages and to the abandonment of the Seven Hours Bill of 1919; and a year later was passed the Trade Union Bill, an extraordinarily reactionary measure. All sympathetic strikes were declared to be illegal; secondly, members of the civil service were forbidden to join unions affiliated to the Trades Union Congress; thirdly, picketing was defined in very harsh terms, harsher than had ever been the case since 1871; and fourthly, it was made more difficult for trade unions to get subscriptions for political funds. This was a serious defeat which has never been retrieved.

Then we come to the fourth offensive, an apparent triumph for the Labour Party. It happened in 1929, the election which gave to the socialists not quite an absolute majority, but something very near it. Then came the world economic crisis, which, superadding itself to that state of chronic depression which Great Britain had been suffering under for years, made things really intolerable. You began to be afraid of seeing the number of unemployed workmen reach the second million; you very soon came to have far more than that number to protect against starvation. Now, the socialists had their explanation of the crisis—at first sight a very plausible one. These crises are crises of over-production, unavoidable in a system based upon wages. With a small minority of profit-makers and a large majority of wage-earners, where is the product of industry to go? If it does not go to foreign markets not yet industrialised, it cannot be absorbed, since the poor are too poor to re-buy with their wages all the products of their industry; otherwise there would be nothing left as profit to the capitalist. Therefore, so runs the argument, the thing to do is to substitute state ownership of capital and start a society made for use and not for profit. But here, in my eyes, lies the tragedy: before the general election it looked as if the leaders of the Labour Party found

it convenient to ignore the problem of unemployment.
They would probably have ignored it if Mr. Lloyd George,
head of the Liberal Party, had not compelled them, in
starting his own programme, to face what should have
been, from a socialist point of view, the main issue at the
General Election. Mr. Ramsay MacDonald appointed a
small committee to study the problem, consisting of
three members—Mr. Thomas (as chairman), Mr. Lansbury
and Sir Oswald Mosley. The latter insisted on something
being done on socialist lines, the only result being that he
made himself very unpopular with his party. You know
what happened afterwards; he left the party in disgust
and became the head of what he calls nowadays the British Fascist Party, while Mr. Ramsay MacDonald, Mr.
Thomas, and Mr. Snowden (now Lord Snowden) vanished into the Conservative Party. Is it not a queer irony
that the party which was supposed to hold the solution
of the problem found themselves helpless and in despair
at the very idea of being asked to solve it? Of course I
know they had their excuse: they could do nothing because
they had not a clear majority, but were they not at bottom
glad not to have it, because they were afraid of the responsibilities of power? I tell you frankly that I shudder
at the thought of the Labour Party ever having a real
majority, not for the sake of capitalism, but for the sake
of socialism.

Such is the difficulty, on which perhaps I have dwelt
too long. I will now try to explain to you my solution of
the problem, dividing my explanation into three parts.

My first explanation is that I think there is a disparity
between the wishes of those who vote for Labour candidates at a general election, and the complicated programme which is the socialist programme. I am not thinking only of those who on sentimental and perfectly respectable grounds went over to Labour, because they were not
socialists but pacifists. I remember a book about this par-

ticular group among the Labour Party, the title of which was *The Mugwumps and the Labour Party;* I confess that I do not know the meaning of the word "mugwumps"; certainly it sounds well and the book amused me. I am thinking of the average workman who normally votes for the Labour Party in Parliament. What is he craving for when he votes Labour? He asks for higher wages, shorter hours and better conditions of work. When the socialist party explains in abstract and, to him, almost unintelligible terms that he cannot have them except through nationalisation of the means of production, distribution and exchange, he does not trouble himself to understand the meaning of these abstract terms at all. He is content to get something of what he wants, through a first form of socialism, which I should call fiscalism rather than socialism, the pre-war socialism of men like Mr. Lloyd George, Mr. Winston Churchill, and even Mr. Philip Snowden. The system consists in allowing the profit-making system to go on, but to take money from the pocket of the profit owners and put it into the pocket of the workers: it was Mr. Snowden's saying in those days that a good budget is one that made the rich less rich and the poor less poor. And the system worked well so long as times were as prosperous as they were just before the war. A portion of the profits went in an indirect form into the pockets of the workmen in old age pensions, insurance against this or that risk to the life of the workman, and so on. But at the same time profits were increasing and it is difficult to assert statistically whether, though the poor became less poor, the rich were really less rich. I very much doubt if even the poor were less poor. In those days there was already a large increase in prices, and while money wages were rising, real wages were decreasing, and it is difficult to say whether the secondary advantages of insurance and pensions made a sufficient compensation for the fall in real wages. Fiscalism does what it can to make the profit-owner's life difficult, but it does nothing to change the profit-making system, while eventually making it impossible to work that system. You must go on, if you really are a socialist, to more socialism in the proper meaning of the word.

The first idea of the socialist malcontents was syndicalism—some in the more extreme form of French syndicalism, some in the new British form of Guild Socialism—according to which trade unions were to capture within each industry an increasingly larger part of the control and to make the workers, through their leaders, masters of the shop. But the whole of this system has been forgotten, even by the very founder of the movement, Mr. G. D. H. Cole, who never mentions it nowadays. Why did the system fail? I think the workmen's psychology accounts for the failure. They do not wish to have the responsibility of bossing the trade. They want better conditions of life, higher wages, shorter hours, but they do not want the responsibility of leadership; they leave that gladly to the captains of industry.

So you fall back upon state socialism, the bureaucratic state which Mr. and Mrs. Webb (Lord and Lady Passfield) call government by experts, eventually taking control of all the capital of the country in the name of the community. But I am sorry to say that I do not see that very much has been done by the Labour Party in that direction, perhaps because the mass of the workmen do not care very much about it, so long as, even under a capitalistic system, they get shorter hours and higher wages. Something has been done towards the reorganisation of the mines, but the work has been done not by Labour, but by Conservative governments. I even think it is a fact that, when the Coal Mines Bill was voted by Parliament while the Labour Cabinet was in power, the Cabinet had quite forgotten to introduce a reorganisation clause into the Bill: the Liberals compelled them to put it in and make it more "socialistic" than the Labour Party had intended.

257

When I say that state socialism does not appeal to the immediate feeling of the Labour electorate, I am perhaps overdoing things; and this brings me to the second part of my observations. I admit that it is possible that a big system of public works, started by the government, controlled by the government, the whole thing being run by government officials, may appeal to the multitude. Think of Stalin in Russia and his Five-Year Plan. Think of Mussolini in Italy and Hitler in Germany. But the thing must come from above. And there, again, the bother in Great Britain and in the whole of the west is that the leaders of the socialist party have not the imagination needed for the starting of such plans. Who are the leaders of the Labour Party in England? Not intellectuals, but trade unionists—a very sympathetic body of men, hard-working, rather timid, very conservative, whose training before they came into Parliament was that of negotiators on peaceful terms with the captains of industry, to extract from them better conditions of work for their clientele. They never had an idea that the secretary of the Iron and Steel Workers Union, or of this or that industry, would be set in the shoes of the captains of industry. Their idea was merely that of a limited monarchy, to control and limit the captains of industry and to get good conditions for those whose representatives they were. They are born parliamentarians. Now, if you go to the root of the idea of Parliament, the system is not one which wants to make the state strong, but one which wants to keep it weak for the sake of liberty. That is the tragedy. The Labour leaders are men whose doctrine requires them to make the state stronger, and whose good British instinct is to make the state as weak as possible.

I was mentioning the tragedy of the Mosley incident. I come to the more recent and equally tragic incident of Sir Stafford Cripps. You may realise that the socialists, not only in Great Britain but all through Europe, have slightly shifted the grounds of their denouncement of capital. In the time of Karl Marx it was industrial capital, the capital in the hands of the industrialists, that was denounced; financial profit was forgotten, since it was weak as compared with the profit extracted in the factories. But as things went on, the captains of industry became less powerful and little by little financial capital grew stronger. The goal of socialist parties all through Europe now is to get hold, not primarily of industrial capital but of the deposits in the big banks. The first thing, therefore, for a socialist government coming into power in this country is to nationalise not only the Bank of England but also the Big Five. Sir Stafford Cripps explained this plan. He explained, moreover, that just as it had only been possible for a Tory government two years ago to put things right for the capitalists by getting emergency powers, in the same way a Socialist ministry in power, on the hypothesis of a Labour majority socialistically minded—of course a big hypothesis—should ask for emergency powers. He observed that the case for the Socialist government would be more difficult than that of the Tory government because the latter was sure to have the immediate consent of the House of Lords to the emergency powers, whereas it would be otherwise with a Labour Ministry. So he proposed that the Socialist government should immediately ask for emergency powers and, this by hypothesis being rejected by the House of Lords, should proceed to do something on the plan that was adopted in 1910 and 1911 to force the Budget and the Parliament Bill through both Houses. There is nothing extremely revolutionary in this point of view. It is slightly dictatorial, but he asked for nothing that, considered as a matter of procedure, was exactly new. However, it was enough to rouse the whole Labour world to anger. Sir Stafford Cripps was denounced as a traitor to English liberties, first by the Trades Union Congress, then by a Labour Party Congress, and, lastly, the Labour Party thought it necessary to have a special conference in January to say the same things once more and to insist that when in power they should confine themselves to the use of strictly constitutional methods.

You may say that the programme itself is dangerous and that you do not care to see the Bank of England and the Big Five nationalised. But this is not my point. The fact is that this has been at the head of the program of the Labour Party. When, therefore, on the one hand they say that they want something, and on the other hand they do not want the means to obtain it, it is legitimate for one to ask what is at the bottom of their minds. I am afraid that rather than socialistic in spirit they are whiggish, eager to protect the individual against the state, not to make the state strong against the capitalists.

I would now go one step further, this making the third and final part of my observations, and ask you whether there is not an inner contradiction running through the whole doctrine of modern socialism. Socialists believe in two extremely different things, perhaps contradictory; on the one hand, liberty, and on the other, organisation. Between them they fall to the ground.

I know that I am addressing an English audience and that no people more than the English are able to understand what Hegelian philosophers call the identity of contradictories. But even for Englishmen I am afraid that logic forces itself in at this point. You have to face what is at the same time a logical and an historical difficulty.

The ideal of English liberty in the eighteenth century was the idea of a Parliament strictly controlling the aristocracy and the monarchy, the paradoxical idea that the basis of society was not to obey those who governed but to disobey them, control them, and make things difficult for them. Then came the political economists, Adam Smith, Ricardo, and their propagandists, Cobden and Bright, who added something to the definition of English liberalism in making the state practically evanescent— through the bold idea of reducing the functions of the state to as little as possible, aiming at what Huxley called "administrative nihilism"—giving the state nothing to do but to abdicate and simply allowing individuals freely to

interchange the products of their respective labour. I think
you will agree that it was in the 'forties and 'fifties of the
nineteenth century that this new idea of English liberalism
reached its acme and England was admired all through
Europe as the center of Western civilisation. Even our
French tyrant, Napoleon III, fell a victim to the propaganda of the English free traders. Then began the rise of
Bismarck and, little by little, as the German Reich impressed the world with its organisation, Bismarckian methods gained the better of the English ideal of liberty and
the Hegelian idea of the state gained the better of the idea
of the evanescent state.

The problem which the socialists find so difficult to
solve is how to reconcile both these ideas. Take free trade.
Well, in a kind of sentimental way, in Great Britain and
all through the continent, socialists like to say vaguely that
they are free traders, possibly to some extent because,
protectionism being agrarian, free trade in industrial states
means cheap bread for the workers, but also because sen-
timentally they are internationalists and free trade means
internationalism. In the last election it might still be said
that the socialists, in some vague way, were fighting for
free trade, but when, not through their votes in the House
of Commons but by administrative orders, in a very ruthless way, you have become a very protectionist country,
have there been any protests from the Labour Party? And
if the Labour Party comes into power, will it not take protection for granted? In fact, why should it not? Once you
admit that you want the state to fix wages and limit profits,
it is difficult not to admit that the state should fix prices
through protection as well as through any other kind of
state action.

But the state you are appealing to is—you have to face
the fact—the traditional national state with its naval and
military apparatus. It is queer in England to observe how
the free trade spirit, with its pacifist implications, has survived the introduction of protection. But you have to rec-

ognise that you have become a protectionist nation, and having become protectionist, you have become nationalist at the same time. I know several socialist intellectuals who profess to be at the same time radical protectionists and radical pacifists. I do not understand how you can be both at the same time. Sir Oswald Mosley the other day in his Albert Hall speech declared that when all nations in Europe have become fascist in spirit and are all self-contained, then peace will be secure. I confess that I do not follow the sequence of his argument. As soon as you have begun to accept protectionism, you are bound to accept something like nationalism, and can you have nationalism without something like militarism? I was struck last winter in reading a speech made at a public meeting by Sir Stafford Cripps in which he declared that he was not "an out-and-out pacifist." I know that just now he is delivering highly pacifist speeches in Canada, but I cannot forget how struck I was by this former declaration of his. I am making a bold, perhaps an absurd, forecast. But who knows? Sir Stafford Cripps's father, after being a Conservative, went over to Labour because he was a pacifist. Who knows whether Sir Stafford Cripps himself will not find himself going over to patriotism and perhaps something like militarism because he is a socialist?

When I was a young man Herbert Spencer had just been writing his book entitled *Man Versus State*. His prophecy was that the world was evolving towards what he called new toryism—protective, socialistic and militaristic. The book is supposed to be old-fashioned; who knows whether the prophecy is not going to be true? You do not call the thing "new toryism"; you call it "the new despotism."

I know that everything I have just been saying is too logical, too clear-cut for the British climate and atmosphere, happily for those who live in it. I know that, though you think you are sticking to parliamentarianism, you are really a country with a strengthened executive.

The process began with the closure; then the closure became more refined; you had the "guillotine," you had the "kangaroo" system, and so on. Then came the war; more dictatorial methods came into use; and you have emergency powers and government by orders-in-council. When you come from France, where parliamentarianism works badly, you feel that in England the machine has been altered so as to work with clocklike perfection and speed. I know that you have the art of sticking to the form, and more than the form, of the old institutions while starting them in new directions. While becoming an extremely democratic country, you have kept the form, and more than the form, of an hereditary aristocracy and an hereditary monarchy. It may be that even if your Constitution becomes more dictatorial you will preserve the form, and something more than the form, of the parliamentary system.

Never mind: the problem remains, a difficult and perplexing one. Returning to England after an interval of a few months, I find that I have to tackle it. Here you have a government which, you may say, has done well. You have a balanced budget, increasing exports, a decline in unemployment; and yet why do I feel everywhere a queer sense of vague dissatisfaction? Why? I admit that the elder statesmen, Mr. Stanley Baldwin and Mr. Ramsay MacDonald on the Conservative side, and Mr. Henderson and Mr. Lansbury on the side of the revolutionaries, are quite satisfied with the present state of affairs. But if you take the younger men, those who are the children of the war, that war which was to make the world safe for democracy but which has apparently taught them other lessons, the attitude is different. Look to the left, you find Sir Stafford Cripps; look to the right, you find Lord Eustace Percy; look—well, not exactly to the center but to a place which is neither the right nor the left nor the center, and you find Sir Oswald Mosley; however differently they think, they all have something in common.

When I was a boy at school in the 'eighties of the nine-teenth century, there was a thing, very much in fashion, which was called "composite photographs." You put the members of one family successively before the same photographic apparatus; a slight exposure was taken, not enough to give more than a dim photograph of each member, but if all the members of the family had some features in common, those features came out strongly, so that you had a "composite photograph" of the whole family, not of any one member. Well, if you took a composite photograph of Lord Eustace Percy, Sir Oswald Mosley and Sir Stafford Cripps, I think you would find this common feature: you would find them all agreeing to say: "We are living in an economic chaos and we cannot get out of it except under some kind of dictatorial leadership." Shall I say that this is a purely superficial phenomenon, a poor imitation of what is going on on the continent, an aftermath of continental phenomena, not to be taken seriously into account? Perhaps, but perhaps also it is due to deeper causes, the same in Great Britain as on the continent, the fact that socialism has risen, but, for the reasons which I have tried to define, has risen as a paralytic and inert party awakening expectations which it is unable to satisfy. That is my problem and my suggestion. I feel that I may have been indiscreet and impudent. I apologise in advance. You asked me to deal with a British subject and I have made this speech to order. I understand that after I have spoken there will be what you call a debate. I decline to call it a debate. I expect you, whom I consider as experts on this British aspect of the problem, to explain to me, who am a layman, what you think of my diagnosis. I am quite ready to hear you qualify my assertions and rectify them, tearing me to pieces if you choose. I have talked long enough. I am glad to resume my normal position in England, that of somebody who comes to learn and not to teach.

THE ERA OF TYRANNIES[1]

Since its beginnings, in the early years of the nineteenth century, socialism has suffered from an internal contradiction. On the one hand, its partisans often present it as the outcome and fulfillment of the Revolution of 1789, a revolution of liberty, a liberation from the last remaining subjection after all the others have been destroyed: the subjection of labor by capital. But, on the other hand, it is also a reaction against individualism and liberalism; it proposes a new compulsory organization in place of the outworn institutions destroyed by the Revolution:

(a) In its original form, socialism was neither liberal nor democratic, but organizational and hierarchical. Witness Saint-Simonian socialism in particular;

(b) By reaction against socialist anarchy and at the same time by the organizational principle inherent in socialism, the socialist revolution of 1848 ended in the caesarism of 1851 (strongly influenced by Saint-Simonianism);

(c) At the source of German democratic socialism stands Karl Marx, an internationalist, the founder of the International, who looked forward to a final stage of the

[1] [Élie Halévy submitted this communication for discussion by the Société Française de Philosophie on November 28, 1936. The communication, the discussion, and the second appendix, which contains further comments and answers, were first published in the *Bulletin de la Société Française de Philosophie*, 1936, pp. 181–253. The communication and the discussion from the floor, without the appendix, were translated as "The Age of Tyrannies" by May Wallas and published in *Economica*, n.s., VIII, 77–93 (February 1941). They have been retranslated for this volume to maintain stylistic consistency.]

265

human race that would be anarchy as well as communism. But there was also Ferdinand Lassalle, a nationalist as well as a socialist, and the prime mover of the "social monarchy" of Bismarck.

These remarks seem to us to be strikingly confirmed by the general evolution of European society since the beginning of the Great War and the opening of what we propose to call the era of tyrannies.[2]

* * *

The era of tyrannies dates from August 1914, that is, from the time when the belligerent nations turned to a system which can be defined as follows:

(a) In the economic sphere, greatly extended state control of all means of production, distribution, and exchange; —and, at the same time, an appeal by the governments to the leaders of workers' organizations to help them in implementing this state control—hence syndicalism and corporatism along with *étatisme*.

(b) In the intellectual sphere, state control of thought, in two forms: one negative, through the suppression of all expressions of opinion deemed unfavorable to the national interest; the other positive, through what we shall call the organization of enthusiasm.

* * *

Postwar socialism derives much more from this wartime regime than from Marxist doctrine. The paradox of postwar socialism is that its recruits often come to it out of hatred and disgust for war, while it offers them a program

[2] I shall say only a little about the reasons that led me to prefer the word "tyranny" to the word "dictatorship." The Latin word "dictatorship" implies a provisional regime, leaving intact in the long run a regime of liberty which, in spite of everything, is considered normal; while the Greek word "tyranny" implies a normal form of government, which the scientific observer of societies must range alongside other normal forms—monarchy, aristocracy, and democracy. One could not, therefore, speak of "an era of dictatorships." It seemed to me, moreover—admit-

consisting in the prolongation of the wartime regime in time of peace. At the outset, Russian Bolshevism displayed these characteristics. Arising out of a revolt against the war, the Russian Revolution was consolidated and organized in the form of "wartime communism" during the two years of fighting with the Allied armies between the Peace of Brest-Litovsk and the final victory of the Communist forces in 1920. Here a new characteristic is added to those we have mentioned above. Because of the anarchical collapse, because of the complete disappearance of the state, a group of armed men, moved by a common faith, decreed that they were the state: in this form Bolshevism is, literally, a "fascism."

* * *

In central Europe, as it happened, "Fascism," a direct imitation of Russian methods of government, was the reaction against socialist "anarchy." But it was led to set up a sort of counter-socialism, under the name of "corporatism," which I am inclined to take more seriously than it is generally taken in anti-fascist circles; it consists in an expanding state control of the economy, with the collaboration of certain working-class elements. The internal contradiction from which European society suffers can, then, be defined as follows. The Conservative parties call for the almost unlimited strengthening of the state with the almost unlimited reduction of its economic functions. The socialist parties call for the unlimited extension of the functions of the state and, at the same time, for the unlimited weakening of its authority. The compromise solution is "national socialism."

What chances are there that these new regimes will

---

tedly without knowing enough of the history of the ancient world, but I am happy to have received the unreserved support of Marcel Mauss on this point—that the complementary analyses of Plato and Aristotle on the way in which the transition from democracy to tyranny took place in the ancient world have a deep relevance to events of today.

spread further? What possibilities are there of internal decomposition? But, above all, have we given a valid explanation of their origin by pointing to the contradictory nature of socialism itself? These are the questions we submit for consideration by the Société de Philosophie.

Report of the Discussion

M. Léon Brunschvicg:[3] Gentlemen, today's meeting is a continuation of a discussion that Xavier Léon organized on March 29, 1902. The subject was historical materialism; the principal commentator was Élie Halévy; the speaker was Georges Sorel. Since then many things have happened that have been influenced by the author of *Les illusions du progrès* (*The Illusions of Progress*) and *Reflexions sur la violence* (*Reflections on Violence*).[4]

M. Élie Halévy: If you like, we are resuming the discussion of 1902. But the subject I have submitted for your consideration is very different from that submitted in 1902 for consideration by the Société de Philosophie. Now as then, much will be said of Marx and Marxism, but it will be from a very different angle. Then, as Brunschvicg said, it was a question of historical materialism, that is, of a certain philosophic interpretation of history not necessarily tied to the socialist interpretation of history. Today it is a question of socialism in and of itself (and not exclusively

[3] [Léon Brunschvicg, 1869–1944. Professor of the history of modern philosophy at the Sorbonne from 1909. *Spinoza et ses contemporains* (1894); *L'idéalisme contemporain* (1905); *Nature et liberté, la génie de Pascal* (1925). As president of the Société Française de Philosophie, he presided at the meeting.]
[4] [Xavier Léon, 1868–1935. Co-founder, with Élie Halévy, of the *Revue de métaphysique et morale*. Georges Sorel, 1847–1922, was the major philosopher of syndicalism, the early twentieth-century mutation of Marxism which so deeply affected trade-union organization.] Élie Halévy's remarks, alluded to by M. Brunschvicg, are reprinted in Appendix I.

of Marxist socialism), of its destiny, and of the kind of influence it will have on the future of the human race.

I intend to be brief, to allow as much time as possible for discussion; and, if Brunschvicg will allow me to usurp the functions of the chair, I shall be so bold as to ask you to follow my example, so that the discussion can develop to the fullest. I do not intend to repeat, still less to elaborate on, the printed text, which has been sent to all the members of the Société. In opening the discussion, I shall limit myself to making some personal observations. Not that I attach any special importance to my personality, but to encourage other speakers to follow my example. In comparing our experiences, perhaps some light will be thrown on the great problem that cannot fail to arouse or at least to trouble the consciences of everyone here.

Let me remind you that, at the time of the meeting in March 1902, to which Brunschvicg has referred, I had just begun several months before to lecture on the history of nineteenth-century European socialism at the École des Sciences Politiques. Once every two years, since November 1901, I have given that course. I have a certain competence, then, in speaking about socialism, not as a partisan but as an historian. Max Lazard,[5] who I see is here and who is no longer a very young man, took that course a good thirty years ago. Now, when I agreed to undertake those lectures, what was my intellectual attitude towards socialism? As nearly as I can remember, it was this:

I was not a socialist. I was a "liberal" in the sense that I was an anticlerical, a democrat, and a republican—to use a word then pregnant with meaning, I was a "dreyfusard." But I was not a socialist. Why? It was, I am sure, for a reason of which I have no right to be proud. I was born five or six years too soon. I was a student at the

---

[5] [Max Lazard, 1875–1953. Economist and president of the Association Française pour la Lutte contre le Chômage et l'Organisation du Marché du Travail, and the author of many works on unemployment.]

École Normale from the autumn of 1889, just after the fall of Boulanger, to the summer of 1892, just before the Panama crisis began. They were years of dead calm. During those three years, I did not know a single socialist at the École Normale. If I had been five years younger, if I had been at the École Normale between, say, 1895 and 1900, if I had been the classmate of Mathiez, Péguy, and Albert Thomas,[6] it is very likely that at twenty-one I should have been a socialist, free to develop in a direction it is impossible for me to imagine. When we apply the methods of historical research to ourselves and come to discover the reasons for our beliefs, we often find that they are accidental, that they spring from circumstances beyond our control. Perhaps there is a lesson of tolerance in that. If we have learned it well, we have to ask if it is worth while to massacre each other for beliefs whose origins are so flimsy.

I was not a socialist, but I already knew quite a lot about socialism, as much from what I could already observe in France as from what I learned through my experience of things English. At that time I had already made long and frequent visits to England over a period of three or four years; I was already drawn to those two outstanding personalities, Mr. and Mrs. Sidney Webb. I have remained their friend; and today I feel that we are contemporaries; but then the ten years that separated us meant a great deal. I was a young man of twenty-five or thirty talking with two older people of thirty-five or forty, who had already written books that are classics today. So I listened to them with respect, and they explained to me the principles of their socialism, which was essen-

6 [Albert Mathiez, 1874–1932, historian of the French Revolution. Charles Péguy, 1873–1914, poet and writer who was both Catholic and socialist. Albert Thomas, 1878–1932, leader in the Socialist Party, Minister of Munitions during the war, and after the war director of the International Labor Organization.]

tially anti-liberal. They were not fighting Conservatism or Toryism, about which they were quite indulgent, but Gladstonian Liberalism. It was the time of the Boer War; and both the advanced Liberals and the Labourites, who were beginning to organize themselves into a party, defended the Boers against British imperialism, out of generosity and a love of liberty and humanity. But the two Webbs and their friend Bernard Shaw were a group apart. They were ostentatiously imperialistic. The independence of small nations could well mean something to believers in liberal individualism, but not to them, precisely because they were collectivists. I can still hear Sidney Webb explaining to me that the future lay with the great administrative nations, where governing was done by the bureaucrats and order was maintained by the policemen.

It may be their fault if I have always been impressed by what was illiberal in the socialist idea. So there is a second accident in the history of the formation of my mind: remember that if you want to understand how my prejudices came to be what they are. In my course at the École des Sciences Politiques, I came to emphasize certain conservative features of nineteenth-century European socialism—authoritarian, monarchical, or Christian socialism; Napoleon III, under the influence of the Saint-Simonians; Bismarck, under the influence of Lassalle. I need not go on: I refer you to the text before you.

About 1910, I admit, I was disturbed by the fact that the Webbs seemed to have been mistaken about England and that their mistake had misled me. A powerful liberal reaction had taken place, which they had not foreseen at all; the new liberalism was strongly tinged with socialism; and the Lloyd George experiment, as they say today, showed that there could be such a thing as a socialistic radicalism, endowed with very great vitality—in short, that reconciliation between socialism and liberalism which the Webbs considered impossible became a reality.

Then the war came. It ushered in what I call the era of

tyrannies. The Webbs and Bernard Shaw have not forsaken their youthful convictions; they find them confirmed by events and divide their sympathies between Russian Bolshevism and Italian Fascism.

I wanted to say this, not to justify my position, but to explain it. To make you understand, I have proceeded, not as a doctrinaire, but as an historian. It is also as an historian—a philosophical historian, if you will, keeping as far as possible above the level of politics (and I hope that you will do the same)—that I have tried to define this "era of tyrannies." After having read the text of my communication, do you agree, first, that the historical phenomenon with which it deals is a reality? And, second, do you think that my explanation of this phenomenon is plausible? The floor is yours.

M. Max Lazard criticized the speaker for approaching concrete social facts "not directly, but as they are reflected in certain doctrines about them." Élie Halévy's reply was as follows:

Max Lazard has made some very interesting observations bearing on the question of method, and it is hard for me to improvise an answer to them. Still, here is what came immediately to mind as I listened to him.

In the first place, I am not inclined to deny, as categorically as he seems to do, the influence of ideas on history and, more directly, on the men who have played important parts in history.

Two examples, which I have given in my communication, and which Max Lazard has referred to, will allow me, I think, to make my meaning clear.

First, let us take the case of Napoleon III. Morny was the real perpetrator of the *coup d'état*, and I grant that, as he saw it, it was inspired only by the political necessities of the time, without any concern with ideas. But he brought about the *coup d'état* for the benefit of the prince-president, who in 1838 had published a pamphlet called *Idées napoléoniennes* (*Napoleonic Ideas*), which was Saint-Simonian in inspiration. The influence of Bazard and Enfantin on his mind is an historical fact; it is an historical fact that he surrounded himself with councillors who had been Saint-Simonians. He was always obsessed by the notion that he was a Saint-Simonian on the throne. The case of Bismarck is both similar and different.

We cannot overemphasize the importance of the part played alongside him, from 1862 to 1864, by a man whose role in the history of European socialism is highly ambiguous. I mean Ferdinand Lassalle. At all the prewar social-democratic congresses, two busts presided over the meetings: one of Marx and one of Lassalle. Rightly so. While Marx gave the party its doctrine, Lassalle was the first man in Germany and the first man in Europe to succeed in organizing a party of socialist action. True; but, at the same time, if by a mishap Lassalle had not been born a Jew, he would rightly be acclaimed as a forerunner in the vast halls where National Socialist enthusiasm is stirred up these days.

In those critical years immediately following Bismarck's accession to power, when Lassalle's workers' *Verein* was being organized, what strange language he was speaking! His bitter attacks were not directed against the Bismarckians, but the progressives who were fighting Bismarck. When a burgomaster tried to stop him from speaking, he appealed to the police for help; and when he was prosecuted for his opinions, he made an eloquent appeal to the judges, claiming to be their ally in defending the state against modern barbarism, that is, against liberalism. We know that he was in active correspondence with Bismarck, and that he had secret conversations with him. When Bismarck founded the North German Confederation in 1866 on the basis of universal suffrage, he was directly following advice given to him by Lassalle. When, later, after 1878, he practiced a sort of "state so-

cialism," "Christian socialism," or "monarchical socialism,"
I am certain that the memory of the lessons Lassalle had
taught him were very much in his mind. Not that there
was anything doctrinaire about him; he was a purely opportunist statesman, with no concern but to create,
strengthen, and maintain the unity of the Empire. He was
ready to use every party and every doctrine in turn; one
of the doctrines he used was Lassalle's.

These are two cases in which, obviously, ideas are
tied up with events, and in which the historian would
make a serious mistake if he ignored the history of ideas.
Having said that in a general way, I should not be inclined to disagree with anything Max Lazard has said. Far
be it from me to reduce history to the history of ideas. Let
me explain myself once more by going back to personal
recollections. When Max Lazard was my student, many
years ago, I was new to teaching; probably the easiest
way for me to approach the history of socialism was
through the study of ideas; probably the lectures that
Max Lazard heard dealt exclusively with ideas. But some
thirty years later, Max Lazard's son was studying under
me: if he will look at his son's notes, he will see that, as
I have learned more, my course has become less and less
a course in the history of ideas and more and more a
course in straight history. That is not to say that I regret
having gone at the history of socialism by way of the
history of ideas. As Max Lazard has very wisely put it,
ideas stylize and schematize events. Nothing I can think
of seems more useful for an understanding of events than
such schematization. When we see what success a doctrine like the Marxian doctrine has had, it is because it
expresses certain striking features in economic development better than anything else, because it answers certain deep needs of the working masses. How can we deny
its utility, insofar as it helps us to understand those striking features and those deep needs?

It is, I think, very easy to translate my ideological language into sociological language, without the slightest logical difficulty or the least modification of my thesis. Let us take the first paragraph of my communication and paraphrase it as follows: "Since its beginnings, the working-class movement has suffered from an internal contradiction. On the one hand, we can see it as a movement of liberation, as a rebellion against the factory system, against the subjection of labor by industrial capital. But, on the other hand, to protect themselves against this oppression, the rebellious workers are obliged to seek out a new compulsory organization, in place of the outworn institutions that revolutionary liberalism has destroyed." So Max Lazard is completely satisfied, and my thesis remains intact.

Besides, does not a major point in my communication —indeed, Max Lazard has admitted it—call attention to the important part played in the recent history of the civilized world by an historical event that has nothing to do with doctrines: I mean the Great War of 1914? On rereading what I have written, I regret that I have not sufficiently emphasized the link between the social consequences of this great event and the earlier evolution of socialism. To explain myself more clearly, allow me to join up the first two sections of my communication. Here is what I should say if I were rewriting it now.

In the economic sphere, I should say, the prewar socialists demanded state control of all means of production, distribution and exchange. In very large measure, this state control was brought about by the war, for reasons that the socialists had certainly not foreseen. If one goes back for a quarter century or so before the war, the socialist program—if you wish, the Guesdist program—called for nationalization pure and simple, the state control of the main industries, starting with the railways, as if that were enough to solve the social question. But in 1914 the syndicalist movement had already been in existence for a number of years; it distrusted the state too much to accept this solution. It called for the general syndicalization of industry without any intervention by the state, and the absorption of all bureaucracy by syndicalist organization —in other words, the radical elimination of the state. The English, however—moderate even in their utopias—worked out a mixed doctrine, looking towards a kind of compromise between the radical syndicalism of the French, Italians, and Spaniards, and a kind of *étatisme*. What were the legitimate functions of the democratic state? What were those of the syndicalist corporations? Such were the questions the Guild Socialists discussed among themselves. When the war had scarcely begun, and because of the war, we see (I am now citing my original text) an "appeal by the governments to the leaders of workers' organizations to help them in implementing this state control—hence syndicalism and corporatism along with *étatisme*." Once the war was over, in all the belligerent countries, we see large numbers of people—who, outside England, probably had never heard of Guild Socialism—working out schemes of "nationalized industry," which, profiting from the experience of wartime socialism, seemed in many ways to be applications of the program of the Guild Socialists.

I turn now to another point that Max Lazard raised at the end. It concerns the prospects for the survival of the tyrannical regimes of today. The last lines of my communication are all that remain of a whole paragraph I had devoted to this question. I eliminated the paragraph on the advice of our chairman, who gave me two different and contradictory reasons for doing so. The first was that I had to keep something in reserve to say in the discussion. The other was that, if the discussion got onto that subject, it could degenerate into a political debate. I gave in to this second reason. I am quite willing, however, to say a few words to answer Max Lazard's observations on this point, to say that I agree with him.

From the standpoint of those who love peace and liberty, I should be almost more pessimistic than he is. The idea of a European federation does not seem to have much life at present, and Max Lazard seems for a moment to have surrendered to a confused hope in an imperialism that, by taking in all of Europe, would bring peace, though it could not bring freedom. That seems to me completely chimerical today. I can think of only one tyranny that could provide this spirit of universality and on which Max Lazard could depend (does he depend on it?) to give Europe such a peace. But the tyrannies closer to us—the tyranny of Berlin and the tyranny of Rome—are narrowly nationalist. They can offer us nothing but war. If it comes, the situation of the democracies will be tragic. If they want to wage war effectively, can they remain parliamentary and liberal democracies? It is my view, which I shall not make you listen to again, that they cannot. When the war begins again, it will consolidate the "tyrannical" idea in Europe.

Speaking of the failure of 1848, M. Célestin Bouglé[7] *attributed it less than the speaker to socialist anarchy and the terror it inspired, pointing to the democratic socialism of Louis Blanc as the first effort to guarantee the progress of political and intellectual liberalism, though at the sacrifice of economic liberalism.*

M. Élie Halévy: We should need not an afternoon, or the end of an afternoon, but, as they say at Pontigny,[8] we should need ten days to give this subject the attention it deserves. But I am going to try to answer the various points raised by Bouglé as briefly as I can.

He criticizes me for using the words "reaction against

[7] [On Bouglé, see above, p. xxvii.]
[8] [At Pontigny, in a Cistercian abbey disused after the dissolution of the religious orders in 1901, Paul Desjardins, in the years following 1910, organized discussions to promote international intellectual co-operation.]

277

socialist anarchy" in describing the *coup d'état* of December [1851]. He is right; my wording has not, perhaps, done justice to what I wanted to say. I should have written "reaction against the fear of anarchy." But, psychologically, doesn't that come to the same thing?

It is a curious fact. Things developed in much the same way in Italy before the march on Rome. In 1920, the year of the occupation of the factories, there was anarchy. It was then that Giolitti armed Mussolini and his Fascists to serve as police, because the army could not be depended on. But when Mussolini seized power, and thanks in part to him, there had been no disorder for two years. What carried him forward was the memory of the fear felt in 1920 and people's persistent feeling that they had been saved from the inability of the parties of order to maintain that order by parliamentary methods.

This helps us to understand better what happened in 1851. At that time there was no more anarchy, except in parliament: in the Legislative Assembly, the reactionary majority could not agree on the form of government to oppose to the Mountain, which was both noisy and frightening to those who remembered 1848 and 1793. The masses threw themselves into the arms of a man who stood for order, without also standing for reaction, as the legitimists and Orleanists in the Assembly were accused of doing. We should not forget that, on the very day when he abrogated the Constitution of 1848, he re-established universal suffrage, which had been badly mutilated by the Assembly. Nor should we forget that when Guizot heard the news of the *coup d'état*, he burst out: "It is the triumph of socialism." The phrase is comic in a way; still it was an accurate enough expression of the feelings of the bourgeoisie faced with a regime not of their own making and pursuing ends other than theirs.

As for my definition of Bolshevism as a "fascism," I agree with what Bouglé has said. But on this point, I do not believe that my wording has failed to do justice to my thoughts. I wrote: "Because of the anarchical collapse . . . of the state, a group of armed men, moved by a common faith, decreed that they were the state: *in this form,* Bolshevism is, *literally,* a fascism." I say expressly that it is only a matter of the form of government. Bolshevism, with its dictatorship, or tyranny, of the Communist Party, was the originator here. But, although Italian Fascism is only an imitation, I think that the word "fascism" is better for describing the common characteristics of the two regimes. It is an old Italian word meaning groups, armed groups of partisans. In Italy after 1870, at the time of the First International, there were *fasci operai,* inspired by the anarchist ideals of Bakunin: they became established in Spain, where we see them in action today. Mussolini seized power by using other *fasci*—the *fasci di combattimento*—in the service of a different ideal.

As to the possibility of a democratic socialism—authoritarian in the economic sphere and liberal in the political and intellectual spheres—I should not want to deny that, theoretically, such a thing is possible. I am only afraid that in using Louis Blanc to support his thesis, Bouglé has found the best way to weaken it.

He must remember (he knows Proudhon better than I do) the violent, concerted attack made after 1848 by Proudhon (who called himself a socialist, but was he?) and Michelet (a republican without being a socialist) against Louis Blanc's socialism. They denounced Louis Blanc for glorifying the Terror, the Committee of Public Safety, and Robespierre, a disciple of Rousseau and an incorruptible, whom he opposed to those immoral republicans who, on the basis of Voltairean liberalism, were leading France to domination by the clergy and to caesarism. Did the event prove them wrong?

Can I ignore the fact that the origins of democracy are ambiguous, since they go back to the Jacobins, and the Jacobins ruled by dictatorship? The Marxist doctrine of the dictatorship of the proletariat comes, does it not, in a straight line from Babeuf, the last survivor of Robespierrism? Was not Karl Marx, in Paris before 1848, very definitely influenced by Blanqui, who revived the theory of Babeuf?

You object. I am reminded of the Marxist formula—really devised by Engels, not Marx—according to which the goal is to substitute the administration of things for the government of persons. That is a transformation of an old Saint-Simonian formula, according to which, when the industrial regime succeeds the military regime, there will no longer be government but only administration. Fair enough; but the doctrine of Karl Marx is also the doctrine of Lenin. I have before me a letter from M. Salzi,[9] in which he criticizes me for having spoken of Karl Marx as "looking forward to a stage of the human race that will be anarchy along with communism." "Nothing could be further from the truth," he writes, "the Marxist system demands a rigorous and total discipline. I see nothing in it that implies any anarchy whatsoever. Look at the Russians, who have applied it with a vengeance." And he sends me to André Gide.

Alas! There lies the tragedy. I am sure that nothing could be truer than my statement. Every socialist government coming to power is forced to use complicated scholastics to explain how it must act when, professing a doctrine of complete socialism, it takes over in a nonsocialist society. Here the Marxist formulas come in. By definition, every state is an instrument of oppression of one class by another. From the advent of capitalism down to the present, the state has been the instrument the bourgeoisie has used to oppress the proletariat. To prepare for and hasten the coming of a society without classes and so without government, we must go through an intermediary period in which the state will be the instrument used by the working class to oppress the bourgeoisie,

[9] [Pierre Salzi, 1889–   . From 1935 to 1947 he taught philosophy at the Lycée Janson-de-Sailly, Paris.]

until the bourgeoisie can be eliminated. Is it a mere suspension of legality? The phrase can have many meanings: Karl Marx certainly did not foresee anything so relentless as the Soviet system; and if it were only a question of full powers given to the government for six months, as they were given to Poincaré in finance, it would be a quite harmless suspension. But if the suspension must last for several decades—why not a century or two?—I cease being interested in the state of anarchy that they tell us will succeed it. What interests me is the present and the near future; beyond that lies what Jules Romains calls the ultra-future. Do not the Nazi fanatics too believe that their regime has an ultimate value, that it is the opening of a new era that will last forever?

Several members spoke, particularly M. Berthelot[10] and M. Maublanc, who objected to the accusation of tyranny made against Marxism and to the assimilation of Soviet dictatorship to the Fascist and Hitlerite dictatorships. Élie Halévy answered as follows:

I must now bring the discussion to a close. I am very sorry to do so, because I find myself in an impossible situation. To satisfy everyone, I should have to discuss the whole of Marxist doctrine in reply to Maublanc, and the whole history of the human race since Tamburlaine to answer René Berthelot. I should have to go outside Europe and say something about the New Deal; in fact, I am sorry that more has not been said about the experiments that Roosevelt has tried, experiments that in some ways resemble Italian or Fascist corporatism, without suppressing freedom.

10 [René Berthelot, 1872–1960, professor of philosophy at the University of Brussels. *Évolutionnisme et platonisme* (1907); *Un romantisme utilitaire* (1911–1922). He was Élie Halévy's cousin and had been with him at the École Normale.]

In answering Drouin,[11] should I bring up the question of predictions? In fact, just now, Max Lazard and I did not evade it. We were in complete disagreement, by the way, with René Berthelot: we saw our only encouragement to hope in a long period of peace, in which the dictatorships would grow less stringent because tyrannical governments cannot continually keep their populations on a war footing without going to war. But are these tyrannical regimes themselves conducive to the maintenance of peace? And if war begins again, and if the democracies are forced to adopt totalitarian methods to save themselves from destruction, will there not be a generalization of tyranny, a strengthening and spreading of this form of government?

I might add that some of you have thought you were criticizing me when the criticism bore only on some possibly imperfect form of expression. I am thinking now of Maublanc and his apology for Marxism. He criticizes me for having presented Marxism "as a liberation from the last remaining subjection, after all the others have been destroyed, the subjection of labor by capital." But when he says that that liberation is "the true liberation, without which all the others are only illusions," his assertion comes very close to mine. After this liberation is brought about, Marx assures us that we shall enter finally (and it is in that sense only that I have spoken of a "final stage" of the human race) into a classless society. In that classless society, the evolution of mankind will certainly continue (I grant that to Maublanc), but it will be according to forms (if Maublanc will grant this to me) that we cannot foresee, since it will no longer be possible to say, as has been true until now, that "the history of the human race is the history of the class struggle."

Rather than dwell on such disagreements, I am trying to find a fundamental point common to several of my

[11] [Marcel Drouin, 1870–1943. He pursued a literary career under the pseudonym of Michel Arnauld.]

critics that would usefully serve as the theme for my concluding remarks. I think I have found it. Is it not the question of whether the Russian tyranny and the Italian and German tyrannies ought to be seen as essentially identical phenomena or as essentially antithetical?

Far be it from me to deny that, in many respects which anyone can see, they are antithetical. I have been to Leningrad, and I know Fascist Italy. When one crosses the Russian frontier, one feels at once that one is entering another world; such an overturning of all values may be thought of, if one wants, as justifying an extreme tyranny. But there is nothing like that in Italy; and the traveler comes to ask if such a huge police apparatus is needed, if the only results are that the roads are better kept up and that the trains are more likely to run on time.

Nevertheless (and everyone seems to have conceded this point), the forms of the systems are identical. A country is governed by an armed sect, imposing itself in the presumed interest of the whole country, which can do so because it is moved by a common faith. But there is something more.

The Russian Communists invoke a system of belief that is valid for the whole human race, and that implies the elimination of nations as well as of classes. But, having seized power in one country only, and becoming more and more resigned to not bringing about the world revolution by propaganda and example, they are forced, by the necessities of their own existence, to set up a military barrier against the threat of foreign armies. By force of circumstances, they are thrown back on a kind of patriotism at once territorial and ideological; and their tyranny, for anyone who looks at it from the ideological point of view, ends up looking very like the German or Italian tyranny. At first, the state was said to be only temporary; it was to be endured because its only purpose was to prepare the way for the abolition of the state and to assure the greatest happiness of the greatest number. Little by little, they began to practice a heroic morality, the nobility of which I quite appreciate: the individual is asked to learn to suffer to do great things in the service of the state. This state of mind bears little resemblance to a hedonism relegated to the distant future. I can only call it warlike.

On the fascist side, in the current sense of the word, in Italy and in Germany, there is no question at all of eliminating classes. The very program of the parties in power is the defense of a society based on class distinctions. But I believe I am right in saying that in these two countries, there has grown up "a sort of counter-socialism, under the name of 'corporatism,' which I am inclined to take more seriously than it is generally taken in anti-fascist circles."

We are told that wages in these countries are very low, lower than in many democratic countries. I am inclined to admit the truth of that. But, in evaluating the total wages of the worker, should we not reckon with the income that he draws indirectly from all the benefits included in what is called *Dopolavoro*—free railway travel, rest homes, and many kinds of recreation? I know that all these benefits are motivated by an ulterior political purpose: the workers' leisure is to be kept occupied to distract them from the possible influence of revolutionary agitators—following my earlier formulation, it is a matter of directing and "organizing their enthusiasm." But in the end all that means a rise in wages, which costs the state money.

And once it costs the state money, I turn around and ask, "Where will the state find the money?" Taking up a formula that some ten years ago scandalized the conservative press, I answer: it can be found and taken only from those who have it. A heavy fiscal burden rests on the wealthy classes; I do not deny that big business benefits from these regimes. But it is not the old capitalism, the free capitalism of Manchester. The captains of industry still prefer such a regime to communism. They are still in charge. But they are no longer the masters, they are highly placed bureaucrats. And the large incomes they draw every year resemble salaries, not profits.

In short, on the one hand, a complete socialism is moving towards a kind of nationalism. On the other hand, an integral nationalism is moving towards a kind of socialism. That is all that I wanted to say.

APPENDIX I

Comment by Élie Halévy during a meeting devoted to discussion of the thesis of M. Georges Sorel, March 29, 1902[1]

M. Halévy proposes not so much to discuss or to refute the interpretation of historical materialism proposed by M. Sorel as to ask him for clarification on certain points. M. Sorel is not a teacher. Consequently it is easier for him to get off the beaten track and to strike out into new paths. But it also means that philosophical exposition is not to his taste. I should not dare to say that his Marxist interpretation is exactly false; I should say rather that it is confused. In clarifying it together, perhaps we can arrive at agreement without too much difficulty.

We are dealing with historical materialism. M. Sorel tells us that Marx and Engels never gave an account of this doctrine. Now, of course, Marx and Engels never devoted a whole work to setting out their materialist philosophy of history; more exactly still, they did not find a publisher for the work on that subject on which they had collaborated around 1845. However, the first chapter of the *Anti-Dühring* by Friedrich Engels and the preface to the *Critique of Political Economy* by Karl Marx are indeed summaries of the principle of this philosophy. We know the current definition of historical materialism, a definition that seems to me to conform to the texts of Marx and Engels: according to these two thinkers, the

[1] *Bulletin de la Société Française de Philosophie*, 1902. pp. 94–96.

evolution of forms of production and exchange is the necessary and sufficient condition of the juridical, political, moral, and religious evolution of mankind. M. Sorel proposes another definition: according to him, the Marxist philosophy of history is a doctrine establishing "the solidarity of theory and practice." To that *new* definition, I have two objections.

In the first place, the terms "solidarity" and "synthesis" are, I am afraid, a kind of treason to Marxist thought. They imply a reciprocity of action between the elements in question which is precisely what Marx, in the name of his historical materialism, thought inconceivable. According to Marx, the action of the "spiritual" on the "material," of the "theoretical" on the "practical" is an impossibility. Marx was originally a metaphysician; with his teacher and friend since the age of twenty, Bruno Bauer, the head of *Die Freien* (The Frees), he belonged to the far left of Hegelianism. For him, as for other post-Kantian philosophers, all metaphysical speculation rested on the fundamental opposition of the ideal and the real; when he first worked it out, his historical materialism consisted in an original definition of the two terms and of the relationship between them. The real is what Marx called "material productivity," economic man as a producer of wealth. But the thinking and reasoning man is powerless to create; he can only understand or reflect the results, once they are given, of his material activity. By definition, the ideal is the reflection (*Wiederschein, Das Kapital,* I, 46) of the real. At the outset, then, Marx thought that action of the ideal on the real was a metaphysical impossibility; the affirmation of that impossibility is the essence of historical materialism; the drawback of M. Sorel's new definition is that it does not make clear this radical impossibility.

In the second place, I am afraid that M. Sorel uses the terms "theory" and "practice" in a quite obscure way. All historical theories, M. Sorel tells us, have consciously or unconsciously a practical end in view (moral improvement, education, etc.); the merit of historical materialism is that it is fully aware of this universal fact. Here I fail to understand. The word "practical" here no longer carries the meaning that until now we have been used to employing with Marx; it is almost a reversal of Marxist terminology; what we now call practice is rather what Marx called theory, and vice versa. How would Karl Marx have reasoned, according to M. Sorel? First, he would have been a socialist by sentiment; he would have followed this "practical" concern (to use M. Sorel's terminology) to eliminate the inequalities of wealth among men. He would then have asked that theory furnish him with information about the means of arriving at this end: and this knowing subordination "of theory to practice" would constitute historical materialism. But then, I should reply, Marx would have been doing exactly what he criticized his immediate predecessors—those whom he called "utopian socialists"— for doing. Perhaps, before he elaborated his theory, Marx had been a sentimental socialist or communist, but he considered this instinctive socialism, this "theoretical" ideal (I believe I am here using a more Marxist terminology than M. Sorel) of a society in which economic inequality would be eliminated as justified only when that ideal would appear as the not yet realized but future and necessary extension of the economic, real, "practical" evolution of the human race. In this sense—entirely different, it seems to me, from that proposed by M. Sorel—historical materialism involves a subordination of theory to practice.

These are the two difficulties which I submit to M. Sorel.

APPENDIX II

Continuation of the discussion at the meeting of the Société Française de Philosophie, November 28, 1936.

I have received a quite large number of letters about my communication on the era of tyrannies, which I should have liked to share with the members of the Society at the meeting. But I did not have the time. I have decided, therefore, to publish lengthy and systematically arranged extracts, adding to them the thoughts that my correspondents' criticisms have suggested to me.

I shall begin with two letters that I believe need no reply; the reasons are, however, different in each case.

The first is from Marcel Mauss.[1] It is a letter completely supporting the thesis I have developed, and I can only thank him for having brought some very interesting additional proof to this thesis or to certain parts of it.

I am in entire agreement with you on every point of your communication. I should like only to add a very few things to which I can testify.

Your deduction of the two Italian and German tyrannies from Bolshevism is quite correct, but it is perhaps be-

[1] [Marcel Mauss, 1873–1950, the nephew and pupil of Émile Durkheim, with whom he founded and edited the *Année sociologique*. He was a specialist in comparative religion and sociology. See the introductory essay by E. E. Evans-Pritchard in the translation, published in 1951, of Mauss's *Essai sur le don, forme archaïque de l'échange* (1925).]

cause of lack of space that you leave it to me to point to two other features of it.

Fundamental to the deduction of all this is the idea of "active minorities," as it was held in syndicalo-anarchist circles in Paris and especially as it was being worked out by Sorel when I left the "Socialist Movement" rather than take part in his campaign. I have watched the spread of the doctrine of the minority, the doctrine of violence, and even of corporatism from Sorel to Lenin and to Mussolini. All three of them acknowledged it. I should add that Sorel's corporatism stood somewhere between Pouget's and Durkheim's,[2] and, finally, that in Sorel it went along with a reactionary view of the past of our societies.

Austrian Christian-Social corporatism, transmuted into Hitler's, is in another class by its origin, but finally, in copying Mussolini, it has become of the same class.

Here is my second point.

I rely more than you on the centrality of secrecy and conspiracy. For a long time I moved in the active circles of the Russian Social-Revolutionary Party; I have followed the Social Democrats less closely, but I knew the Bolsheviks of Parc Montsouris, and, finally, I lived with them for a time in Russia. The active minority was a reality there; a conspiracy was always going on. The conspiracy lasted through the whole war and through the Kerensky government, and it won out. But the structure of the Communist Party has remained that of a secret sect, and its essential organ, the OGPU, has remained the combat arm of a secret organization. The Communist Party is camped in the heart of Russia, just like the Fascist Party and the Hitlerian Party, without artillery or fleet, but with the whole apparatus of police.

2 [Guillaume Pouget, 1847–1933, a priest of the Lazarist order and a professor in the seminary of the order's mission in Paris, 1888–1905; after his retirement he had a powerful effect on many young intellectuals. Émile Durkheim, 1858–1917, the most important of French sociologists.]

These events seem to me to be very like events that often took place in Greece, which Aristotle has described very well, but which are particularly characteristic of archaic societies and perhaps of the whole world. It is the "société des hommes," with its brotherhoods, public and secret at the same time, and in the société des hommes it is the young who act.

Sociologically, perhaps it is a necessary form of action, but it is an anachronism. Still, that is no reason why it should not be popular. It satisfies the need for secrecy, influence, action, youth and often tradition. I might add that the pages of Aristotle can still be cited on the way in which tyranny is normally linked to war and to democracy itself. One could think oneself living in the time when the young men of Megara swore secretly not to stop before they destroyed the famous constitution. So things begin all over again, and the course of events is the same.

The second letter, from Roger Lacombe,[3] is a different matter. It is a rather sharp and very lucid criticism of my thesis. If I do not answer, I hope that Roger Lacombe will not take it amiss. But I think I have answered his arguments to the best of my ability, either in my reply to Bouglé's objections or in my final remarks.[4] To the best of my ability, which is not necessarily to say in a manner satisfactory either to Roger Lacombe or to the readers of this *Bulletin*. But I can only allow them to judge between Lacombe and me.

To maintain that socialism "suffers from an internal contradiction," you must give the same importance to currents of thought whose influence on the socialist movement, as it emerged at the end of the nineteenth century, are not

[3] [Roger Lacombe, 1896–   . *La psychologie bergsonienne: étude critique* (1933); *L'apologétique de Pascal: étude critique* (1958).]
[4] [See above, pp. 277–285.]

at all comparable. From the first, socialism has been an extremely confused movement; many different trends have appeared in it, but not all of them have survived. Unquestionably, authoritarian, organizational, and hierarchical socialism existed side by side with the emancipationist socialism founded on the will to destroy "the subjection of labor by capital." But the first has been progressively eliminated and has exercised almost no influence on the political movements that, in the last half-century, have called themselves socialist. You talk about Saint-Simonianism, whose impact may indeed have been great in 1848 and 1851. But there is only an indirect and distant link between Saint-Simonianism and the socialism of today. You talk about Lassalle, who certainly stands with Karl Marx at the source of that German social democracy which in turn inspired all the socialist parties of continental Europe. But while Marx's influence has grown, Lassalle's has been quickly eliminated, or nearly so: what French socialist, or even what German socialist still reads Lassalle? On the contrary, all the doctrines that have directly affected modern socialism look to the liberation of man. First of all, Marxism itself, which you recognize as looking forward to "a final stage of the human race which would be anarchy as well as communism"; and, along with Marxism, the conception of Jaurès and that of revolutionary syndicalism, Fabianism and Guild Socialism, and, finally, the thesis of Henri de Man.[5] And if one considers not doctrines but the popular aspirations expressed in the socialist movement, there is no doubt that they arose from

[5] [Henri de Man, 1886–1953, a Belgian socialist. After the first world war, he deserted the far left, criticizing Marxism for its immersion in nineteenth-century assumptions and preferring to find the source of the socialist impulse in the alienation of intellectuals rather than in the grievances of the workers who are inevitably growing more *bourgeois*. He was a minister in Belgium in 1935–1938, and in 1946 was condemned *in absentia* for his role during the German occupation.]

a revolt against employer domination, from a desire to be free and not from a desire to submit to authority.

I do not think one can speak of a "contradiction," if by that you mean a conflict between antagonistic tendencies within modern socialism itself. But I admit that there exists, if not a contradiction, at least a contrast, not between goals pursued, but between the proclaimed goal (the liberation of man) and the recommended means (the taking over of economic functions by the state). Certainly there is no insoluble conflict there; we must not forget that the state can play and, historically, has effectively played a liberating role vis-à-vis the individual. I will not deny, however, that socialism here encounters a difficulty that its most original thinkers, since Marx, have tried to evade.

This distinction between means and ends, I believe, allows an interpretation of postwar events different from yours.

When you say that "postwar socialism derives much more from this wartime regime than from Marxist socialism" (that seems to me applicable only to Russian Bolshevism, for even though the socialist parties in our democratic countries have taken wartime experiences into account, they have made no significant change in the direction of their activity), you must in fact distinguish between the means used—the wartime regime—and the goal pursued, which unquestionably came from Marxism. For the Russian Bolshevists, Marxism seems to me to have been something quite different from an ideological cloak; they owe to it that faith, that firmness in action, without which they would not have been able to accomplish that remarkable task—bringing about, in a huge country and under difficult conditions, not the institution of socialism (granted it has not been realized in Russia) but the disappearance of private capitalism, the creation, for the first time in history, of a highly industrialized modern economy without capitalists. The movement for peace and land which made the Russian Revolution could have resulted only in anarchy or even in a truly fascist dictatorship, if that "group of men" of whom you speak had not drawn from Marxism a very clear idea of the road to follow in transforming society, if they had not wanted, no matter what the obstacles, to make reality fit a preconceived doctrine.

Again, when you compare Fascism to socialism, you must recognize that the similarity bears only on the means employed, not on the end. In today's economy, one finds a whole series of facts which impose themselves on every doctrine. Fascism and socialism seek to use these facts, but that is certainly not to say that they are running in the same direction. These facts are, first, the scars left on the economy and in men's minds by the last war; then the spontaneous evolution of the capitalist economy, with its tendency to destruction of competition and with the crisis of overproduction, both of which bring about state intervention; and, finally, the preparation for a new war which, in a time when war is formidably mechanized, demands greater and greater state domination of production. These facts impose themselves on all governments, whatever their political orientation. Under the pressure of the crisis, Weimar Germany, in the time of Herr Brüning, went further in the direction of state intervention than Fascist Italy in the same period. But socialism seeks to take advantage of and to benefit from this spontaneous evolution, since it sees in it a preparation of the economic structure that it must bring about (as formerly the Marxists benefited from the development of cartels and trusts). As to Fascism, it looks to the exaltation of the national will, not to the taking over of economic functions by the state. At the outset, Fascist Italy made hardly any effort to bring the economy under the direction of the state. But because Fascism creates a strong state that suppresses all internal resistance, it is relatively easier for it than for a democracy to extend state power indefinitely. But first of all, the preoccupation with war being dominant, it is naturally led, more than any other political system, to control all production. But this take-over by the state, leaving the capitalists to their good life, is very different from that of Bolshevism, which eliminates the capitalists.

I do not believe, therefore, that National Socialism can be seen as the compromise solution of the conflict between conservatism and socialism. The Fascist goal is the same as that of the conservatives, but pushed to the extreme— "the almost unlimited strengthening of the state"; it is only because of circumstances that it tends to expand the economic functions of the state. On the contrary, the socialist goal is the freeing of man; the taking over of economic activity by the state is only a means, necessary no doubt, but fundamentally regrettable. Socialism and Fascism look to opposite ends; the fact that, confronting the same world, they are led to use the same means—in a very different way, it should be said—can give rise to only a superficial parallel. National Socialism is not a synthesis retaining one of the contradictory elements in socialism as one of its essential components. It is a movement directly opposed to socialism, resembling it only because, like socialism, it has been adapted to the modern world.

Now I come to other letters, which demand some comments in addition to what I said at the meeting.

First, a letter from Albert Rivaud.[6] At first sight, it is an unqualified endorsement of my ideas. Unfortunately, it is written in terms that lead me to ask if Albert Rivaud has interpreted my ideas in a way entirely satisfactory to me. After congratulating me for advancing ideas very close to those arising from his own thinking, he continues:

I have been studying the history of Marxism for quite a long time in connection with a book I am writing on Germany. As I see it, socialism—a system of organization

6 [Albert Rivaud, 1876–1956, professor of philosophy at the Sorbonne, 1927–1945. *Les grands courants de la pensée antique* (1930); *Histoire de la philosophie* (1948–62); *Le rélèvement de l'Allemagne, 1918–1938* (1939).]

*applicable only within narrow limits, as the ancients un-
derstood—and internationalism are antagonistic. On the
other hand, the idea of the class struggle renders any
organization impossible. But the Marxists have used it only
to destroy the existing order, which they see as evil. It is
a weapon and nothing more. Marxist socialism had finally
to begin in one country. This country, having turned communist, works to bring about the revolution in other
countries. Having put an end to the class struggle at home
by violent means, it sets about propagating it abroad, to
weaken other countries. In the end, this Marxism leads
to a national imperialism, served abroad by the methods
of traditional statecraft, made worse by the ideology of
the class struggle. Marxism must lead to the formation
of tyrannical states of the classical type, practising a realistic policy of expansion. This evolution has been made
easier by Marxist materialism; this materialism is not
original with Marx. It has been used in foreign or enemy
countries as a means of destroying from within the moral
and charitable feelings that, in the last analysis, are the
foundation of society.*

I shall not dwell on the parts of this letter that in effect
repeat my thoughts exactly: my readers will have no difficulty in finding them. Rather, I shall draw their attention
to the points where I have a right to say that he seems to
me to misconstrue them. It is in concentrating the whole
force of his denunciation on the personality and doctrine
of Karl Marx. Mussolini and Hitler spoke this way when
they came to power in Italy and Germany, eleven years
apart: they offered themselves as saviors of a liberty
threatened by Marxist tyranny. Albert Rivaud's language
differs on only one point: in his last sentence, if I understand him correctly, he presents Karl Marx as a panger-
manist agent, working to demoralize other nations in the
interests of a greater Germany: Hitler certainly would not
say that, and on that score, as I see it, it is Rivaud who

is wrong, not Hitler. To clarify the disagreement between Albert Rivaud and myself, let me say that, in the one sentence in my communication that mentions Karl Marx, I set him on the side of internationalism and freedom as against Ferdinand Lassalle, who was an authoritarian nationalist. No more than an advanced radical when he came to Paris to discover socialism and communism, Karl Marx subsequently—through Friedrich Engels at first and then through the effects of a thirty-year stay in London—was very greatly influenced by English liberalism, in the strongly internationalist form of the free trade of the political economists. René Berthelot very properly brought this to our attention. Thoroughly hostile to the notion of "fatherland" (see his *Critique of the Gotha Program*), he looked forward to the world crisis that would wipe out capitalism, the victim of its own excessive development, and that would assure at a blow the triumph of socialism throughout the world, because of the physical impossibility of the continuation of capitalism.

Now, what about the dictatorship of the proletariat? The Marxist has to ask what will happen if he gains power before the economy is ready for the triumph of communism. The problem was raised in 1848 when Marx and Engels wrote the *Communist Manifesto* to serve as a program for an imminent revolution. It was raised much later when Engels gave his name to the theory of the dictatorship of the proletariat (a theory that was French, Jacobin, and Blanquist in origin) to serve as a program for the Marxist parties organized nationally in the various European countries. It was raised, but in a much vaguer way, for Karl Marx when he was working on *Das Kapital* in the fifties and sixties. If one reads the portions of the *Communist Manifesto* corresponding to what later came to be called the dictatorship of the proletariat, it will be seen that what is at issue is no more than a very advanced fiscal radicalism, with only the most remote resemblance to the Muscovite tyranny. What was needed to produce that was

not the spread of the Marxist idea, but the experience
of four years of world war and its revelation of the powers
with which the progress of militarism, bureaucracy, and
science had invested the modern state. From this state of
war (and, in the support he is willing to give to my thesis,
Albert Rivaud takes no account whatever of what I regard
as its essence), I have deduced first the emergence of
Bolshevism and then the emergence of Italian Fascism
and German National Socialism (about which Albert Rivaud says not a word). These *"frères ennemis"* (to use
the happy expression of another of my correspondents,
Maurice Blondel) had a common father—the state of war.

On this point I am happy that Maurice Blondel[7] agrees
with me, while advancing some criticisms very worth considering:

*For a long time you have studied and thought about
the dialectic of political and social history, disentangling
from it the influence of the irresistible necessities of war
and its consequences. I do not know but that I should
prefer the old word "dictatorship" to the word "tyranny,"
which you use to characterize the present era in which,
on the contrary, we see an honorable and all the more
fervent dedication to liberty and to the recognition of
spiritual values. You say, in effect, that military demands
have contributed much to creating, imposing, and making
acceptable the authoritarianism that the political sense of
the Romans had invented and limited to times of extreme
danger. You will object, no doubt, that the autocracy now
in existence in a good many countries no longer resembles
a dictatorial power of six months' duration; but perhaps,
if the scale and complexity of events extend and prolong*

7 [Maurice Blondel, 1861–1949, professor of philosophy at
Aix, a Roman Catholic modernist and voluntarist; *La Pensée*
(1934); *L'Être et les êtres* (1935); *L'action* (1893 and
1936–37); *La philosophie et l'esprit chrétien* (1944 and
1946).]

certain systems of force and repression, their domination, uncertain as to duration, will not be able ultimately to maintain itself as the normal form or at least to remain long viable for civilized societies. The perpetuation of classical tyrannies no longer seems possible, for whatever services they render are bought at the price of the true civic energies, spiritual freedom, and the higher personal and moral impulses.

Among the great currents troubling the world today, therefore, there are other things than the effect of war psychosis, economic crises, and scientific and cultural revolutions. There are questions about the human ideal, the organizing principle, the eternal and ultimate end to set to social effort, the political order, and the whole human problem. It is here that your analysis is so valuable in pointing to the internal contradictions and dynamic paradoxes forcing opposed conceptions from one extreme to the other, conceptions that, through this very opposition, are still species of the same genus, forms entrapped in the same insufficiencies or mutilations. You say, for example, and not without reason, that our second Empire, like the first, was a reaction against revolutionary demagogy and a socialism tending towards anarchy. Inversely, organizing and hierarchical socialism always runs the risk of oscillating from the dictatorship of a mass to the dictatorship of a man, so long as the organization of the means of production, employment, and possession ignores the individual dignity of men and their legitimately infinite aspirations. You very powerfully help us to see it ourselves when you sum up that hidden logic of the political and social repercussions as an internal contradiction between individual liberation and totalitarian organization.

From that formula you derive the dual inconsistency from which the society of all Europe suffers and perhaps the society of all the world will soon suffer. On the one hand, the parties that call themselves conservative of the established order demand "the almost unlimited strength-

ening of the state," but it is to protect established situations against being taken over by the state or against the creation of a juster order, which presently seems to them to be disorder; they call out the police against it. On the other hand, "the socialist parties call for the unlimited extension of the functions of the state," and for its intervention in the economic sphere, while weakening more and more its coercive power as between all the social classes, some of which are less numerous and whose work, necessary though it is to the spiritual welfare of the nation, is more easily misunderstood and sacrificed; so that the very extension of the functions of the state and the displacement of its role result in the opposite dictatorship, that of the "proletariat," substituting itself for the just balance of all the values needed to maintain order in liberty.

The following passage, taken from another letter which he wrote to me subsequently, seems to me to define still more clearly than the beginning of the first the point on which Maurice Blondel and I disagree.

1. *The concentration of authority demanded by the war of 1914–1918 does not seem to correspond to the idea either of tyranny or of Fascism or of proletarian domination. It was, in effect, a matter of saving by military action the independence, the integrity, and the very life of the threatened countries. It was for just such analogous cases that Rome invented the dictator.*

2. *If the repercussions of the war have given rise to authoritarian and totalitarian governments, it was from ideologies and so-called utilitarian seizures of power that repressive regimes emerged in different countries, but not among all the belligerent nations, whatever analogous difficulties arose among them all. There have been quite opposite reactions, which prove the absence of logical identity between the state of war and the totalitarian state.*

3. *It seems to me that there is a formal heterogeneity between the classical and theoretical notion of the tyrant, drawing everything to himself, and the Duce, the Führer, and even Lenin or Stalin, claiming to act and to exist only for the people, the nation, political grandeur, and the vital interests of a herd-like and depersonalized mass. Practically, no doubt, as Gide has shown, Stalin gathers all adoration to himself, and Hitler and Mussolini are apotheosized like Nero; but, after all, their despotism is of a very different color from a tyranny declaring "L'État, c'est moi" and practicing not only the "Paucis vivit humanum genus," but the total oneness of the people incarnate in a man.*

If I understand him correctly, Maurice Blondel refuses to admit the close connection I have drawn between contemporary tyrannies and the dictatorial regime of the war years. To support his thesis he argues: (1) that once the war was over, not all the belligerent states adopted the tyrannical regime of Fascism; these regimes, therefore, lack the universality necessary to allow us to speak of an era of tyrannies following the Great War; and (2) that in the countries where Fascist tyranny has come to power, it has come to power at different times, responding to different needs in each country, needs that can be only temporary, just as the necessity of defending the threatened nation in wartime was temporary. When the needs they are meeting cease to be felt, they will pass away. The regime therefore displays neither the necessity nor the universality needed to sustain my thesis. To emphasize this transitory and precarious character, Maurice Blondel would prefer that I speak of dictatorship rather than tyranny.

That being the case, I should like to group with Maurice Blondel's letter two other letters that, in very different ways, seem to me to imply reservations quite similar to his.

Raymond Lenoir[8] objects to the excessive simplicity of my schemes. The sociological method is more realistic; sociology considers social phenomena too flexible to permit their being imprisoned in the rigid framework of an abstract system.

Georges Bénézé,[9] convinced that the final victory of liberalism is tied to the influence of the middle classes, refuses to believe in their irremediable defeat, as the Marxist scheme would have it.

I cannot [he writes] *allow Maublanc's statements*[10] *to pass without protest. Perhaps the Soviet regime deserves the greatest praises. But to present it as the entry to paradise is to exaggerate: tomorrow you will be happy; today hold yourself back.*

But even leaving aside this too easy dialectic, the picture of the present state of the USSR cannot be accepted. How can we fail to see that that state is encouraging the emergence of a new class, a class that will finally restore to Russia the ruling and middle classes? How can we not recognize the important fact that rewards and salaries are distributed not according to needs but according to labor and "capacities"? How can we not foresee tendencies arising from this to hereditary wealth or position and, whatever its juridical disguise, to familial or individual appropriation? These are the facts, easily sustained by the

[8] [Raymond Lenoir, author of *Condillac* (1924), *Les historiens de l'esprit humain: Fontenelle, Marivaux, Lord Bolingbroke, Vauvenargues, La Mettrie* (1926). Lenoir's letter is a long, rambling series of reflections, difficult to understand and nearly impossible to translate with any hope of faithfulness to his intentions. Since Halévy did not comment on or reply to the letter, except for a passing remark about the dangers of oversimplifying in writing history, it has seemed wise to omit it here.]

[9] [Georges Bénézé, 1888–   , taught philosophy in the provinces and in Paris; *Sur le transcendental* (1936); *La méthode experimentale* (1960); *Le nombre dans les sciences expérimentales* (1961); *Généreux Alain* (1962).]

further fact that the Bolshevik Party works like an aris-
tocracy in the great empire. It is the unquestionable nu-
cleus of these new developments.

I do not want to be told that we ought not to compare
them to our bourgeoisie. Why not? Our capitalist bour-
geoisie took its rise from the organization of industrial
production. Why, by the same token, should not the or-
ganization of that intensive production of the USSR result
in the creation of privileged groups analogous to ours? Has
the moral education of the Bolshevik leaders and sub-
leaders been carried to the point where they will unani-
mously reject this prestige of an authority "founded on
the general interest"? In short, quite to the contrary, Rus-
sia is going to school to the West. She was quite far
behind.

That partially answers the questions in your statement
circulated prior to the meeting of the Société de Philoso-
phie.

Yes, there is an internal contradiction in socialism, and
it would seem clearly fatal to the socialist ideology, if
socialism were to come to power. But it will not come to
power. The middle classes, without whom nothing can be
done, have not allowed it yet; they are not taking that
road, in England, France, Germany, or Italy. Even if they
are pauperized, they remain at the service of the ruling
classes, their natural allies. Besides, it should be noted that
socialism has never proposed a consistent plan for renew-
ing the continent's economy.

Liberty remains an ideal and a characteristic of the
middle classes. It perishes with them, a fortiori *if war*
comes.

To reply to these comments, I shall go back to some
questions asked by Charles Seignobos in 1927 of readers
of an American journal.[10] "Is the representative system,"

[10] [Charles Seignobos, 1854–1942, professor in the Faculté
des Lettres in Paris, and a distinguished historian.]

he asked, "going to be replaced by arbitrary government? Let me answer by a question—or rather by two questions. Can anyone imagine the establishment of a dictatorship, even a proletarian dictatorship, in Switzerland, Great Britain, the United States, Canada, Norway, or Holland? Can anyone guarantee ten years of existence to dictatorships in Spain, Italy, or even Russia? . . ."

Let us leave Spain aside, for reasons apparent to everyone: she has escaped from one dictatorship, from two dictatorships, only to be threatened by a third. But the system of "dictatorship" (to speak like Charles Seignobos; but is a dictatorship lasting twenty years, six years longer than the *grade mortalis aevi spatium* of Tacitus, still a dictatorship? Is it not a tyranny?) still exists in Russia, at least if the Constitution of 1936 is not looked on as the beginning of the end. By all appearances, the Italian tyranny is more stable than it was ten years ago. Finally— and this is very serious—a Fascist regime has taken root in a great country of more than sixty million inhabitants who can be considered in many respects to stand at the forefront of European civilization.

The rest of Europe? I shall not speak of the Balkan tyrannies. They offer nothing new. In those countries, tyranny was once commonly considered as an inferior form of government adapted to the needs of peoples of inferior culture; a decade or so ago, a good many Englishmen did Italy the injury of tolerating Mussolini's tyranny because it was adapted to the needs of a people who, in their eyes, had not risen much above the level of Balkan civilization. But this much is new in the Balkan tyrannies of today. The tyrants no longer excuse themselves to western nations by pleading the necessity of governing their people by autocratic and barbarous procedures. They are under the impression that, in doing so, they are raising themselves to the level of German civilization.

In another respect, the last ten years have verified Seignobos' predictions. There is no dictatorship, even a proletarian dictatorship, in Switzerland, Great Britain, Norway, or Holland. But we should note, in the first place, that Charles Seignobos said nothing about France or Belgium, and that, without questioning the extreme stability of representative democracy in those two countries, one cannot say that either of them, large or small, is not more threatened by the prestige of arbitrary government than they were ten years ago. In the second place, we should note that those countries with representative governments have become the timid countries, eager to protect a past that is dear to them rather than to work for a future of which they are sure. Their attitude towards the arbitrary governments is the attitude of fear: need we give examples, which spring immediately to everyone's mind? The prestige and the power of intimidation are on the other side. Even if the territory of the arbitrary governments should not be expanded, it is sufficiently large, and the prestige of these governments is great enough, that we can consider this form of government as constituting, in Fourier's phrase, the "pivotal" feature of the historical era through which Europe is passing.

I am, however, inclined to agree with Bénézé that the future of the middle classes is less desperate than Marxist orthodoxy would have it. I admit only in passing to feeling disturbed to see Bénézé, after having identified the cause of the middle classes with that of liberalism, presenting —not without reason—what is happening in Germany and Italy as a victorious reaction of the middle classes. I am also in full agreement with Raymond Lenoir in recognizing that historical reality is too complex, the life of societies too flexible, to be forced into the simplicity and rigidity of our systems. It came to mind as I thought back over the meeting of November 28 and noted an aspect of the problem that none of the speakers, myself included, had touched on: I mean the conflict of Church and State. For imperial Rome had two heirs, the Church and the Empire, both totalitarian in their ambitions. Sooner or later, here and there or perhaps everywhere, it seems, these two powers must clash. And who knows if this conflict, which goes on entirely outside the field of my communication, may not be the fundamental fact of the century that is opening, with consequences for liberty of conscience it would be interesting but difficult to imagine.

Be that as it may, I shall dare to say that a new age really has opened, with new characteristics, which appear to be permanent. That is why (I am now answering Maurice Blondel) I have preferred to use, instead of the Roman word "dictatorship," the Greek word "tyranny," which signifies a lasting regime, arising from the degeneracy of democracy, for reasons that the "sociology" of Plato and Aristotle tried to define. Greek tyranny ended in the great world tyranny of the Roman Empire, which gave the Mediterranean world some centuries of peace, if not with freedom. Maurice Blondel disputes the too close connection that I claimed to establish, in corresponding with him, between the new tyrannies and the "anthropolatry" of imperial Rome. But I am convinced that, just as today there is anthropolatry in the new regimes, so ancient Rome under the Caesars displayed a social character more marked than its aristocratic opponents liked to admit, opposed as they were to this government of the masses. I had occasion in the last volume of my *History of the English People* to cite this curious passage from a young Englishman, an enthusiastic convert to state socialism: "I was wondering yesterday why the devil the world didn't found a religion on Caesar instead of on Christ. . . . To me it also seems that Caesar was a far greater personality. . . . Perhaps it wasn't so incongruous as it was made to appear by damned Christian scholars. Worship isn't the same thing as prayer."[11]

[11] [Frederick Hillersdon Keeling, 1886–1916. Letter to Mrs. Townshend, July 6, 1912, in *Keeling Letters and Recollections,* edited by E. T. (Emily Townshend) with an introduc-

As I see it, this new age began with the end of 1914 and the proclamation of a state of siege in the great belligerent nations of the West. The connection between that state of siege and the systems of arbitrary government is disputed by Théodore Ruyssen,[12] with regard to that regime in which the connection seems evident to me. "I believe," he wrote me, "that Russian Bolshevism, even if it had not had to fight for two years against foreign armies or armies under foreign influence, would have developed according to the Marxist scheme and, still more, according to the Lassallean scheme. We must not forget the enormous influence Prussian authoritarianism had always had in Russia, even in the time of the Tsars." I grant that there is something in that last observation: it was, I believe, Miliukov[13] who said "Bolshevism built on the solid base of Tsarism." The fact remains that Bolshevism could have sunk into anarchy, and order could have been restored in Russia by its adversaries. In that period of Bolshevik history from the October days to the signing of the treaty of Brest-Litovsk, I see only a competition in anarchy with the social-revolutionaries. It was after the signing of that treaty, when socialist Russia had to undergo enemy attack from all points of the compass that I see appearing this "wartime communism," which, in its most intense form, is certainly an authoritarian nationalism and

tion by H. G. Wells (1919), quoted in *History of the English People: Epilogue, II* (1934), p. 262.]

12 [Théodore Ruyssen, 1868–   , professor of philosophy at Bordeaux and secretary-general of the International Union of Associations for the League of Nations, 1921–1939; *Kant* (1900); *Schopenhauer* (1911); *De la guerre au droit: étude de philosophie sociale* (1920); *Le caractère sociale de la communauté humaine* (1938); *Les sources doctrinales de l'internationalisme* (1954).]

13 [P. N. Miliukov, 1859–1943, professor of political science at Moscow who was forced into exile in 1907; he served briefly as minister of foreign affairs in the provisional government in March 1917, and, after breaking with the Petrograd Soviet, fled to France.]

in which it is difficult not to see a combination between Communist ideology and the necessities of the conduct of the war.

To prove that the same observation holds for the tyrannies of Italy and Germany, we need only point out that, so far as the form of government is concerned, Rome imitated Moscow before Berlin imitated Rome. But the wartime regime affected the two nations of Central Europe still more directly. The philosophy common to Mussolini and Hitler, before they seized power, was a philosophy of former soldiers, humiliated to see their countries in military and diplomatic decline, and holding the mediocrity of the representative government responsible for that humiliation. Whatever is socialist in the two regimes has not been fused with nationalism in the same way. When he came to power, Hitler put what socialist elements there were in his "national socialism" at the head of his program. For, in order to gain power, the mass of the people had to be allowed to hope, not that the shame of Versailles would be erased, but that work and bread would again be given to six million unemployed. But when Mussolini marched on Rome nine years earlier, he had declared himself brutally antisocialist; only four years later, when his slipshod financial and monetary policy had precipitated a very serious crisis, did the internal logic of his system lead him to the formulation of "corporative socialism." But, in both cases, it was the same mixture of a proletarian ideology with a military ideology. Labor camps. Labor front. Battle of this and that. And the regime itself took on what can only be called a permanent state of siege, under the control of a militia moved by a common faith.

I have just spoken about corporatism. That gives me a chance to answer the objection made to me by Félix Pécaut.[14] "Is corporatism," he asks, "the expansion of state

14 [Félix Pécaut, 1866–1946, inspector-general and later director of the École Normale Supérieure de Saint Cloud; he had great influence on French primary education.]

control? I thought its essence lay in giving the force of law to decisions taken by a majority of the corporation (has not England gone very far in that direction, for milk, butter, etc.?). In that case, corporatism could be called state control, but it could also be called dismembering the public power. As to the part played by the workers, is it anything but a sham in Italy? For the worker delegates are not elected by their union but appointed by the Fascist authority." And I shall join to this quotation another taken from letters I have received from Charles Appuhn,[15] in order to answer my two correspondents together. "In France, the more the state intervenes in the production and the distribution of wealth, the more incapable it seems of carrying out its principal functions, which I believe to consist in maintaining order, respect for persons, freedom of labor, etc. Is this what you mean by the weakening of authority? I should like to be sure that we understand each other on this point. That leads me to another question. Does not the weakening of authority—I should say of government rather than of the state—if it has the character I have just indicated, arise from the growth of an institution claiming in some way to take the place of government and aspiring to tyranny? You will know that I am speaking of the trade union."

My answer is yes, exactly, and I was thinking of that weakening of state authority by union interference. In this precise case, however, I should hardly like to talk about union tyranny, although I recognize that the expression can be used, with a pejorative implication, to refer to that discipline imposed by union leaders on rebels, to force them to obey the rules. I should rather speak of unionist anarchy to designate the paralyzing effect imposed by workers on the discipline of production when they feel themselves more or less masters of the factory. To counteract this anarchy, the state is appealed to "to maintain

15 [Charles Appuhn, 1862–1942, translator of and authority on Spinoza.]

order," as Appuhn put it, but not, as he put it less happily, to maintain "respect for persons" and "freedom of labor." In Soviet Russia, after many shifts of doctrine, the union has ended by becoming, in official doctrine, not an organ of struggle against tyranny from above, but a governmental organ for the systematic organization and intensification of production. According to Mussolini's or Hitler's interpretation, the corporation has nothing to do with the corporations of the Middle Ages, which were spontaneous creations of the economy to which the state gave only the seal of legality (and the same would be true of certain corporations—still very fragile by the way—in liberal England): they are creatures of and emanations from the state, run by leaders whom the state has chosen, and to whom it grants only advisory powers. The whole system is no more than a shadow of deliberative institutions, within a general state control of the economy. Pécaut tells me that it is the degeneration of true corporatism. I agree; but it is a degeneracy, so to speak, normal to corporatism. It is one aspect of what I call the internal contradiction of socialism.

Socialism is a reaction against the anarchy and waste in production. As a result, it is a doctrine of organization and state ownership. But at the same time it is a doctrine of struggle against all authority, of complete emancipation. Now, with some difficulty, the two tendencies are compatible. What in state ownership of the railways, mines, and banks contradicts Caesarism, the doctrine of arbitrary or tyrannical government? As I write these lines, Hitler has just brought about a degree of state control of the Reichsbank much more sweeping than what was done with the Banque de France last summer by the Popular Front. Let us go a step further. The state to which socialism appeals to bring order into production is necessarily the national state: all *étatisation* is necessarily nationalization. The socialist who also wants to be a liberal is an internationalist. He tries to superimpose the formulas of classical free trade on the formulas of orthodox socialism. Yet how can the freedom left to producers to exchange the products of their industry with whomever they want, inside or outside the borders of the country, be reconciled with the nationalization of all production? As can be seen in Russia, socialism's last word is the complete suppression of foreign trade, with the state reserving to itself alone the right to execute advantageous barter agreements with foreign states. No more do I see the possibility of reconciling freedom of exchange with the policy of general regulation of all internal prices, towards which socialism necessarily tends. But where there is nationalism, there is also necessarily militarism; and can one imagine militarism without a limitation of freedom of thought? In the west, liberal socialists would like to speak the language of Gladstone and the language of Lenin at the same time. I ask if that is possible.

To this thesis, however, two of my correspondents have entered an objection, the weight of which I confess not to understand, but which is perhaps more serious than I believe it to be, since two of them have brought it up. "I do not see," writes Félix Pécaut, "the contradiction you speak of in the concept of socialism. Certainly, the establishment of socialism would have to overcome a tremendous difficulty; but that difficulty arises not from an internal contradiction, but from external conditions." So, too, Théodore Ruyssen: "Is there really an *internal* contradiction in socialism? Is not the contradiction rather between a necessarily simplistic abstract system and the resistance of a complex reality which cannot be mastered by liberal procedures?" If I understand Pécaut and Ruyssen correctly, what they call external difficulties I should myself call internal in human nature, and so the necessity of fighting against both of them—the proprietors' need of liberty as well as that of the workers—forms part of the intrinsic nature of socialism. Am I going to be told about a future state of the human race, when a perfect socialism will be

313

united with perfect freedom? What freedom? The freedom to do nothing, as in the abbey of Thélème, or the absence of obedience to a master, along with incessant labor like an ant or a bee? This ultra-future, as I said at the meeting, goes beyond the limits of my vision. And when I see men giving themselves up to these dreams, I cannot help but think of Kant's dove trying to fly in the void or of Hegel's swimmer without water.

A question raised by Dominique Parodi[16] moves me more. He asks:

if the conflict of the two tendencies, liberal and authoritarian, is peculiar to socialism, and if it does not appear in democratic doctrine itself? Is it not already apparent in Rousseau and in the Contrat social? *Is not the fundamental postulate that all citizens equally resign all their individual rights to society? And against the general will— the expression of his own sovereignty united with that of all his fellow citizens—the individual has no recourse but exile. It is very striking, in reading Rousseau's correspondence, to see him, in connection with internal dissensions in Geneva, dominated by the fear of demagoguery and anarchy and favoring the most moderate schemes for reform, those most careful to maintain the strength of the central power by checks and balances. If democracy is specially concerned with individual liberty, it is with the liberty of all individuals, of an equal liberty for all—"men are born free and equal in rights." Logically, then, democracy implies equality from the very beginning: it is pregnant with socialism. The connection, long believed*

16 [Dominique Parodi, 1870–1955, inspector-general of national education, 1919–1938, after a career of teaching philosophy; *Traditionalisme et démocratie* (1909); *Les bases psychologiques de la vie morale* (1923); *Le problème moral et la pensée contemporaine en France* (1925); *En quête d'une philosophie* (1936); *La conduite humaine et les valeurs sociales* (1938); *Le problème politique et la démocratie* (1945).]

indissoluble, between economic liberalism and political and moral liberalism is a true historical accident and a manifest ambiguity. But authority can never be anything but a means and a pis-aller, *with the end remaining the respect for justice and the promotion of humanity in all its members. In that democracy is clearly different from all the Fascisms and, undoubtedly too, from those socialist ideas that are explicitly Marxist, if it is true that for Marx the class struggle becomes a historical necessity and that the materialist and determinist inspiration masks or at least obscures the preoccupation with justice as well as freedom.*

Without taking up this or that point in Parodi's letter on which I could make some reservations, I declare myself in agreement with him that the internal contradiction I observed in the idea of socialism is already present in the idea of democracy. Indeed, one might ask what socialism is, if it is not the extension of the formulas of political democracy into the economic sphere? The problem, however—if I may be allowed to note the slight difference between my position and Parodi's—is to know why the democratic idea tends to take on a less liberal, less parliamentary form when socialism is at issue than it does in political democracy. If Parodi will admit the reality of this fact, I should suggest the following explanation. Radicalism originally viewed all men, rich and poor, as belonging to a single class. Inequalities of wealth were only individual accidents in the same class. Everything changes if we admit that there are classes in society arising from the natural evolution of the economy and constituted in such a way that, in one, all individuals are hereditarily favored by fortune and, in the other, all are hereditarily disfavored. The Saint-Simonian formula—"improving the lot of the most numerous and the poorest class"—has a much more definite meaning than the Benthamite formula —"the greatest happiness of the greatest number." It sets two armies against each other as on a battlefield. One can imagine that, in order to bring off victory, the leaders who have been given power to lead the battle for the most numerous and the poorest class or who invest themselves with that power, will demand military discipline from their troops, if they want to be victorious. One can imagine that the opposing party will turn against its adversaries the very method that they recommend and will demand the same revolutionary authority in the name of a different "socialism," proclaiming the union of classes in the same country. Before 1914 the possibility of a man or group of men exercising that power seemed doubtful; and the revolutionary syndicalism of the first years of the century after 1910 began to get bogged down in parliamentarianism. They forgot that in 1793 the state of siege created the Jacobin regime, from which, by degeneration as well as reaction, was born the Caesarism of succeeding years. It belonged to the world war of 1914 to show the men of revolution and the men of action that the modern structure of the state put almost unlimited powers at their command.

A NOTE ON
"THE WORLD CRISIS OF 1914–1918"

Élie Halévy was forty-four years old when the Great War broke out. He was too old to fight, too austere a patriot and a philosopher to stay at home. He volunteered for the ambulance corps, preferring the companionship of common soldiers to that of Paris intellectuals who led the chorus of chauvinists. "In wartime, if pacifistic eloquence sounds false, martial eloquence sounds falser still. At the present time, only one writer satisfies me and that is Joffre. The rest is, or should be, silence."[1]

Halévy had sensed the coming of the war and he quickly sensed its revolutionary character. His wartime letters to friends—moving testimony to an abiding patriotism tempered by wisdom—reveal his constant efforts to apprehend the meaning of the war. Gigantic issues had brought on the war, he thought, and these must be solved before the war could—or should—end. Anything less would signify only an armistice, and the slaughter would have to be resumed after a brief pause. In his published correspondence he did not identify these issues, and it may well be that they remained obscure in his own mind. All he knew was that the war marked a terrible *caesura* in the life of Europe, that that life would never be the same, that a new era was being born amidst the collective exertions and sufferings of the war. In March 1916, before any revolutionary movement had become visible anywhere, he

[1] December 15, 1914, Halévy to Xavier Léon, in Alain (Émile Chartier), *Correspondance avec Élie et Florence Halévy* (1958), p. 343.

wrote: "I always come back to my thesis. The day when Jaurès was assassinated and when the conflagration of Europe was lit, a new era opened in the history of the world. It is foolish to believe that in six months this could be extinguished, and that the same parties, the same groups, the same individuals could resume the same rhythm of their combinations as if nothing had happened in the interval. Don't make me say, in the fashionable style of the day, that Europe is going to emerge regenerated, purified by this baptism of fire. I say she will emerge changed; and I say that she is not at all near emerging from all this."[2]

Over a decade later, when for a fleeting moment Western Europe thought itself secure, as it had not since 1914 and as it has not since, Halévy, invited to deliver the Rhodes Lectures in Oxford, returned to the task of interpreting the war. In three deceptively simple lectures, he presented a model of explanation which in its profundity and suggestiveness has never been rivaled. The lectures exemplified perfectly his historical method, as analyzed in Mr. Webb's preface. By bold hypothesis and intelligent and honest marshaling of facts, he presented a new interpretation of an intractable subject.

The subject had become the most controversial of the postwar decade. The Treaty of Versailles had injected into European politics the issue of responsibility for the outbreak of the war; the so-called war-guilt question intrigued historians and incited peoples. The search for alibis and culprits had become an all-consuming passion, especially among the defeated nations. What side had started the war, what nation, what statesmen? How to distribute the proper measure of responsibility? In this search, no one asked whether one was looking in the right places or asking the right questions. The race was on, and each man ran roughly over the same course.

[2] March 24, 1916, Halévy to Xavier Léon, in *ibid.*, p. 358.

As a consequence of this fascination with immediate origins, people lost sight of questions about the deeper forces that plunged Europe into war and determined the course and meaning of that war. They explained the causes of the war in categories that were either excessively concrete or excessively abstract. Historians fastened on the principal statesmen of the crisis of July 1914 and scrutinized their every move and telegram as if reality could be recovered by the more or less objective compilation of those minute facts. Marxists, on the other hand, insisted that the war was the necessary result of capitalistic contradictions and imperialist rivalries, while nationalists in every country blamed the war on the inherent rapacity of the opposing side. Historians were captivated by the ever-swelling supply of available minutiae, as every major government published some of its prewar records. Other writers fell back on generalities of doctrine or expressions of resentment that would readily appeal to the already converted. The great tomes of historians and the empassioned outpourings of publicists provided little enlightenment to a generation that wanted to know what had happened to Europe during those catastrophic years.

Halévy offered an entirely different perspective. He abandoned the search for immediate causes because that search would never be able to uncover the nature of the war or its historic meaning. "The object of my study is the earthquake itself. I shall attempt to define the collective forces, the collective feelings and movements of public opinion, which, in the early years of the twentieth century, made for strife."[3] His hypothesis was that the strife of the prewar years exploded into the great war, and that once the war had started it consumed many of the remaining barriers to violent changes. In seeking to identify the forces making for strife, Halévy, true to his habitual style of analysis, pursued the social career of great ideas.

[3] *Supra*, pp. 210–11.

Socialism in its many forms constituted the principal force making for revolution, and nationalism and the nationalist grievances in East-Central Europe the principal force making for war. The two forces, he argued, were closely related, and both were responsible for the outbreak of the war. The Austrian Empire was threatened by revolutionary nationalist agitation, and the European diplomats could neither banish the threat to Austria nor preserve the peace of Europe while a great power was in danger of disintegration. In the early stages of the war, the revolutionary forces within nations were contained; as the war dragged on, these forces became ever stronger, because they now added the urgent plea for peace to their older revolutionary aims.

For Halévy there was no merit, then, in the prevailing, nostalgic view that a peaceful, stable Europe had been overwhelmed by the outbreak of the war which then raged senselessly until the energies of nations had been burnt out. From his vantage point, the "good old days of before 1914" appeared as a foolish myth and an obstruction to right understanding.

He had wanted to study "the earthquake itself," and his metaphor helps us to understand the extraordinary scope of his interpretation. He had pointed to the deep stresses and strains that finally led to a series of eruptions called the world crisis. In this way, he illuminated the continuities between prewar and wartime society, but he also was one of the first to understand the discontinuity that the war had brought about. The very image of an earthquake suggests that while the tremors had built up for a long time, the final eruptions did create something new, even if the rubble did not at first allow a clear view of the new landscape.

His wartime letters and his later essay which furnished the title to this volume clearly express what is only hinted at in "The World Crisis": the new order in Europe, which was characterized by an accommodation of socialism and nationalism, was built more on force than freedom. The war had left a terrible legacy of constraint, and the ever precarious balance between liberty and authority had tipped in favor of the latter. No wonder that he had singled out Jaurès' assassination as signaling the opening of a new era: in the world after 1914, the humane socialism of Jaurès was all but extinguished by the ruthless Soviet socialism and the equally ruthless national corporatism of Italy or national socialism of Germany.

His three lectures were beguilingly neat and modest. He did not celebrate his own originality by denigrating his predecessors. He had sketched a new interpretation which offered a unified explanation for the various phases of the war. In this new view the traditional distinction between diplomatic and political history, between a nation's external relations and internal order, lost relevance. The relationship between domestic and foreign politics has always been closer than historians have grasped; in Halévy's view the two are so closely intertwined that to separate them is to understand neither. In these lectures, he did not fully work out the many connections between the forces making for revolution and those making for war. Only in one case did he say that "it is legitimate for historians to ask, whether one of the reasons—we are far from saying the main reason—why the German military aristocracy decided, in July 1914, to run the risks of a great European war was not a growing sense of discomfort under the increasing pressure of Social Democracy, and a surmise that a bold attempt to give a set-back to socialism, by asserting themselves once more as the party of war and victory, might prove the wisest course."[4] It is likely indeed that this conscious or, far more likely, unconscious, fear of revolution played a considerable role in the prewar conduct of foreign policy everywhere in Europe, and it

[4] *Supra,* pp. 215–16.

seems incredible that questions of this sort have rarely even been asked by historians since Halévy.

Halévy's achievement has yet another dimension. Somewhat like Tocqueville in his work on the French Revolution, Halévy—who in his conservative defense of liberty, his austere moral outlook, and his astounding historical perspicacity resembles Tocqueville—discovered the underlying continuities between an *ancien régime* and a revolutionary upheaval. He lifted a recent historical process which people were still treating politically and in isolation to the level of past history. He connected the war with the great recognized stream of past events.

Today's reader may not at once recognize the novelty of Halévy's approach and insight. His interpretations of many details have finally filtered down to us and have become common coinage. It is worth recalling, however, that his interpretation of prewar socialism in Germany and of the impact on Europe of the Russian Revolution of 1905, his comprehension of the overshadowing importance of the year 1917 and his sense of a kind of ideological rivalry between America and Russia in 1917, were startlingly new when he delivered these lectures.

We may be surprised, on the other hand, that Halévy said relatively little about Germany's role in prewar Europe. Before and during the war, he acknowledged the fact that her striving for hegemony posed a threat to the established balance of power, just as the France of Louis XIV had done two centuries earlier. Germany's foolish and intermittently aggressive policy before the war merely exacerbated the fears of her neighbors which were initially aroused by her mere strength and existence. Indicative of a more serious misreading, perhaps, is Halévy's erroneous assertion that the world crisis came to an end in August 1920 "when the last of the postwar treaties was signed at Sèvres, when the Bolshevik army was defeated in Poland, when an attempt at a Communist revolution in Italy proved abortive, and the rise of Fascism began."[5] Halévy's exceptional perspicacity seems to have failed him when he was first confronted with the phenomenon of fascism. He saw in it at first only a new form of *étatisme* and a new ideological mixture of socialism and nationalism. Only later did he see that it embodied a power of unreason and hatred, more violent and dangerous than he had imagined possible. But his judgment in 1929 about the end of the world crisis reflected the happy glow of the Locarno spirit. That spirit evaporated a year later, and the world crisis reappeared in still uglier form. The forces of revolution and war were once more on the march.

The greatness of Halévy's lectures cannot be measured by the accuracy or inaccuracy of details. The enduring value of these lectures lies in the totality of his vision, in the fact that every thought could have inspired a separate study, while the conception as a whole could lead to a better understanding of the world since 1900. Few historians, unfortunately, have followed the path he laid out, preferring instead to tread familiar tracks or ruts. One of the reasons for this failure may have been the fact that, paradoxically, Halévy had gained more distance from the great war, from violence and revolution, than any historian since. In the nearly forty years since he wrote these lectures, historians have lived with war and revolution and in their political engagement may not have found his detached and supra-national analysis to their taste or within their grasp. The lectures, moreover, have been difficult to obtain, and this too may help to explain their relatively limited influence. Perhaps we have now regained the necessary distance, and the new availability of these lectures together with his other writings on contemporary history will at last stimulate students to go back to the tasks which he long ago perceived.

Halévy had meant to be more than an historian's his-

[5] *Supra*, p. 245.

torian. In these lectures—as in much else he wrote—he had a moral purpose as well. "In looking for the 'causes' or 'responsibilities' of the War, not in the acts of individual statesmen, but in collective anonymous forces, against which individual statesmen were powerless," Halévy had meant to show that "the wisdom or folly of our statesmen is merely the reflection of our own wisdom or folly."[6] Hence every citizen shares political responsibility, and Halévy hoped to fortify that sense of civic virtue. In this, too, he was right. For the wars and revolutions of our time have been made possible not so much by a few leaders or sects as by the multitude of passive citizens who smugly thought that politics was the responsibility of statesmen.

Fritz Stern

[6] *Supra,* p. 245.